I Belong to This Band, Hallelujah!

D1600998

I Belong to This Band, Hallelujah!

Community, Spirituality, and Tradition among Sacred Harp Singers

LAURA CLAWSON

The University of Chicago Press   Chicago and London

LAURA CLAWSON is currently senior writer at Working America, the community affiliate of the AFL-CIO. This is her first book.

The University of Chicago Press, Chicago 60637
The University of Chicago Press, Ltd., London
© 2011 by The University of Chicago
All rights reserved. Published 2011.
Printed in the United States of America
20 19 18 17 16 15 14 13 12 11   1 2 3 4 5
ISBN-13: 978-0-226-10958-9 (cloth)
ISBN-13: 978-0-226-10959-6 (paper)
ISBN-10: 0-226-10958-5 (cloth)
ISBN-10: 0-226-10959-3 (paper)

Library of Congress Cataloging-in-Publication Data
Clawson, Laura, 1976–
    I belong to this band, hallelujah! : community, spirituality, and
    tradition among sacred harp singers / Laura Clawson.
       p. cm.
    Includes bibliographical references and index.
    ISBN-13: 978-0-226-10958-9 (cloth : alk. paper)
    ISBN-13: 978-0-226-10959-6 (pbk. : alk. paper)
    ISBN-10: 0-226-10958-5 (cloth : alk. paper)
    ISBN-10: 0-226-10959-3 (pbk. : alk. paper)
    1. Shape-note singing—Social aspects—United States.
    2. Sacred vocal music—Social aspects—United States. 3. Folk
    music festivals—United States. 4. Folk music—Religious
    aspects—Baptists.   I. Title.
  ML3188.C53 2011
  782.270973—dc22   2010040491

♾ The paper used in this publication meets the minimum requirements of the American National Standard for Information Sciences— Permanence of Paper for Printed Library Materials, ANSI Z39.48-1992.

R0432000608

Contents

Preface

In 2001, two vanloads of twenty- and thirtysomethings drove from the small towns of Western Massachusetts to the much-smaller towns of northeastern Alabama. Staying four to a motel room and arriving en masse at little country churches, they were a highly visible contingent contributing to an electrifying weekend of participatory singing. Of the Fuller Cemetery singing, Alabama singer Susan Harcrow said, "I know that something happened there that night that is a once in a lifetime thing." That visit solidified a new tradition of travel between Western Massachusetts and northeastern Alabama, allowing members of both groups to develop pathways connecting the locations so that future journeys have become easier, for themselves and for others.

In the late 1990s, at a mid-Atlantic singing organized by relative novices, the one man from Georgia was accorded pride of place as he audibly deployed his southernness. In fact, he, too, was a relatively new singer, but his southern accent and religious demeanor brought him deference, as it was assumed to bespeak Sacred Harp authenticity and expertise in a room where he was far from the most experienced or knowledgeable.

Throughout their sixties, Coy and Marie Ivey opened their Henagar, Alabama, home to Sacred Harp singers from around the country. Their four-bedroom ranch house and their son's small garage apartment, and sometimes even their younger son's house down the road although he does not sing Sacred Harp, were stretched to accommodate visitors from Alabama and Georgia, from Minnesota and Illinois, and from Maine and Rhode Island. In addition to bringing food for an army to every day of singing—barbecue, fried chicken livers, coleslaw, potato salad, deviled eggs, punchbowl cake—Coy and Marie fed their visitors morning and evening. Their hospitality was boundless in service of bringing people in from afar to sing Sacred Harp on Sand Mountain.

At the Huntsville, Alabama, stop of the Great High Mountain tour, Alison Krauss, Ralph Stanley, and other greats of bluegrass shared the stage with nearly a hundred Sacred Harp singers, amateur musicians of highly variable levels of talent and experience, many of them children who had only recently shown interest in the old music sung by their parents and grandparents. The previous December, they had watched family members and friends appear with Nicole Kidman and Jude Law at a televised concert of music and readings from *Cold Mountain* and with Alison Krauss and Elvis Costello at the Academy Awards. And now they had the chance to be onstage with the stars of the *O Brother, Where Art Thou?* and *Cold Mountain* sound tracks. Suddenly Sacred Harp was more exciting.

These vignettes illustrate the major and interrelated themes that animate this study: they are the making of music, of authenticity, and of community. As a musical tradition, and a contemporary musical practice, Sacred Harp singing straddles borders of place, identity, and meaning. Predominantly rural southern singers typically regard Sacred Harp as religious in character, while more recent, largely urban northern adherents tend to regard it as a form of folk expression with the religious content seen as incidental rather than central to its meaning. These differences, of religion, politics, region, class, and education, make the question of how Sacred Harp works to construct community a challenging one and point to the role of music and authenticity in motivating and maintaining such boundary crossings. For, despite such differences, Sacred Harp singing produces, at peak moments, a shared experience that singers, both northern and southern, religious and secular, describe as transcendent.

Community

Achieving community may seem a simple task among southern Sacred Harp singers whose families have sung the music for generations, who live in the same communities where they were born, and who are related to, work with, and live in proximity to other singers who share an understanding of the music as sacred. Coming together to sing in a church associated with the family, with singers connected by dense networks, may not seem to be much of an accomplishment. Such togetherness fits neatly with two strands of sociological theory, one emphasizing homophily, or shared demographic characteristics,[1] and another that emphasizes the importance of shared networks.[2] Paradoxically, however, singing is dying out in many such communities. It turns out that in the South as well as the North, community is by no means automatic and requires a constant effort, including active outreach to involve a new generation.

Given the lack of tradition, achieving community in northern Sacred Harp singing is more obviously a challenge. Singers, who are a tiny minority within a large metropolitan area, lack overlapping networks and bonds with other singers. There is also a mix of reactions to religion and an absence of any common space to call their own.

More surprising is Sacred Harp's ability to bring together, from around the nation, North and South, people with very different backgrounds and lives—religious and secular, traditional and alternative, conservative Republicans and ultraliberal Democrats—to achieve *both* a meaningful community *and* an openness to difference. This community is deep enough that a northern singer living in New York would be buried in a rural Alabama cemetery and open enough that the singer's gay father and his partner would be welcome in an Alabama Baptist church.

That ability to create deep and meaningful community, while still leaving room for major differences, is central to *I Belong to This Band, Hallelujah!* Community is created through practice and through a shared commitment to the music, a participatory music that is best sung in large groups and thus benefits from drawing in more people.[3]

The emphasis on common rituals and practices is consistent with the analysis of religion as a means of building community.[4] Participants share a commitment to the music; their pursuit of the collective experience it offers, together with the practice of singing, unifies them. Contrary to Vaisey and Etzioni, however, in important ways singers do *not* share a "moral order"[5]—they agree on the importance of the rituals of singing but have very different understandings of what the music means and of the character of the community it produces. This argument, developed in this book, both challenges and specifies understandings of the basis underlying community, while contributing to a growing recognition of the sociological significance of music.[6]

Music

Though they tend to remain religiously, culturally, politically, and sartorially distinct, an important spiritual meeting ground is afforded by the music and is re-formed each time any group of singers meets to sing. Especially in its peak moments, Sacred Harp works as a hybrid form in which the religious, the spiritual, and the wholly secular interact to produce a collective experience that singers, both northern and southern, secular and religious, describe as transcendent, an exaltation that emerges from the making of music. An attempt to capture that experience, within the limits of written prose, is a necessary part of this text's analytic purpose.[7]

Central to that effort is a conception of music as an activity, what Christopher Small has called "musicking."[8] Within this framework, music is never just a stable object, but the product of relentlessly social doings.[9] As Roy and Dowd observe, the activity of music is contained not just in its performance, "but also in the efforts that precede and enable such performance . . . the rendering of these musical texts involves a considerable process, containing both musical and nonmusical elements." They also note about Small's analysis of a classical concert, and as I find in my study of Sacred Harp, "the meanings created by a classical music concert, including the architecture of the concert hall, the physical relations of participants, the conventions for behavior, and microsocial interaction" all "frame the music and the discourse around it."[10]

Building on this insight, this study enables us to see the ways in which music and spirituality are grounded in a more or less visible, but always complex, material and social infrastructure that produces etiquette, authority, and food, all of which are fundamental to the Sacred Harp experience and to its continued survival. Central to Sacred Harp is a set of practices, above all around the music but extending beyond that to a larger set of agreed (and at times enforced) expectations: all-day singings or conventions will run for five or six hours, stretching from morning until midafternoon; singers will be dressed as for church; the singers will sit in a hollow square, with one musical part on each side of the square; people will take turns leading the music and the leader of each song will stand in the hollow space in the center of the square; experienced, attentive singers will sit in the front row of the square; every person—regardless of skill—will be equally entitled to lead; the best/most-honored singers will be called on to lead at certain traditional times; no song may be sung twice on the same day; there will in most cases be a "memorial lesson" honoring singers who have died and those who through reason of illness are not able to attend; and, crucially important, in the middle of the day there will be "dinner on the grounds" with food for all provided by the people hosting the singing. This routinization of Sacred Harp practice enhances visiting between singing communities, as a singer from Chicago can expect to walk into a singing in California or Georgia confident that he will not violate local etiquette in any significant way.

Unlike many other genres, such as blues and country,[11] which have been reproduced and disseminated as performance genres via the recorded music industry, club owners, and concert promoters, the infrastructure of Sacred Harp resides in an almost totally volunteer effort. Southern singers can rely on the availability of certain churches on the weekends singings are held, on local singers to bring huge quantities of food and lay it out as the noon hour approaches, and on other actions that are routine for people who have been singing their entire lives, although, as Ruth Finnegan observes in regard to English Methodist traditions, "It is easy . . . to forget that for a tradition of this kind to remain active it had to be passed on and learnt by a whole series of congregations, year after year after year."[12] In the North, however, these efforts are more visible, and Sacred Harp in the North is distinctive in its reliance on formal committees and other bureaucratic structures that build on social practices rooted in southern traditions but are shaped by the particular class culture of its northern adherents as well as by the practical difficulties of reproducing it in the North. It thus offers insight into the way practices may be altered and amplified in different social contexts, even when the intent is to reproduce them exactly.

Music is, moreover, an activity that rests on, produces, and orders relationships. "When we perform," Small writes, "we bring into existence, for the duration of the performance, a set of relationships, between the sounds and the participants, that model ideal relationships as we imagine them to be and allow us to learn about them by experiencing them."[13] In Sacred Harp, because the more participants there are the better the music sounds and the more powerful the experience, all participants have an incentive to welcome and draw in new singers. In this sense they intentionally seek out and produce new relationships. But Small's specification of "*ideal* relationships" (emphasis added) is important. The relative standardization of practices from one singing community to the next enables singers to be familiar as they travel; singers also face the expectation that while they may adapt some traditions, if they are to travel and sing in other cities—as most serious singers do—they cannot stray too far and still expect to be fully accepted at other locations. The centrality of practice in the experience of Sacred Harp as *music* therefore foregrounds the question of authenticity.

Authenticity

"Issues of authenticity," as Richard Peterson notes, "most often come into play when authenticity has been put into doubt."[14] When Sacred Harp singing expanded from the South to become a national movement, when it moved from those who sang as a family tradition to those for whom singing was a post-childhood discovery, authenticity emerged as a central issue. Most of the literature on authenticity, however, examines the way it is used to "sell" a product (and producer), whether that be blues clubs, luxury wine, a tourist destination, or country music.[15] Sacred Harp has never been a performance music or a commodified product; that does not mean issues of authenticity are not central, but they take a somewhat different form.

In telling this story it would be easy to romanticize the southern "folk," the white residents of rural Georgia and Alabama whose families have sung Sacred Harp for generations and whose churches were often built with Sacred Harp in mind. The easiest form of authenticity is that which is ascribed to someone on the basis of their identity (born in the South to a singing family).[16] Northerners find it far more difficult to make claims of authenticity based on their ascribed characteristics and thus must create claims for themselves or their friends. "It clearly takes an effort to appear authentic,"[17] requiring "authenticity work" and an active process of social construction.

As Roy and Dowd note, the American folk music tradition has been "valorized . . . precisely because it is the music of common folk, both black and white." As a result, "the more marginal, humble, and unsophisticated the makers of the music, the better for these enthusiasts."[18] My study of Sacred Harp confounds this assumption in several ways. First, while novice singers may see it as simple and natural,[19] observation of southern singers reveals that they frequently engage in evaluative judgments about singers and singings and operate with a developed knowledge of the etiquette and practices that produce a satisfying or "authentic" day of music-making. Moreover, it was not the northern folk revivalists who reached out to a closed-in South, seeking its authenticity and validation, but singers from the South who insisted that if those in the North were to sing Sacred Harp, they could not appropriate it piecemeal. Rather northerners needed to be taught, and to follow, the entire tradition: singing the shapes as well as the words and participating not just in the music but also in a communal meal, a democratic and egalitarian practice of leading songs, and the use of a memorial lesson to honor the dead. Above all, they resisted the performer/audience divide that characterizes most Western music and insisted that Sacred Harp could not become a performed music. The more visible contestations that characterize this history enable us to see the ways in which "authenticity" is always a negotiated process, a "representation of reality" that must be actively constructed.[20]

For some singers, especially but not only those in the South, the music is unequivocally religious, and it is offensive to deny or gloss over this. To others, especially newer singers in the North, the unequivocally Christian religious words are merely a metaphor, the Christianity something that can be set aside. Many such northern singers would insist, however, that something transcendent takes place, at least during the best singings. What different groups understand by religion, or—as others would put it—spirituality, and how they navigate these differences is one of the themes of *I Belong to This Band, Hallelujah!*

For many years, Sacred Harp flew almost entirely beneath the media radar. Since it is a participatory rather than a performance music, it was known primarily to participants, despite its occasional inclusion (by those new to the music more than by traditional singing families) in a folk festival or other performance, despite its having been recorded by Alan Lomax, despite an occasional news article. But in 2003 two Sacred Harp songs were included in the Miramax film *Cold Mountain*, directed by Anthony Minghella and starring Nicole Kidman, Jude Law, and Renée Zellweger, with music produced by T Bone Burnett, which resulted in some Sacred Harp singers (including me) performing onstage at the Academy Awards and other concert events. What might be seen as a one-way appropriation of a folk culture instead emerges as a multidirectional exchange. Sacred Harp's character, the fact that it was not a performance music and not remotely commercial, served the producers as an authenticator of the film's historical accuracy and high-culture ambitions. Singers, for their part, self-consciously mobilized to use this moment of mass media attention to garner press coverage and acquire a different kind of validation, that of contemporary popular culture and mass media.

Cold Mountain revealed something about Sacred Harp communities as well. When the media spotlight was turned on, it had the potential to create tensions and disrupt community, possibly even changing the music itself. However, the media spotlight on Sacred Harp was not that bright and did not last that long; moreover, the Sacred Harp community was stronger and more resilient than many groups facing media attention. This book attempts to uncover the sources of—as well as challenges to—that resilience.

Acknowledgments

The debts one accrues in the process of writing a book are remarkable, even if you are often accused by friends and family of being unwilling to ask for help. This process destroyed that unwillingness at several key junctures, often in surprising and wonderful ways. And even at the times when I attempted to go it alone, my debts continued to pile up. But the standard disclaimer that mistakes and omissions are my own is unusually true in this case.

As an ethnographer, I racked up an enormous debt to my subjects for their time and ideas, their hospitality, and, in many cases, their friendship. Without the singers of Sand Mountain, West Georgia, Chicago, and Minneapolis-St. Paul, I wouldn't have had singings to attend, food to eat, interactions to observe. But most importantly the love with which this book was written was not only for the music and the communities, it was for individuals in them: Kelly and Karen House, Tim Eriksen and Minja Lausevic, Rodney and Cheyenne Ivey and many other members of their family, Jeannette and Scott DePoy, Richard DeLong, Karen Freund and Jerry Enright, Lynne deBenedette, Susan Harcrow, Martha Henderson, Dana Borrelli, Betty Shepherd, and too many others to name.

As I describe in the first chapter, Karen House was present at the moment the ideas in this book began to come together, and her memorial service nine months later was foundational in my thinking. The community of Sacred Harp singers has since lost two more singers named in the preceding paragraph, both of whom gave me thoughtful interviews on Sacred Harp as well as the occasional use of a spare bedroom: Minja Lausevic passed away in the summer of 2007, and Jerry Enright in the summer of 2010. Both are very much missed.

As for the writing of this book, first I have to thank Bob Wuthnow and Paul DiMaggio who not only let me go ahead with what must have seemed like a crazy idea for a book but also provided incredible support, guidance, and patience at every stage. Mitch Duneier and Judith Gerson were also invaluable sources of insight and encouragement. Each of these colleagues has a distinct personal and intellectual style, all of which have proven to complement each other in the best possible way. At the University of Chicago Press, Douglas Mitchell and Tim McGovern, as well as two anonymous readers, provided thoughtful guidance throughout.

Ann Heider generously provided me with interviews she had done with Chicago and Georgia Sacred Harp singers, which greatly informed my discussion of Chicago in particular. At key moments, Tim Dowd and David Grazian provided me with helpful feedback and the incredible reassurance that comes when someone who doesn't know you likes your work anyway (I think I stole this line from Clawson 1989).

I was lucky to have financial support from the Center for Arts and Cultural Policy Studies, the Center for the Study of Religion, and the American Studies program at Princeton University, as well as a fellowship from the Louisville Institute.

Through graduate school I was equally lucky to have other kinds of support from many people, including Alice Goffman, Eszter Hargittai, Carol Ann MacGregor, Alexandra Murphy, and Chris Wildeman.

The preliminary manuscript was finished after I left Princeton and the book after I had moved on yet again, after my intellectual and social worlds had changed radically. Jake McIntyre, Barbara Morrill, DavidNYC, Markos Moulitsas, Susan Gardner, Dana Houle, and many others were not only supportive through my periodic book-related disappearances, they also gave me a lively intellectual life even as I moved on from academia. Arjun Jaikumar in particular made the final rounds of revisions go (relatively) smoothly by being always sweet and even tempered, but perhaps most crucially by thinking well of me even when I didn't think very well of myself.

But after all those names, three people have most made this book possible. Joan Walling is the kind of friend who seems too good to be true in works of fiction, and her intellectual contributions have been as great as her personal ones. My greatest debt, though, is unquestionably to my parents, Dan and Mary Ann Clawson. After spending my graduate school years managing what must have been an excruciating balancing act in providing me with guidance in their field without trying to run my life, they then, at my request, all but dragged me across the finish line when it came time to wrap up this book. Their intellectual and personal contributions to this project are immeasurable.

ONE

Onto Sand Mountain, Into Sacred Harp Community

If there is an originating moment in which the thoughts woven together in this book began to come together, it is the second Sunday and Saturday before[1] in September 1999. That year's United Sacred Harp Musical Convention was held at Liberty Baptist Church in Henagar, Alabama; forty years earlier, Alan Lomax had recorded the United Convention when it was held some seventeen miles away at Fyffe, Alabama. A handful of Sacred Harp singers were present at both the 1959 and 1999 United Conventions, and a commemorative recording was done of the 1999 singing. Although I had first been to a Sacred Harp singing six years before, and to a southern Sacred Harp singing two years before, this was my first exposure to Sand Mountain.

The hotels closest to Liberty are about twenty miles away in Fort Payne, and on the weekend of a big singing, most breakfast locations become impromptu gathering spots of singers. When we entered the Fort Payne Waffle House Saturday morning, there were already several singers from New York, New Jersey, and other northern states, heightening the sense that the area and the weekend were entirely pervaded by singing and singers. Henagar barely registered to me as a town at all when we passed through its single traffic light on the way to the singing, but there was no mistaking that something was happening at Liberty, which was surrounded by cars and trucks well in advance of the opening song at nine o'clock in the morning. The church was packed, not just with singers from thirteen states other than Alabama but with many listeners from the area drawn in by announcements in the local papers and by social ties with local singers promoting this singing in particular—early in the day the singers were welcomed by the head of the county commission, highlighting the importance placed on this convention by local singers.

The atmosphere was exceptionally relaxed and not merely hospitable but genuinely friendly. The southern singers at Liberty were more mixed in age than at most southern Sacred Harp singings I had attended, particularly in comparison to those in Georgia; unusually, I did not stand out as one of the youngest people there, and attendees' ages ranged from toddlers held on their parents' laps to people over ninety years old. Some singers led in groups of two and three, usually with relatives but sometimes with friends; this was partly out of concern for the size of the crowd but also because it is common in places with such strong kin- and friendship ties for singers to lead with their loved ones. On both Saturday and Sunday, songs were led for Virgil Phillips, a beloved Alabama singer who was in the hospital. Friends called him from cell phones so that he could hear the church full of singers singing for him.

The lunch provided by local singers on both days was exceptional, even by the high standards of southern Sacred Harp singing (more on this later). Coy and Marie Ivey, pillars of the local singing community, had made over a hundred pounds of barbecued pork, as well as fried chicken livers, dressing, and other dishes; Willard and Betty Wright brought homemade ice cream; Bud Oliver made lemonade; and dozens of others brought ham, chicken, macaroni and cheese, green beans, creamed corn, casseroles, pies, cobblers, and cakes. Pictures taken that day show the long concrete table entirely covered in food and dozens of arms outstretched, piling the food onto plates.

Saturday after the singing a general invitation was issued to the home of longtime singers Jap and Joyce Walton to visit with Jap, who had had a stroke and was unable to attend singings. His wife Joyce brought him to the singing briefly to visit and then put out the invitation for afternoon and evening visitors so that he would not be deprived of the company of other Sacred Harp singers. Afterward, my traveling companions from the Northeast—Kelly and Karen House, who had introduced me to Sacred Heart, and Lynne deBenedette, a newer friend—and I were invited to Coy and Marie Ivey's house where we spent time with them and with their two singing sons,[2] David, clean shaven, quiet, and every inch the middle-class professional, and Rodney, bearded with a mullet haircut and a broken front tooth, winkingly flirtatious, and a working man to his core; grandchildren ranging in age from three to sixteen; and a few other singers. At Coy and Marie's house that evening, much of the breadth of the Sacred Harp singing community was on display, in the contrast between brothers David and Rodney as well as in the gathering of northern and southern singers, of high-school students and graduate students, of a technical writer and a construction worker, of a farmer and a lawyer.

At Sunday's singing, the memorial lesson, held to remember singers and their loved ones who had passed on in the previous year, was conducted by a committee that had clearly been chosen to be geographically representative, consisting of Elene Stovall from Alabama, Marcia Johnson from Chicago, and my traveling companion Kelly House from Rhode Island. Elene and Marcia gave brief speeches that were a study in contrast, with Elene quietly drawing on the Bible and memories of her father, a lifelong singer, while Marcia orated more dramatically, without mention of the Bible and with reference to older southern singers unrelated to her as well as to a deceased son who had not been a singer. When Elene and Kelly led the closing song of the lesson, I looked across the square and saw that the entire front bench of the tenor section, all adult southern men, was crying unashamedly. On the last verse of the song, which uses the words of Newton's "How Sweet the Name of Jesus Sounds"—"Dear name! the rock on which I build, My shield and hiding place; My never-failing treasury filled With boundless stores of grace"—all the singers rose spontaneously to their feet, and I looked over to the treble section and saw that, like me, Kelly's sister Karen House was close to tears, though neither of us knew any of the singers on the memorial list.

By the end of the weekend, I knew that a significant part of my manuscript lay here; whether "here" was the United Convention, Liberty Church, or Sand Mountain more generally remained a mystery, and the importance of community in what I was witnessing escaped me completely, but I was on fire with ideas. Though I had attended singings throughout the Northeast and in Georgia and Alabama, the weekend's singing was well beyond anything I had experienced, both in the quality of the music produced and in the way it brought together the loose threads of my thinking on interactions between northern and southern singers and on what constitutes "real" Sacred Harp singing. There was a great deal that was new—and somewhat exotic—to me, as well. The sheer number of people sharing the last name Ivey, the fact that among the singers there were people who had been recorded by Alan Lomax in 1959, that Coy and Rodney Ivey offered us moonshine on Saturday evening all highlighted the distance between the lives of singers on Sand Mountain and my own. Both the specifics of what I witnessed that weekend and the path that it set me on have shaped my research since: How do people form community not around structural forces, such as geography or occupation, but around a shared interest? How is community formed despite differences of religious or political beliefs, or despite regional, educational, or class differences? How is community shaped by shared (or not) notions of what is authentic or real?

A number of theories exist to explain why certain groups of people do not interact much with each other; while the culture wars thesis has been cast into doubt by engagement with empirical data,[3] its persistence in the public debate and the emergence of related concepts, like the opposition of "red" and "blue" states suggest that it continues to speak to a widely held perception of cultural conflict. Network theories and patterns of class, status, and religious endogamy are widely cited in explaining social segregation.[4] Similarly, many recent studies have suggested a decline in community or social capital.[5] What is less certain is how such barriers are overcome in forming community across difference.

I Belong to This Band, Hallelujah! shows how one such community (composed of many smaller communities) is created and maintained around a shared practice, joining a growing body of work insisting that the *doing* of music be attended to.[6] In theorizing this doing of music, Tia DeNora stresses that

case studies provide a means for describing the mechanisms of culture (music) in-action—for specifying *how* music works. Such a focus on practice leads us further away from a focus on musical textual objects and toward a focus on the materiality of music as event—its relations, its uses, and its circumstances and technologies of production/reception.[7]

Music can shape social life in many ways—and mine is not the first work to suggest that community or solidarity may be formed around music.[8] Sacred Harp is distinguished, though, by its participatory nature and the fact that people come together solely for the purpose of singing it, rather than using it to create solidarity to a specific other end, such as a political one.

———

The Sacred Harp is an 1844 tune book that gives its name to a tradition of a cappella singing practiced continuously in the southern United States since the book's publication; it originated as only one of a number of nineteenth-century tune books set in shape notes, a late-eighteenth- or early-nineteenth-century system designed to make sight-reading easier. Today, though a few other shape-note books survive, *The Sacred Harp* is the one most actively used.

Shape notes were part of one of several waves of music education initiatives in the early United States. The noteheads are literally shapes, with each shape corresponding to a syllable in a solfège system, much like the more famous "do, re, mi"; Sacred Harp singing uses four shapes, a triangle called "fa," a circle called "sol," a rectangle called "la," and a diamond called "mi." With only four shapes, some notes repeat in each scale—the major scale runs "fa, sol, la, fa, sol, la, mi, fa," and the minor scale is "la, mi, fa, sol, la, fa, sol, la." At Sacred Harp singings, the names of the notes are sung before the words, both because the notes continue to be a useful tool for singing new or difficult songs and because doing so is a tradition of many generations' duration.

The Sacred Harp was published in Georgia and used most heavily there and in Alabama, though its use did spread to other states through the South, including Florida and Texas. It contains a number of styles of song popular at the time, including hymn tunes, such as "Amazing Grace" (called "New Britain" in *The Sacred Harp*) and "Wondrous Love"; camp-meeting tunes, in which well-known verses are joined with a chorus that can be picked up quickly by large gatherings at which there are more singers than books; fuguing tunes, in which the vocal parts begin the song together, then split off, one continuing while the others rest and then reenter in succession, before all finish together; and multipage anthems, with time changes, internal repeats, and unmetered texts often drawn more or less directly from the Bible. The book has been revised several times—most recently in 1991—each time adding songs by living composers.

Sacred Harp singing is a participatory, rather than performance-oriented, genre of music, ideally sung in large gatherings. As the term "sacred" suggests, the lyrics are religious, but *The Sacred Harp* songbook itself has not been adopted as a church hymnal by any major religious denomination (though it is used in a handful of independent Baptist churches). Neither is the music intended for formal performance. It is participatory congregational singing, and while some may come to listen rather than sing, the singers themselves and, for believers, God, are its main audience.

Participants sit in a hollow square, with tenors facing altos and trebles (sopranos) facing basses; the space in the middle is where the song leader stands. Both tenor and treble are sung by men and women in doubled octaves; the melody is carried by the tenor, but the harmony parts are unusually complex. Similarly, the words are not for the most part the self-referential texts of gospel and Christian contemporary music; instead, many of the texts are drawn from the eighteenth- and early-nineteenth-century religious poetry of Isaac Watts, Charles Wesley, and Philip Doddridge, focusing less on the individual than on the grandeur of God. In these ways, Sacred Harp is less akin to contemporary Christian, folk, or gospel music, and more to classical choral music, despite the "folk" context in which it is sung.

Every attendee of a singing, from children too young to read to adults too old to stand unaided, is given an opportunity to lead a song by standing in the middle of the square facing the tenors and beating time. The entire group sings the leader's song choice at his or her chosen tempo and following the chosen verses and repeats; no song is led more than once in a day[9] and no one leads a second time until all have had an opportunity to lead once. An all-day singing begins between nine and ten in the morning and runs until two or three in the afternoon, with hourly breaks and a potluck lunch, or "dinner on the grounds," provided by local singers at noon. The day begins and ends with prayer.

In its traditional home in the South, Sacred Harp singing tends to be concentrated in predominantly white, rural areas and is often associated with extended families of singers, many of them with Primitive Baptist backgrounds, although some Independent Baptist and Methodist churches also have longstanding ties to Sacred Harp. These churches historically only held services one or two weekends a month, depending on the availability of circuit-riding preachers who served several churches over a large geographic range; singings were scheduled on weekends with no services. Most churches in a community had their own singing conventions—all-day participatory events lasting from one to three days—which singers would join as they would join a church.[10]

Through the twentieth century, the number of singings dwindled as some churches lost interest, or replaced congregational singing with instrumental music or choirs, but many churches continued to hold singings, and as transportation improved, visits between singers increased. As a result of this history, many if not most southern singings are associated with particular families who have been members of the host church and supported the singing both within the church and by visiting other singings, thereby incurring reciprocity. In some cases these family connections are tenuous, the singing continuing through the force of will of a bare handful of singers, while in other cases the connections are thriving and immediately obvious to a visitor—dozens of usually nonsinging members of the host church show up to their church's annual singing, carrying food for dinner on the grounds; the names of the song leaders called are echoed on the tombstones in the cemetery behind the church; and groups of family members stand together to lead a deceased mother's or grandfather's favorite song.

Over the past twenty to thirty years, Sacred Harp singing has spread to many states outside its traditional home in the South, following the folk revivals and early music movement of the 1960s and 1970s. Although Sacred Harp never achieved the widespread popularity of more performance-oriented musics, such as ballad singing and fiddle tunes, it was made available in small quantities by folk-revival institutions, including recordings by Alan Lomax and features at the Newport Folk Festival. Over the years, therefore, relatively small numbers of participants in folk revivals came to Sacred Harp singing. Some continued to participate in Sacred Harp only occasionally, at folk festivals perhaps, while others became active Sacred Harp singers. As they built local singing communities, some people came to those groups along other pathways, but the origins of most Sacred Harp singing groups outside the South are nonetheless rooted in folk revivals and their adherents. More recently, two Sacred Harp songs were used in the film *Cold Mountain*. Following this, Sacred Harp singers were one of several groups performing in a concert that became a special on the A&E channel and is included on the *Cold Mountain* DVD. They also sang backup for Alison Krauss on a non-Sacred Harp song at the Academy Awards and were included on a concert tour of musicians from the *Cold Mountain* and *O Brother, Where Art Thou?* sound tracks. All of this has provided unprecedented publicity for the tradition, with a small but noticeable upsurge of participation resulting in some areas. It also provided a test of community strength, as some singers and not others were chosen for these events in contravention of the inclusiveness of day-to-day Sacred Harp practice; though some hidden tensions came to the surface, the encounter with commercial culture did not produce any serious ruptures and may indeed have added to its cultural capital and enhanced its recruiting efforts, especially among young people.

The new northern singings are concentrated in urban areas and college towns, and the new singers are a religiously diverse group composed largely of highly educated professionals. Though southern singers tend to come from the property-owning middle class and most are comfortably well-off (especially given the relatively low cost of living in the small towns and rural areas many of them live in), northern singers have more elite occupations. Southern singers I have interviewed include a chicken farmer, a feed store owner, a backhoe and bulldozer operator, a mailman, and a secretary, while northern singers include college professors and students, an architect, a Russian translator, and a librarian. The class distinctions are not clean—there are many elementary and secondary school teachers in both the North and the South, there are secretaries and tenuously employed people in the North and executives in the South—and southern singers are probably more socially and politically influential in their areas than northern ones, but there are broad occupational and educational differences.

Singers in both the North and the South are overwhelmingly white. In the South, the demographics of areas in which Sacred Harp is traditionally strong, such as Sand Mountain, are similarly white, but even in areas with substantial African American populations, Sacred Harp singers are white. This is certainly a persistence of earlier patterns of segregation; such patterns were partially responsible for the emergence of a parallel songbook, *The Colored Sacred Harp* and its associated (though now fading) tradition. Today, there are a few singings a year at which the so-called Denson and Cooper *Sacred Harp* books, used by white singers, and *The Colored Sacred Harp* are all sung from on the same day, with singers from the different communities joining together, but there are significant musical differences. In the North, singers often find Sacred Harp through institutions of largely white folk revival traditions, the racialized history of which has been beautifully detailed by William Roy.[11] Singers, both northern and southern, are likely to accord particular attention and emphasis to nonwhite people who join them, perhaps in an effort to show that despite the whiteness of their communities, they are nonracist and welcoming, but this does not extend to a sense of pressure to seek out and recruit people of color in particular.

Unlike southern singers, who tend to come from and sing with large families, many northern singers do not have strong family ties.[12] Though they typically ask their nonsinging (or non-Sacred-Harp singing) friends to attend, few northern singers were acquainted with each other before their involvement in Sacred Harp. The singing conventions these people have established are held in rented spaces—churches of which no more than one or two, if any, are members; college event rooms; community centers; or any acoustically acceptable, moderately affordable spaces. Responsibility for these spaces begins and ends on the day of the singing.

New and lifelong singers[13] therefore have both different cultural backgrounds and differently structured relationships to the Sacred Harp singing tradition, yet they do speak of it as one tradition. While Sacred Harp is indeed one tradition, it is also many. Each singing community has its own habits, differing slightly from those of its neighbors, and each community is structured around slightly different understandings of what they are doing when they sing and of what is most important about that. Singers of differing backgrounds bring divergent ideas to the singing, and the diverging structures of local singing communities create further differences of ideas. For many singers, northern and southern, notions of authenticity structure what they value in their communities, but because authenticity is itself "a socially agreed-upon construct,"[14] there are many possible forms of authenticity to choose from. Which are chosen, and how those choices are justified, can create cohesion or separation.

These local communities are then layered into a national community in which the question of which local norms take precedence must be dealt with. Sacred Harp is most often characterized by what I'm calling "strategic silence," in which people understand where difference exists and often subtly acknowledge it or defer conversation of it until they are in small groups in private settings, without publicly confronting possible sources of controversy. These silences, though, do not prevent contestation over meaning from being enacted as singers from different local communities gather to sing together.

These social and cultural differences point to a major problematic of this book. As the sociologist Mitchell Stevens observes,

An ideologically diverse movement creates considerable uncertainties among activists and constituents about who thinks like they do and who does not. Cooperation is greatly enhanced if people share assumptions about who one another is and how they are to work together.[15]

Ideological diversity, of course, can be general or specific—differences can exist in many areas of daily life and belief or can be relevant with regard to a particular movement or activity, Sacred Harp in this case. By either measure, Sacred Harp is extremely ideologically diverse nationwide; within-community ideological coherence varies from place to place and at least partially accounts for the success, in membership and musical terms, of those communities.

On a national level, the ideological diversity of Sacred Harp is tenable, not producing excessive uncertainty, because of a "group style" that promotes silence on potentially controversial issues (Sacred Harp singing itself occasionally included) and relentlessly focuses the community and its discourse on the act of singing itself and a few, restricted and fairly general, ways of talking about Sacred Harp singing and religion that echo the eighteenth-century Freemason dictum to follow "that religion in which all Men agree, leaving their particular opinions to themselves."[16] In recent theoretical work, sociologists Eliasoph and Lichterman define group style as "recurrent patterns of interaction that arise from a group's shared assumptions about what constitutes good or adequate participation in the group setting."[17] In the case of the Freemasons, this went beyond assumptions into formal doctrine, which meant "that men could enter the order, and relate to one another, as individuals, without reference to their identities as members of confessional communities."[18] But for Sacred Harp singers, who are not guided by a constitution and among whom there is no formal hierarchy, this pattern of behavior and expression of opinion is a group style that is generally adhered to but not formalized.[19] Although many subjects are restricted or prohibited, communities and the relationships between singers are not experienced as being shallow or without content because of the depth of the participants' commitment to singing Sacred Harp.

This avoidance of controversy is not the avoidance of politics described in Nina Eliasoph's 1998 study of political discourse among members of volunteer, activist, and recreational groups. Eliasoph describes how, even in groups that had political goals, "in a strange process of political evaporation . . . what was announced aloud was less open to debate, less aimed at expressing connection to the wider world, less public-spirited, more insistently selfish, than what was whispered."[20] By contrast, while political talk is actively proscribed in the front stage of Sacred Harp singings, how the act of singing itself is structured and the enduring community Sacred Harp provides create a substantial new backstage area in which many potentially controversial subjects—including politics—can be addressed, in voices louder than a whisper, even between people who might otherwise have little to say to each other.

In addition to the broad Sacred Harp style, characterized by strategic silences and observed in some form in almost every location in which people identify themselves as singing Sacred Harp, there are also more defined local styles in most areas. The overall Sacred Harp style reduces the visibility and salience of ideological differences regarding Sacred Harp itself and issues from the outside world, such as religious and political beliefs. The group styles of local singing communities, though, vary widely in what can and cannot be discussed and may allow for more explicit discussion of potentially controversial topics, depending in part on the diversity of the community. Such local styles are rooted, in part, in the era in which that singing was founded and formed its identity. In his classic work in the sociology of organizations, Stinchcombe argues that "the organizational innovations that can be made at a particular time in history depend on the social technology available at the time," and, once established, "the basic structure of the organization tends to remain relatively stable."[21]

Although Sacred Harp singing communities, with their lack of formal institutionalization, do change with time, the historic roots of each community nonetheless continue to shape them. On Sand Mountain, where singing grew up within a church context and where women did not even lead songs for years, church dress is considered appropriate; in some churches a woman wearing pants to sing risks a public rebuke, and convention officers are overwhelmingly male. In Vermont, where many singers come to Sacred Harp as a "folk" form and participate in other folk music and dancing, women in not just pants but blue jeans are common. Likewise, the degree of similarity among singers in a given area determines a great deal about what can be discussed. In a place where most people share backgrounds and beliefs, more subjects can be considered safe than in a place where people differ more or are unsure of the beliefs of their fellow singers.

Despite these local variations, singers from local communities around the United States and in England and Canada can attend each other's singings and never feel at a loss for what is going on, and people from many communities can gather together for a large convention, as they did at Liberty in September 1999 for the United Convention, and sing in powerful harmony, experiencing themselves not as members of many local communities but of one national and international community of Sacred Harp singers. Differences and similarities alike contribute to this sense of community, which develops through and around the act of singing.

————

While Sacred Harp is, for the purposes of this study, a *practice* that constructs and maintains community, it is important to recognize that the music itself—its sound, its aesthetic qualities—is a central component of that community formation. Sociologist of music Simon Frith has argued that "the exercise of taste and aesthetic discrimination is as important in popular as in high culture but is more difficult to talk about,"[22] with many studies of popular culture focused on the politics of consumption to the exclusion of aesthetic questions. As I show in chapter 4, some Sacred Harp singers do discuss aesthetics regularly; often, though, they do so in relatively technical terms, explaining *why* a singing was good or bad without really attempting to engage the question of *how* good or bad it was and what those categories actually sound like. The best singings are generally agreed to be beyond words, leaving singers helpless to describe them, even to others who were there.

All that said, though, such a description of the Sacred Harp sound must be attempted. The sound of Sacred Harp singing can be difficult for the first-time listener to penetrate, composed as it is of four vocal sections, two of them divided between men and women singing in different octaves, with the three harmony parts being substantially more complex, more similar to melody, with greater vocal range, than is the case in most Western choral music. Add to this that many songs involve the different sections entering and exiting at unpredictable intervals and singing different words at the same time, and the overall effect can seem cacophonous. Sacred Harp is *loud* too, sung in what singing school master David Ivey describes as "full voice." This full voice is straightforward, without vibrato, more like an extension of the singer's speaking voice than like classical singing. Dynamics are rare, with almost all songs sung in this full voice, a firm and aggressive sound well suited to the highly developed rhythm of Sacred Harp, which when done at the level desired by many southern singers has a shuffling feel that approaches syncopation. Many singers pat their feet gently to the beat (a few stomp more aggressively, a somewhat controversial habit).

The sound of Sacred Harp singing is strongest in the middle of the hollow square, where the voices of all the singers converge. As Buell Cobb writes, "In the center, in the midst of the terrific volume, it is as if the imperfections are burned away. When the singing is at its best, the timbre of voices on each part seems to fuse, and the chords that come through then are rich and true."[23] This sound is often analogized to instrumental music, whether voices "ringing out like bell tones" or a church that "sounds like the inside of a banjo."[24] Such analogies, I believe, reflect the way the individual voices become submerged in a greater sound, one in which the number of voices being blended becomes impossible to guess, in which it is even difficult to guess which vocal part is producing which sounds, as the different harmony lines cross over and under each other. Occasionally one section reaches up above the others, popping out clearly in that moment; singers in that section with especially good vocal range may sound above the others before retreating back into the mass on the next, lower note.

The Sacred Harp songbook contains songs conducive to many moods, and at a good singing, the songs chosen and the tone of the class[25] and singing mesh. One fast, exhilarating song may follow another, leaving the singers breathless and excited, reaching higher and singing harder with each ensuing song, only to have that accumulated energy harnessed into a slow, focused, intense song just at the moment at which greater speed would have become impossible, producing chaos. At such a time, the singing may develop such an intense rhythm that sustained notes—and even, somehow, rests—have internal pulses.

Sacred Harp singing, existing so fundamentally in action rather than objects, exemplifies the understanding of music argued for by music educator and scholar Christopher Small in his book *Musicking: The Meanings of Performing and Listening*. Small writes, "The fundamental nature and meaning of music lie not in objects, not in musical works at all, but in action, in what people do. It is only by understanding what people do as they take part in a musical act that we can hope to understand its nature and the function it fulfills in human life."[26] *The Sacred Harp* is an object, a book containing a specific set of compositions, but unlike the classical compositions whose uses and meanings Small analyzes, *The Sacred Harp* is understood by its practitioners to have importance and power not because of the individual genius from which it originated but because of its routine use, because of the set of traditions and understandings that have grown up around and through it.[27]

Sacred Harp singing, then, must be understood as action, in which we can find not only answers to the question "What does it mean when this performance (of this work) takes place at this time, in this place, with these participants?"[28] but also understandings of religion and spirituality, community, history, tradition, and authenticity as well as of music. These understandings are not simply part of the meaning of the music; they are produced by it in ways that extend outside the hollow square of Sacred Harp. As Tia DeNora argues, music is a "resource for—rather than medium about—world building" that "affords," or "helps to structure such things as styles of consciousness, ideas, or modes of embodiment."[29]

The important role of music as a shaper and solidifier of social solidarity or community has been addressed in many studies, in contexts ranging from Depression-era southern textile workers involved or potentially involved in labor disputes to the adoption of national anthems.[30] Similarly, Wuthnow suggests that music and the arts are an important part of spirituality and religion for many—indeed, the relationship between religion and the arts is one reason that religious participation in the United States has remained so high over the past half century. The development of spirituality requires "carriers, vehicles of expression to help people make sense of their [spiritual] feelings, to become more aware of them, to talk about them, and to realize that other people are having similar feelings,"[31] and art and music may function as such carriers. Many people also approach art and spirituality in similar ways, as involving "devotional effort" such as praying, meditating, or using contemplation of art forms to achieve effects similar to prayer or meditation.[32]

Wuthnow shows how people's personal, private experiences of music lead them to engage seriously with spirituality in ways that often, though not always, lead to engagement with organized religion and religious communities. This is importantly true of Sacred Harp, in a way that highlights the communal rather than individual aspects of both the arts and religion; for if Sacred Harp is most obviously music, defined by the act of singing, it is also importantly religion, sitting at the nexus of grounded community and individual spirituality. Studies of congregations provide one way of understanding Sacred Harp singing communities, which are both similar to and different from congregations. On the one hand, they are religious communities operating in particular locations for decades and even generations. They must cope with many of the difficulties sociologist of religion Nancy Ammerman finds church congregations responding to: aging participants, changing local populations, and challenging structural or financial problems.[33] On the other hand, they differ from churches in their lack of formal structure and leadership and lack of an official theology binding people together. As Ammerman argues, "The small things of everyday life give shape and identity to a particular congregation, and those small things will prove the most resistant as the congregation faces new challenges and incorporates new constituencies."[34] Group style, in other words, operates in formally structured entities such as churches as well as in looser groups and, in addition to its role as a binder and solidifier of solidarity, can be a hindrance to an organization's ability to adapt to change in ways that allow it to survive.

American religious life is by no means fully defined by congregations, however, and turning to recent work on spirituality, and particularly spiritual seeking, points to another divide between the worldviews of southern and northern singers. In *Habits of the Heart*, Bellah and his co-authors argue that a new form of individualism has emerged, a modern "individualism in which the self has become the main form of reality,"[35] and that this points to a "profound impasse."

Modern individualism seems to be producing a way of life that is neither individually nor socially viable, yet a return to traditional forms would be to return to intolerable discrimination and oppression. The question, then, is whether the older civic and biblical traditions have the capacity to reformulate themselves while simultaneously remaining faithful to their own deepest insights.[36]

Prior to their involvement with Sacred Harp singing, many northern singers, living unconnected to traditional communities such as churches and families, would seem to meet this picture of the individual who "can only rarely and with difficulty understand himself and his activities as interrelated in morally meaningful ways with those of other, different Americans,"[37] while southern singers, with their relatively small, closed communities, might represent the other end of this continuum.

Sacred Harp singing communities at least partially bridge this divide, "remaining faithful to [the] deepest insights" of the older traditions without "return[ing] to intolerable discrimination and oppression." That is, they create a setting and structure in which people from these widely differing backgrounds can come together and share a common ground, as they did at the 1999 United Convention. People from thirteen states came together that weekend, and the memorial lesson—one of the most extended statements of belief and community made at any Sacred Harp singing—was given by people not just from three different states but from three different regions of the country with thirty years separating their ages.

While the sociology of religion or spirituality points to one of the crucial divides between the backgrounds of northern and southern singers, it also suggests a way to understand how this divide may be bridged. Wuthnow identifies three modes of spirituality: dwelling, seeking, and practice. "A spirituality of dwelling emphasizes *habitation*," while "a spirituality of seeking emphasizes *negotiation*."[38] Southern singers have tended to come from dwelling modes of spirituality, with their singing and their religious practice rooted in small churches often associated with particular families, such as Liberty Baptist Church and the Iveys, or, ten miles down the road from them, Antioch Baptist Church and the Woottens. Northern singers, on the other hand, are often seekers, with the folk revival involvement that led them to Sacred Harp having been part of spiritual seeking that in various cases encompasses Eastern and New Age religions as well as therapy, other types of music, and historical research intended to connect them with their forebears. These spiritual orientations are mirrored in the generally more mobile lives of northern singers. The pitfalls of each orientation remain similar to those identified by Bellah—excessive constraint in the case of a spirituality of dwelling, and shallowness in the case of a spirituality of seeking.[39]

What significantly occurs in Sacred Harp singing communities, though, is that singers from different places and backgrounds move toward the common ground of a spirituality of practice, in which "people engage intentionally in activities that deepen their relationship to the sacred."[40] While Wuthnow elaborates this idea of practice as a way that individuals can worship in a meaningful way without full participation in a community, I suggest that it can also be fruitfully applied to the dispersed and ever-shifting communities of Sacred Harp singers.

If community is one central theme of this book, the concept of authenticity is a second, which both complements and complicates understandings of Sacred Harp. Rejecting notions of authenticity as that which is intrinsically "real" or "genuine," sociologist David Grazian points to its character as a set of "idealized representations," "a shared set of beliefs about the nature of things we value in the world."[41] Studies of musical performance genres such as Richard Peterson's analysis of country music and Grazian's ethnography of the Chicago blues world emphasize the role of authenticity as a component of commercial or critical success, in which authenticity becomes one of the axes on which a genre is assessed by consumers. The noncommercial nature of Sacred Harp singing transforms but does not lessen the importance of authenticity, which emerges as not only an idealized value but also a resource to be actively contested between and within local singing communities.

For northern singers, authenticity and the effort to achieve it are expressed more explicitly and regularly, but similarly provide a locus point around which community can not only be intentionally constructed to promote the valued tradition of Sacred Harp but also to support identities for themselves apart from the commercialism and social atomization they perceive as characterizing contemporary American life. At the same time, the language of authenticity can be used to cover over moments in which Sacred Harp practices are altered or reinvented to maintain the ethic of connection to tradition even where direct replication of rural southern practices, or practices of decades past, would not be tenable.

Finally, struggles to define and appropriate authenticity may operate to produce hierarchy and assert status. "Once the signs of authenticity have been agreed upon," Grazian notes, "people can vie for all sorts of intangible rewards made more attractive by their meaning than their economic value."[42] Though Sacred Harp brings seekers and dwellers together in musical practice and in close-knit community, the interplay between the rural and small-town southerners, who have sung Sacred Harp for generations and consider it worship, and the college-oriented and urban northerners, who have been singing it for perhaps twenty years and consider it social singing, leads to a constant, if unspoken and subtle, contestation over the meanings of Sacred Harp—over whether the music is sacred, secular, folk; over whether authority within the tradition is a product of lifelong participation, religious faith, or of a degree in music theory or history; over North and South. This contestation is rarely spoken; rather, it inheres in people's use of particular group styles at particular moments, invocations of specific local traditions and well-known singers, and subtle status demarcations.

Such contestation was evident at Liberty in September 1999 in the silent struggle for control of the front bench of the tenor section, which is considered the most important seating in the square. A singer, whose understanding of herself as an authority on the tradition and who is generally respected in her home area of New England, spent too much of Saturday sitting in the front for the taste of local singers. Though any singer can take a turn on the front row, doing so for extended periods without offering others the opportunity is frowned on. In this case, local singers apparently felt she was neither a strong enough singer for her extended presence there to benefit the singing as a whole, nor a regular enough traveler to singings in the area to deserve the reward of special seating for an entire day. Through the afternoon, she was squeezed into the corner of the bench in attempts to make room for more people, and Sunday morning a local singer arrived early enough to mark the front bench as occupied before she could claim a seat. That local singer and others then controlled that prime seating for the rest of the day, inviting favored singers up whenever someone moved to another row, rather than leaving the empty seat to chance. Other visiting singers tried to claim forms of membership or authority for themselves through actions, such as publicly thanking the cooks who had brought food for the dinner on the grounds or using song dedications to link themselves to well-known singers who could not be there.

Particular claims about the southern Sacred Harp tradition were also made through the weekend, mainly in the songs that were included in this singing. A year before, at one of the first Alabama singings I attended (having spent more time to that point in Georgia), I sat slightly bewildered as most of the class sang a song not in *The Sacred Harp*[43] from memory, not having drawn any distinction between this and other songs. Next to me, a woman from an area in Georgia where Sacred Harp singers sing exclusively from *The Sacred Harp* fanned herself silently, then leaned over to me and noted that the Georgia State Convention had written into its bylaws that only *The Sacred Harp* would be used; for the first time, I realized that the very songs that constitute Sacred Harp singing are contested. At Liberty, one song from the Cooper Book, one song from an almost entirely defunct version of *The Sacred Harp* referred to as the White Book, and one song from another source entirely were sung, all on Sunday. While nothing was said at the time, some Georgia singers and others who follow the more purist, Denson-revision-oriented version of Sacred Harp practiced in western Georgia, did complain privately. Such variation in what is considered to be properly included under the umbrella of the Sacred Harp convention is a key difference from one singing community to another. This is one of the occasions for explicit debate over what constitutes authentic Sacred Harp even among southern singers: For some, the Denson revision (also called the 1991 revision) is primary not only as a personal preference but as a matter of principle; for others, the Cooper fills this role; for still others, a mix of songs from both books and from other sources belong to the tradition in which they grew up. Northern singers often display their allegiance to a particular southern singing community through the canon of songs they draw on.

Similarly, the place of religion is so variable that even the name by which the tradition is referred to varies from place to place, singer to singer, moment to moment. In some places, particularly regions of New England, singers refer to "shape note" rather than "Sacred Harp" singing. This can be used to describe singing songs set in shape notes but not from *The Sacred Harp*, but as often it is intended to avoid use of the word "sacred," and though they rarely, if ever, challenge its use, southern singers understand it as such. Lifelong Alabama singer Shelbie Sheppard says, "I cannot emphasize enough about religion; it's upsetting to hear Sacred Harp referred to as folk. When you get up there and you treat it like secular music, it offends." In addition to the issue of naming, she points to song leaders who, in her words, "dance" or "gyrate" in the square, often in specifically contra-dance style.[44] Similarly, at one Chicago singing, local singers conducted the convention's business session (at which officers are elected) jokingly, doing a send-up of the typical business session. This caused Richard DeLong, a lifelong Georgia singer and member of the music committee of the 1991 revision of *The Sacred Harp*, to publicly rebuke the class, saying that if they understood the tradition and had respect for the singers who had nurtured it through the years, they would not mock even the nonsinging aspects of it. At the same time, while they had held the business session jokingly, the joking had come in the course of explicitly observing the tradition as they had been taught it, rather than simply abandoning it as unnecessary, while southern singers, despite their religious understandings of Sacred Harp, have consistently sought to extend the tradition, despite their awareness of northern newcomers' differing motivations.

Despite such conflicts, singers from different areas and approaches to the tradition do welcome each other and form deep communities. Northern Sacred Harp singers are on average younger than southern ones, and when I attended the 1999 United Convention in Liberty, our group was young even by the standards of northern singers. Karen and I were graduate students, Kelly was a technical writer, and Lynne was an adjunct Russian professor—occupations fairly typical of northern singers. Although—and perhaps to some extent because—we stood out, we were welcomed at the singing and afterward at singers' houses.

Over the next several months, I attended several more singings, both North and South, with Karen, Kelly, and Lynne as well as with others. The United Convention had made such a strong impression on us all that, with little coordination, we all returned to Liberty the next time it hosted an all-day singing, in January 2000. This time, we spent the entire weekend at Coy and Marie Ivey's house—their hospitality to visiting singers is legendary—and went out Saturday evening with Rod Ivey and Elene Stovall. Sunday at the singing, the local singers were all discussing the carbon-monoxide poisoning deaths of a local couple; the fact that seemingly all the local singers knew this couple although they were not themselves Sacred Harp singers strengthened my impression that the social networks here were substantially different from anything I had encountered before.

The connection with singers from Liberty continued and was strengthened when David Ivey gave the singing school that opened the Western Massachusetts Sacred Harp Convention and when he, his wife Karen, Rodney, Elene, and a number of singers from Georgia spent Saturday evening at my parents' house. A similar group of people spent the weekend together at Chicago's Midwest Convention the following month, and Karen House formed plans to spend the summer living in Birmingham with Elene and singing every weekend.

On June 12, 2000, Karen House died suddenly as a result of a congenital heart defect. She was thirty-two years old, days away from moving to Birmingham, months away from beginning a PhD program, and she had spent the last afternoon of her life at a Sacred Harp singing. Because her heart condition was not widely known, her death came as an enormous shock to most of the Sacred Harp singing community. Within two days, Rodney Ivey called Kelly to offer space for Karen in the cemetery at Liberty. Karen had lived in Brooklyn, Kelly lived in Rhode Island, their father in Washington, DC, their mother in Massachusetts—the offer made a kind of geographic sense, but more, it made spiritual sense. Kelly later said that one of her first thoughts as she processed her only sibling's death was "I have to get Mom and Dad to the National Convention," which was being held that week in Birmingham; the e-mail message Kelly sent to inform the Sacred Harp community of Karen's death was addressed to

"Karen's beloved family of singers." At the National Convention, both Karen's biological family and that beloved family of singers mourned together as Kelly spoke in her sister's memory, and many singers dedicated songs to Karen.

The next day, Karen's family and friends attended the small singing she would have been attending had she lived, rested briefly at Coy and Marie's house, and then drove to Liberty. The funeral was planned as a small service by the grave Rodney had risen before dawn to dig by hand, but when the little caravan arrived, the churchyard was filled with members of the church and local singers who had come to remember Karen, though few had sung with her more than a bare handful of times.

The planned graveside service was put aside as the church was opened and its benches moved to form Sacred Harp's traditional hollow square, with Karen's family, including her father's male partner, on the front tenor bench. An hour of singing and brief remembrances by some of her closest friends was followed with preaching by Elder Ricky Harcrow, a Primitive Baptist preacher and lifelong Sacred Harp singer whose wife and daughter had shared a hotel room in Chicago with Karen not two months before. After this, the service moved to the graveside for a few last songs, including a tune written by Karen and fitted with words by her friend Tim Eriksen after her death.

This event, emotionally trying as it was and as its memory remains, provides a view of several crucial themes of this manuscript and reinforces my almost immediate sense that Liberty is a central location for understanding Sacred Harp singing in the past ten years, at least. The event itself was a hybrid of a southern funeral and a northern memorial service, with a traditional sermon preached and a graveside component, with the burial accomplished beforehand and with some friends offering remembrances. Karen's family accommodated some aspects of southern tradition in their farewell to a beloved daughter and sister; the people of Liberty gracefully adapted to an unfamiliar style of event being held in their church. The very fact that it happened is also revealing of the depth of the bonds between singers; southern singers are almost universally welcoming of northern visitors—seeing in them not merely fellow singers in the present but the future of a cherished tradition—but the particular emphasis placed on this at Liberty is given a permanent physical form by Karen's grave in the small cemetery behind the church, which is otherwise filled mainly with family members. Most years, Kelly and her mother, Sally, attend the Decoration Day singing at Liberty, reconfirming the bond with the singers there at the same time as they remember Karen. Simultaneously, the event revealed the especially close-knit character of the local community at Liberty, as many of the church members and singers who attended Karen's funeral would not have known it was even taking place without active lines of communication.

This event also had far-reaching implications for Sacred Harp as a whole, though it could not have been predicted at the time. Karen House's funeral was the first time her friend Tim Eriksen sang at Liberty; almost exactly two years later, still never having attended a regular singing at Liberty, he was hired to provide the singing voice of a character in the film *Cold Mountain* and brought the film's director, Anthony Minghella, and sound track producer, T Bone Burnett, to record Sacred Harp singing there. The relationships that began at the 1999 United Convention contributed to the decision to give Karen a place in the cemetery at Liberty, which in turn contributed to the relationships through which the *Cold Mountain* recording was done there.

Sacred Harp singing was a personal topic to choose to write about even before Karen's death, and my grief at the loss of a friend remains a potent symbol of the difficulties and the benefits of such a personal topic. Scribbling down field notes through tears as Kelly and her mother Sally lead a song in Karen's memory and thanked the Liberty congregation for giving Karen a place in their family is a uniquely difficult thing to do. However, my heartfelt involvement at that moment and others provides insight into things that otherwise might have remained half understood, as when, at the 1999 United Convention, I looked at that row of tenor men crying.

That heartfelt involvement hardly stands alone, however. First and foremost, I have conducted extensive ethnographic observation, including two summers spent in the Sand Mountain, Alabama, region (where Liberty Baptist Church is located) and numerous shorter trips to west Georgia, east Alabama, Chicago, and the Twin Cities of Minneapolis-St. Paul. From 1999 to 2003, I attended 111 all-day singings or multiday conventions. Additionally, I have attended local afternoon or evening singings, informal gatherings and convention-sponsored socials following singings, singing schools, and four sessions of a five-day summer camp. Attending singings means not only seeing singers at the actual event, but, often, also staying in their houses, carpooling on multihour drives, and spending evenings in restaurants and hotel rooms, often singing loudly enough to have the managers of those locations complain. I was also present for all of the major events connecting Sacred Harp and *Cold*

Mountain, from the initial sound track recording session to the *Words and Music of "Cold Mountain"* show, the Academy Awards, and three concerts on the Great High Mountain tour.

My fieldwork does not end with attendance at public or formal events; rather, I have come to know (and be known by) my subjects in a much more pervasive way. (My two summers on Sand Mountain were especially fruitful.) Because most singing events happen on weekends, weekdays provided valuable time to become familiar with the daily lives of singers, whom I have visited in their homes and workplaces. In their homes I may sit and visit, or watch the televisions that are always on in the homes of southern singers, but I have also helped prepare many meals, washed dishes, painted walls, and cared for children. Rodney Ivey's daughter Cheyenne has spent more than one night sharing a bed with me, and we have made many trips to Walmart together with her cousin Jessica. I have also been asked to events such as the weddings and funerals of singers—Sacred Harp is very often part of the funeral services of singers—and have seen two singers appear in plays, one as a professional, one in community theater.

Visiting singers at their workplaces has given me more exposure to heavy machinery, septic systems, and the life cycle of the cow than the average sociologist gets: I have ridden on a backhoe and numerous tractors as well as varying sizes of trucks, and Alabama singer Shane Wootten has said, "Laura lays pipe as well as anyone," while the septic tank delivery man and the pumper have been known to ask after me. Stillborn calves must be removed and their mothers cared for; calves and the occasional bull whose fertility is declining get taken to the sale barn; cows that escape from their pasture have to be herded back in; and when a cow collapses in the middle of a pasture, it can mean a rather harrowing backhoe ride down a muddy hill to bury its bloated corpse. More mundanely, I have spent time in numerous offices.

Such activities lend me valuable perspective on the lives of singers and make me ever more part of the community rather than an occasional observer whose presence is cause for changes in behavior and routine. Because of this active engagement in the community and with individuals, some singers have become active informants for my study rather than mere subjects, sharing anecdotes about and analyses of particular singings, answering my more awkward questions, and helping me gain access to relatively aloof or insular singers.

Additionally, exposure to the day-to-day existence of Sacred Harp singers can help make clear the salience of Sacred Harp in their lives. An interview subject answers the questions asked; if those questions center on a specific topic, that topic may become more central in their accounts of daily life. Similarly, Sacred Harp singers will be disposed to talk about Sacred Harp singing in each other's presence. Going to their homes and jobs provides a different view, one in which they may be more likely to talk about different things.

Most Sacred Harp singers do, indeed, have lives that are otherwise very full, with jobs, families, nonsinging friends, churches, and hobbies. But Sacred Harp is also very clearly embedded in their lives, not simply a persona they put on around other singers. Coy and Marie Ivey's home may be the most organized around Sacred Harp, with a bookshelf filled almost completely with videos of singings and copies of *The Sacred Harp* that Coy has worn out, a cross-stitch of the song "Amazing Grace" in shape notes, and a refrigerator on which all the pictures not of family members are of Sacred Harp singers, but such signs are not absent from other people's houses. When the songbook was converted to computer typeset for the 1991 revision, the old printing plates were sold to singers as a fundraiser, and many singers have a plate as a decorative element in their home. Elene Stovall has a verse of a Sacred Harp song taped to the monitor of her computer; Tim Eriksen and Minja Lausevic have a small quilt, made for them by another singer, with a representation of people in a hollow square and a song verse. Many singers have e-mail addresses referring to Sacred Harp—"FasolaMan," "HarpQueen," "LindaSacredHarp"—and singers in several states also have license plates saying "fasola" or some variation thereof. People's children pick up on the centrality of Sacred Harp in their parents' lives: When Luka Eriksen was first beginning to speak, he looked at an illustration of a bear rearing up and raising one paw in a manner resembling a Sacred Harp song leader and said, "Bear sing fasola," while Coy and Marie Ivey's young granddaughters Cheyenne and Jessica use a chalkboard easel to teach make-believe singing schools. Sacred Harp may be only one of several activities or identities in people's lives, but it is clearly not an identity casually donned around other singers and shed in their absence, and the depth of my fieldwork allows me to consider this aspect of their participation in a way that interviews alone or even participant observation that began and ended with the singing events themselves would not do.

I rely mainly on this fieldwork, first because I am most interested in how communities of singers function rather than in what individual singers say about their involvement, and second because Sacred Harp singing is a tradition defined by participation. Without participating—not just singing, but leading songs and bringing food to singings local to me—I would certainly have faced greater difficulty getting singers to agree to be interviewed and to be forthcoming in those interviews. Such difficulties have been pointed to repeatedly as I sought out interviews. A Chicago singer responded to an e-mail I sent out by writing:

Well, I'd be willing to entertain this, in part because the last time anyone from the outside tried to analyze Sacred Harp he got it so wrong that I could hardly believe he had ever been to a singing. If you see any reluctance at this stage in the game, it would mostly be because of what one of your predecessors did. So be aware of that as you conduct interviews.

Despite this abrupt response to my initial e-mail, our correspondence and ensuing interview quickly became very cordial when I was able to list several singings we had both attended; without such credentials, I might have faced a very suspicious interview subject. Similarly, more than one southern singer expressed willingness to be interviewed specifically as a favor to me as a singer familiar to them. My participation therefore enriched the formal semistructured interviews I have done with eleven Alabama singers, four Georgia singers, seven Chicago singers, and seven Twin Cities singers.[45] But even had I been able to obtain identical interview data without participation, I would have lost out on the richness of the informal conversations and e-mail correspondences I have had with dozens of singers. How the community functions when it is gathered together, how singers interact with each other and at what moments particular behavioral norms are invoked or plays for authority are made, cannot be easily learned from interviews, and these are the central foci of this manuscript.

My interest in Sacred Harp singing as a research subject originally stems from my love of the music—because, as Sacred Harp singer Buell Cobb writes,

At a Sacred Harp session when the singing has reached a certain level—when the singers respond wholly to the music—it is almost as if they are only receptacles, vessels for something age-old which lives through them again. As the old songs well up through and around them, the singers submit to the effects of the music with a kind of awe.[46]

Sacred Harp music is at this point an inextricable part of me; to deny that would be false, while not feeling it would, I believe, deprive me of an important understanding of the people I am studying. Sacred Harp singing, to singers, engages with the transcendent if not the formally sacred; many times during interviews when I asked singers to recall the best singing they'd ever been to and try to describe what made it so, they simply began to cry. Minnesota singer Martha Henderson explains, "Words fall so far short—it doesn't really exist as words exist—so when you put it in words it makes it sound really small and kinda boring maybe, like what's so great about that?" Although my words, too, will inevitably fall short of explaining that aspect of Sacred Harp singing, my awareness of it deepens my understanding of the dynamics of the community formed around it.

I have also come to count many singers among my friends. I have, however, chosen as my research areas locations in which I had not spoken at any length with many, if any, local singers before I was actively engaged in research. For almost all of my subjects, then, even or perhaps especially those with whom I have developed friendships, I was engaged in sociological research from the beginning, and I have given copies of my work, on this and other subjects, to anyone who expressed interest. And while Cobb notes of George Pullen Jackson, an early scholar of the tradition, "A few of the older Sacred Harp singers have related Jackson's eventual disappointment that the body of singing folk did not respond more actively to his publications. . . . [P]lainly, these people would rather make music than read about it,"[47] on occasion a singer, likelier to be a lifelong than a new one, will lean over to me at a singing, indicate a particularly bad leader or some other form of inappropriate behavior and say, "Put in your book not to do that."

Such comments aside, a day of singing offers relatively few opportunities to explicitly discuss the tradition or, really, much of anything. The chair may make some welcoming remarks, the chaplain offers prayer, and the memorial committee remembers the deceased and the sick, but individual leaders rarely speak when they stand to lead, and in most places seated singers do not address remarks to the class as a whole. Singers may lean over to their neighbors and comment on a song or leader, but such exchanges are brief. During the hourly breaks and the lunch hour, there are opportunities for more extended conversations, but it is as likely that singers will spend these times speaking briefly to a number of people rather than to a few at length. Eliasoph and Lichterman define "group boundaries" as "put[ting] into practice a group's assumptions about what the group's relationship (imagined and real) to the wider world should be while in the group context,"[48] and the boundaries drawn for public interaction between Sacred Harp singers include a widely shared consensus that a singing, even during the breaks, is not a time to raise issues that may be points of disagreement between singers.

Yet while these disagreements are rarely acknowledged publicly, many singers are aware that they lurk beneath the surface. Because the tradition remains largely structured as it was in the South before northerners began singing, and the worldviews of southern singers are more built in to what is acceptable during a singing, northern singers may be more frequently aware of these disagreements. A Jewish singer, for instance, can hardly fail to notice when she finds herself surrounded by people enthusiastically singing "Yet God hath built His Church thereon, In spite of env'ous Jews."[49] But such moments occur for southern singers, as well, as when northern singers make public statements attributing a nonreligious character to Sacred Harp singing, or when one wore an antiwar button to a southern singing. The informal prohibition of controversial conversation reduces the frequency of such moments and the amount of overt conflict they can provoke; however, they remain a component of the communities and relationships formed.

––––––

In chapters 2 and 3, I introduce the four communities on which this manuscript focuses: Sand Mountain, Alabama (and Liberty specifically); west Georgia and east central Alabama; Chicago, Illinois; and Minneapolis-St. Paul, Minnesota. Each site has a different history and composition of singers, which are the foundations of their community differences. I move from these foundations to how the groups function as Sacred Harp communities specifically, considering structural questions, such as the availability of locations to sing, as well as questions that bridge structure and culture, such as the calendar of singings, and more purely cultural issues, such as who brings what types and amounts of food for the dinner on the grounds, what type of clothes are worn, and the demeanor and behavior of singers and leaders.

Chapter 4 considers how behaviors and organizational forms come out of the beliefs and ideals people bring to Sacred Harp. Five themes—musical genre, religion, authenticity and tradition, authority, and history—structure the preconceptions singers bring to Sacred Harp and how those preconceptions themselves are reshaped through engagement with Sacred Harp practices and communities. It is through this that local communities form in ways reflecting both their immediate cultural contexts and the broader Sacred Harp world.

Chapter 5 takes the local communities discussed in the preceding chapters and examines how they and other singing communities combine to form a nationwide (and even international) Sacred Harp community.

In particular, I focus here on large singings that draw visitors from many areas; at these events, the norms of different areas can come into subtle conflict, with the norms of local singers or of visitors taking precedence at different moments. The necessary reverse side of the question of community norms is the question of individual singers: some are frequent travelers who form the core of a nationwide community by being familiar with the singers and traditions of many areas, while others may be marginal to the broader community yet central to their own local singing groups. Still others are marginal even to their local groups, attending no more than once or twice a year; yet the meaning of marginality is distinctly different for a third-generation, if infrequent, singer from Georgia than it is for an equivalently infrequent singer whose first exposure to Sacred Harp came as an adult in Chicago.

The sixth and final chapter examines the effects of the inclusion of two Sacred Harp songs in the film *Cold Mountain*. The unprecedented attention this brought to Sacred Harp created something of a natural experiment, introducing new pressures and new opportunities to singing communities. In the process, some existing but largely hidden tensions were exacerbated as small groups of singers were chosen to appear at events, such as the Academy Awards, excluding others, but the resiliency of Sacred Harp practices and communities was also demonstrated as these tensions quickly subsided back to their original invisible states. More lastingly, the ability of singers to mobilize publicity for the tradition was expanded, and routes into singing were created or expanded.

TWO

The South: Family
and Community

In her rich ethnographic study of amateur music-making in Milton Keynes, England, in the 1980s, Ruth Finnegan writes of participation in amateur music as happening along a series of pathways. These pathways are simultaneously ways *into* particular practices, providing the means by which one person takes up rock and another takes up Sacred Harp, and the ways those practices are *carried out*—the social practices associated with a musical form, the geography that gets defined as familiar and appropriate, and the cycle of the musical calendar. "These pathways of music-making are not 'natural' ones that cut their own way through the bush," Finnegan writes, "but were opened up and kept trodden by those who worked them."[1]

Perhaps the most obvious approach to understanding a community of singers is examining how and along what routes these pathways are "kept trodden" by singers. What is the daily practice that brings people back time and again? What cultural frameworks do they bring to Sacred Harp that inform their participation in the tradition? Following Stinchcombe,[2] if we know how the group emerged, we may better understand how the form in which it emerged continues to shape its organizational structure today.

But it is first important to uncover how individual singers in each area found entries to their Sacred Harp paths. Whether a person found Sacred Harp through active family practice or distant family history, through an institution or product of folk music revivals, through a church or a historical society event; whether they came to it as a baby, a teenager, or an adult; whether they entered a singing group composed of people who had come along a similar path or felt alone in their approach; whether the singing in their area is done by a relatively cohesive community or by a loose association of people—these have far-reaching implications for their continuing the practice of Sacred Harp, for the pathways they take will in turn open up or keep trodden.

Each Sacred Harp singing community has its own history, its own place in a local population, and its own place in the broader Sacred Harp community. By 2004, all-day singings or conventions were held in thirty-one states and an even greater number of metropolitan areas and rural locations. Of the four communities of singers that constitute the focus of this book, two, Chicago and Minneapolis, represent major sites of northern Sacred Harp practice, while two others, west Georgia, in particular Holly Springs, and Sand Mountain, here represented by Liberty, stand as exemplars of the tradition's southern core. For many years, and to many singers, both northern and southern, Holly Springs represented the iconic center of Sacred Harp tradition, but it now struggles to maintain itself as a viable community, even as Sand Mountain, Alabama, a rural area with a number of interconnected sites, flourishes. Of these, I focus on the singings held at Liberty Baptist Church, which now plays a central and generative role in the region.

All of these communities assert, and predicate themselves on, the idea of a singular tradition, an ideal of authenticity that may be called upon to justify particular local practices, organizational structures, and personal investments.[3] That ideal, combined with the material reality that many singers attend singings outside their home region, maintains a coherence and unity to Sacred Harp. At the same time, my case studies demonstrate that there is no such thing as one Sacred Harp tradition, or even one southern Sacred Harp tradition, and that each set of local traditions is a product of context, history, and individual personalities as well as of the existence of more than 150 years of history and the ever-changing traditions surrounding it.

Although I chose four locations as my research sites, the reality of this study is more complicated. While my most systematic participant observation and all of my interviewing has been done in these locations, I have attended many singings in other places and do draw on that experience.[4] Such experience has been particularly invaluable in considering the difficulties of holding a singing convention in the North, which I might have been less attuned to had I not helped to organize the first several years of the convention in Western Massachusetts.[5] Additionally, each location has complexities and variation such that even talking about singing in Chicago or on Sand Mountain as a unitary phenomenon is problematic; I will try to unveil those variations when possible and appropriate but will at other times make broader generalizations about the areas.

Finally, my research process has produced certain tilts. Although I initially planned to address each of the four locations equally, perhaps it was inevitable, given that the 1999 United Convention at Liberty Church was such a central moment in shaping this project, that Sand Mountain, and Liberty specifically (for there are a few distinct sets of singers on Sand Mountain), would remain central. There are many reasons this focus emerged, which will become clear as I progress. The fact that the recording for the *Cold Mountain* sound track was done at Liberty provides a nice narrative consistency, but it is not coincidence that I chose Liberty for my manuscript and Tim Eriksen chose it for *Cold Mountain*—those choices were made for many of the same reasons.

———

In what follows, I introduce these communities of singers and the pathways along which they formed, paired with a detailed description of a weekend of singing in each site, all four of which play host to more than one all-day singing annually and to shorter, more frequent singings held just for local singers. This chapter focuses on two southern singings; the next on two northern singings.

The most obvious comparison is between South and North. In the South, in many families singing is a tradition of many generations, and people learned singing somewhat as they learned language, because it was all around them and an integral part of growing up. Even those who do not sing are likely to be aware of Sacred Harp and to regard it as a recognized part of the community. In the North, people were introduced to singing as adults, singing was an active choice and choosing to sing Sacred Harp makes singers different from, rather than similar to, most of the people they know. In the South, numerous churches have longstanding connections to Sacred Harp and are available whenever a singing is to be held; in the North, arranging (and paying for) space poses difficulties. In the South, a culture of massive cooking is established, and "dinner on the grounds" is a recognized part of church activities outside of Sacred

Harp; in the North, most singers have no experience with such practices. In the South, religion, and indeed particular forms of Christianity, is taken for granted, and the religious character of Sacred Harp is assumed. Among northern singers, religion is less salient, less agreed upon, and has an unclear and contested relation to Sacred Harp music. In both North and South, it is taken for granted that authentic Sacred Harp music comes from the South and that those from the South speak with authority on the tradition.

If I simply contrasted "the South" with "the North," there would be a tendency to romanticize and naturalize southern singings. Comparing Sand Mountain and west Georgia helps show the variation within the South as well as the common elements. In both locations there are family histories of Sacred Harp and lifelong singers, but at Liberty younger singers have been drawn in, while in west Georgia there are no replacements. In both locations, churches are available for singings, although at Liberty the area churches are still in active use and attendance, while in west Georgia the churches that traditionally held singings have fallen into disuse. In both locations active efforts have been made to maintain and indeed to spread Sacred Harp music, but initially Liberty did so primarily in its own immediate area, whereas west Georgia put its main outreach effort into spreading singing nationally.

West Georgia was remarkably successful in its national campaign, and successful as well in insisting that if Sacred Harp was to be sung, the entire tradition should be replicated—participation not performance, democratic turn-taking in song leading, dinner on the grounds, and singing the shapes before the words. In many cases, the revival of a folk practice involves "the reinvention of tradition."[6] In this case, "the folk" were still actively singing the music and enforced the need to preserve the tradition in its entirety. The irony is that in the process of doing so, west Georgia may have sacrificed its own singings, putting its effort into national outreach instead of local continuity.

Sand Mountain

Because of its centrality to my work, it is appropriate to begin the detailed discussion of sites with Sand Mountain. Sand Mountain is a large plateau in the northeast corner of Alabama, which runs approximately eighty miles southwest from the northwest corner of Georgia, just below Chattanooga, Tennessee. For many miles it runs parallel to the more famous Lookout Mountain, separated by a valley. In fact, the two mountains are

both part of the much larger Cumberland Plateau. The area was inhab-
ited by the Cherokee until their forced departure in 1838 on the Trail of
Tears; DeKalb County seat Fort Payne was named after a fort established
in the cause of Cherokee removal. The area was then open for a growing
white population, though the valley was settled first and the mountain
remained relatively sparsely populated into the twentieth century, giving it a reputation as one of Alabama's more rural and remote areas. This
reputation was solidified in recent years by Dennis Covington's 1995
book, *Salvation on Sand Mountain*, which takes as its starting point the
attempted murder trial of a snake-handling preacher in the area and goes
on to consider snake-handling congregations themselves.[7]

Since the mountain is divided between three or four counties, each of
which covers neighboring areas as well, census data for Sand Mountain
alone and as a whole is not available, but data for the three counties—
DeKalb, Jackson, and Marshall—that comprise much of the mountain,
provide some picture of the people living there. Perhaps most strikingly,
the populations of all three counties are over 90 percent white. Moreover,
all three counties show much lower levels of education than the United
States as a whole or the entire state of Alabama, with both high school
diploma and BA rates more than ten percentage points under the US
averages. Henagar and Ider, where many singers live, are both more than
96 percent white and share the relatively low rates of completion of high
school and college of the counties as a whole.[8]

Sand Mountain does have a largely rural character, but it is in fact dot-
ted by small towns. Running north and south along Alabama Highway
75, they feed into each other "city limits on city limits," as Rod Ivey says.
Most of the towns only seem like *towns* at a single crossroads, where there
will be one or two gas stations, a beauty salon, some sort of farm-related
business, and perhaps a grocery or family restaurant—tellingly, Henagar's
lone traffic light was the only cue I had that it was a town the first time
I rode through.

Away from the main state highways, the roads are about as likely to
be dirt as paved. Here there are virtually no commercial, nonfarm estab-
lishments, but numerous small churches can be found, most of them
independent rather than members of the major national denominations, whose churches tend to be located nearer the center of town.[9] It
is in these churches—Liberty, Antioch, Chestnut Grove, Zion Hill, Pine
Grove—that Sacred Harp music flourishes.

On the main roads between the crossroads town centers, and on side
roads, the way is lined by occasional houses or trailers, chicken farms, crop
fields, and beef cattle grazing in rolling, tree-lined pastures. Potatoes were

a common crop into the 1980s, but today there are few potato farmers left in the area. Perhaps the most common crop is hay for the cattle; through much of the year, large round hay bales dot the landscape. Cows are kept for as long as they remain fertile; calves graze for several months before being sold on to feedlots to be fattened on corn and pharmaceuticals.[10]

In contrast with the cattle grazing freely, chicken farms are highly modernized factory settings. Chicks are hatched in hatcheries owned by large corporations, such as Tyson and Perdue, then transported by made-over school buses to chicken houses on locally owned farms. The chicks arrive in large, flat crates and are dumped into the stiflingly hot, humid chicken houses, where they spend the next six weeks constantly serviced by automatic feeders and waterers. Every day, those that don't survive are cleared away, and periodically an employee of the contracting corporation arrives to test one chicken's fat levels. Although when the chicks arrive, the newly cleaned houses smell overpoweringly of ammonia, that smell is quickly replaced by the stench of chicken "litter," which hangs in an almost-tangible haze over surrounding areas on humid summer days. A few large hog farms also cover their immediate surroundings in a heavy odor.

It is somewhat tempting to understand Sand Mountain as a relic of a way of life that has disappeared for most of the rest of the country. The education levels are reminiscent more of the 1960s than of today, though there is a community college in Rainsville; the prevalence of manufacturing and agricultural employment and the rarity of service work is striking given the American economy's general shift away from those industries to service and technology industries; the boundedness and homogeneity of the overwhelmingly white, Protestant community is closer to stereotypes of small-town life in the 1950s than today; and the importance and size of the social networks I have observed among singers is greater than it is believed to be in much of the rest of the country today.[11]

Despite these reasons to see Sand Mountain as a throwback to an earlier time, it is important to remember that the area exists fully in the present in many ways. Residents of Sand Mountain have and freely use cable television, e-mail, and cell phones. Though more likely to work in manufacturing and less likely to work in communications or personal services than people in other areas of the country, they are definitely participants in and affected by the national economy. Local chicken farmers are contracted to large corporations; potato crops have become less important as the national potato chip companies stopped purchasing much from the area. Drug problems over the past couple of decades, and law enforcement responses to them, have followed national trends. And though the area remains extremely white, and though there is certainly substantial racism, it too has felt the impact of the civil rights movement. Thus, though there are certainly ways in which Sand Mountain echoes an earlier time, this view must be complicated by an understanding of the ways it is fully in the present.[12]

Sacred Harp singers in the area are for the most part well-established, influential, middle-class people—far removed from Covington's snake handlers or even from Charismatic and Pentecostal church members, who are, and are understood by singers as, of lower socioeconomic and cultural status. Most are property owners, several owning in the hundreds of acres, and while a few live in trailers, at least as many live in lavish, newly constructed houses. More common are modest, neatly kept ranch-style houses on multiacre lots. At the same time, they are well-established middle-class people in a context with a class structure that is compressed relative to that in most urban areas, and they generally fall into the working class or lower middle class occupationally.

Some singers, like brothers Shane and Wayne Wootten, farm as a primary income source (though Shane added working in insurance to his six chicken houses during my research period). Others, like Rodney Ivey, do some farming as a sideline to other work—in Rod's case, as a self-employed backhoe and bulldozer operator—or, like Rod's father, Coy, as a form of partial retirement. Some own small businesses: Coy Ivey was a self-employed well driller for years and then owned a restaurant; Terry, Levon, and Dewayne Wootten own a lawnmower and feed store in addition to having chicken houses. Women are likely to either stay at home or work at office jobs: Susan Harcrow is an insurance company office representative and Donna Wootten is a receptionist, while Teresa Bethune is an elementary school teacher.

Singers are also well represented in local elected offices: Terry Wootten has been on the county school board, Wayne Wootten has been on the Henagar City Council, and Ricky Harcrow is a county commissioner. Singers in this area are almost universally Republicans, some of them from families that were Republicans prior to the New Deal, others more recent converts.

Sand Mountain is the most generationally integrated of my four sites. Most singings there are attended by a number of young children and teenagers brought by their parents, and adults attending of their own free will span people in their midtwenties and early thirties, like Joel and Sarah Jenkins or Shane and Donna Wootten, and many from their forties up to some in their eighties. The presence of elderly people is common in the

South, a product of a tradition stretching back generations in particular churches and towns, but the presence of younger adults—even those in their forties—is not universal, and the population of younger singers on Sand Mountain rivals that in even some northern communities that are oriented to colleges and universities.

Given the racial composition of the area, singers do not define themselves primarily in opposition to a racial other, for the other does not enter their lives enough to require such definition. It is precisely lower-class whites—Covington's snake handlers, in the time since that book was released—against whom they define themselves, when their own identities come into question.[13] Susan Harcrow, for instance, makes a point of saying, "We're not all rednecks, sitting on the front porch dipping snuff, your typical southerner as it's portrayed in books and movies. That is not typical of people in this area." While she is correct that area Sacred Harp singers do not conform to this stereotype, it is also true that they engage in active boundary work against it. The wife of a local singer has on occasion described someone to me as "low class" or "white trash," then self-consciously amended it by saying that maybe she herself is white trash. The initial description appears to be a way she habitually makes social distinctions, and her subsequent retreat suggests that she feels it to be a harsh designation, an unkindness that she is uncomfortable with, but also that she feels some class anxiety. This anxiety is perhaps exaggerated in the presence of northern singers, some of whom she has identified as having condescended to her in the past.[14]

Many singers—especially the men—engage in some conversational code-switching, a fact demonstrated on one occasion when a classmate from Princeton spent a few days on Sand Mountain with me. In direct conversation, she could understand Coy and Rodney Ivey's accents reasonably well, but upon hearing Rod talking to some local friends he ran into, she leaned over to me and said, "Can you understand what they're saying? Because you could tell me it was German and I'd believe you."[15] Apart from conversational changes made in talking to northern singers, singings are treated as a place to wear their best clothes and drive their nicer vehicles, in part because this is considered appropriate for church, but also partially related to boundary maintenance, which is also expressed via a more contained demeanor.

At both singings and church, particularly emotional displays by attendees may be greeted with polite silence and private disapproval, for reasons stemming both from recent Sacred Harp culture and from longer-standing denominational styles. A few singers in the area are Primitive

Baptists, a relatively strict predestinarian denomination; more are Independent Baptists, defined by their very lack of denominational structure but affiliated into associations composed of a handful of churches. These Independent Baptists do altar calls and other practices resulting from a belief in conversion experiences but are, as a result of historical and geographical proximity to Primitive Baptists, less conversion oriented than Southern Baptists or most evangelical denominations. Preachers are drawn from and trained within the community and do not go to seminary. Sermons are not supposed to be prepared in advance but should be inspired directly by God at the moment they are delivered. Nor are preachers salaried—they may receive love offerings on some occasions and fill a social and religious role beyond Sunday sermons, but for most being a preacher is more of a status or place in the community than it is an occupation.[16]

Independent Baptist and Primitive Baptist churches alike, if to varying degrees, remain tied to the older practices while being gradually influenced by the spread of charismatic and even evangelical cultures. The practice of raising one's hands into the air during prayer or song, common in charismatic churches, for instance, is frowned upon by some members of Liberty (albeit politely), and excessive proselytizing is considered inappropriate, if not nearly as much as it would at a predestinarian church. In July 2002, at a revival service at Liberty, a young woman called on everyone in the congregation who had been saved to stand during the singing of a song, leaving me the only seated person in the church (some children who hadn't been listening to what she said stood when they saw everyone else standing). Rod Ivey subsequently told me that Liberty's preacher had wondered if he should speak to me personally to be sure I wasn't upset; after saying he'd talk to me, Rod reported invoking a class as well as a denominational distinction, saying that such things were characteristic of Pentecostal services such as Church of God, but not of Liberty. My conspicuously seated presence without question heightened or produced the discomfort, but it did so in part by pointing to an ongoing cultural shift away from the older practices of independent churches in the area.

These shifts are constantly ongoing, and during the course of my fieldwork, the churches on Sand Mountain saw significant change. Since 2000, Antioch and Shady Grove have held Bible studies, but Liberty still eschews Bible study.[17] As of the end of my research period, none of these churches had Sunday schools, but that would be a logical extension of the move toward Bible study. Shady Grove, which is probably the most religiously conservative and most charismatic-leaning church attended by singers in the area, began holding services every Sunday during my research period, but as late as the summer of 2002, one of its members noted that since each weekend they held services involved spending Saturday evening and all day Sunday in church, it was about all the church he could stand. Other churches hold services one or two weekends a month; while this may be a relic of the days of circuit-riding preachers, today it allows people to attend more than one church, whether they are a member of one and visit at another or are not formally a member of any church, membership being a weighty process that some people never go through despite a lifetime of fairly regular attendance at a given church. Most churches hold a weeklong revival each summer, again in staggered weeks so that people can attend revivals at more than one church.

Other special events include Decoration Days at each church, in which the graves in the cemetery behind the church are topped with flower arrangements by family members, and a reunion-style gathering is held. Liberty holds a singing on Decoration Day, which is attended by nonsinging family and church members and, increasingly, by nonlocal singers. Rather than holding the traditional Sacred Harp memorial lesson before lunch, the singers gather in the cemetery and sing a few songs there while the nonsinging locals look on; during breaks and lunch, all socialize together.

Though there are moments of minor tension over what is appropriate, for the most part, singers in the area not only form a community as singers but also participate in several overlapping communities—many are kin to each other, attend the same churches, share local town concerns, share political affiliations, or have professional involvement of some kind. This is central to the differences between the Sand Mountain singing community and the others I examined.

For local singers, then, Sacred Harp fits relatively neatly into church and kinship structures; indeed, some degree of involvement with Sacred Harp is incorporated into those. Dedicated church-goers may go to the services of more than one church to fill every Sunday in the month, but Sacred Harp singers can use the Sunday services that are not held at their church to attend singings. The most dedicated singers reverse this, attending singings when possible and church when there is no convenient singing, and while I have heard church-oriented people say that they considered church most important, I have never heard condemnation of someone for choosing Sacred Harp over church. In fact, while Liberty's three annual singings are all scheduled for weekends on which services are not normally held, when they host the United Convention (which travels between locations), they have to cancel or reschedule their usual second Sunday of the month service. When the United is held at another nearby church, Liberty sometimes shortens the Sunday service or shifts part of it to Saturday evening so that people can attend church Sunday and still get to the singing without having missed too much.

Some years Easter and relatively large singings coincide, and attendance at the singing does not suffer noticeably; when the singing at Pine Grove, on neighboring Lookout Mountain, coincided with Easter in 2003, chairman Bud Oliver acknowledged the significance of the day, while defending the choice of singing over church, by saying, "I don't know any better that we could have done than to meet and sing His praises." Other people in the area might make a different choice in attending church, but few would directly argue Bud's claim.

The central fact, then, of people's choices regarding church versus singing is that both choices are supported by the structure of observance and by a reasonably broad local consensus. It is important to be clear, though, that choosing singing over church is a *choice*, not a natural result of living in the area or even of being raised in a singing family in the area. For every active Sacred Harp singer on Sand Mountain, there are probably two people who were exposed to Sacred Harp in their childhoods but do not participate in the tradition beyond one or two annual singings of particular importance to their family. Some do not like to sing, some do not like Sacred Harp specifically, some prefer church, some are too hung over on weekend mornings to be around loud noises, and some have family commitments. Sacred Harp is a more available option than it is in Chicago or Minneapolis-St. Paul, but it is not a default position. Rather, it is a pathway that is open and lies close beside other paths taken by kin and friends, but it must be chosen. Similarly, it is tempting to understand the singing community on Sand Mountain as a natural expression or outgrowth of kinship, shared church membership, or geographic proximity, but it too is chosen, not automatic. A look at the annual Decoration Day singing at Liberty exemplifies this point.

Liberty's Decoration Day is one of the singings attended by many people whose families have Sacred Harp singing histories but who are not themselves regular singers. It is publicly listed as beginning at ten o'clock in the morning, but for the last several years, it has started earlier, around nine thirty, as soon as enough singers have arrived. At ten past nine on June 5, 2005, nearly a dozen cars were already parked outside the church, and the temperature was just hitting 80 degrees, with a haze beginning to lift. A bucket filled with a couple inches of brown water and sitting on a mat of paper towels beneath one of the air-conditioning vents was an ominous sign given the early heat.

The stones in the cemetery behind the church were covered in bright silk floral arrangements, and many had natural flower arrangements standing in front of them. Rod Ivey was standing by Karen House's bright-pink-topped grave with LaRue Allen, a singer from a part of Alabama several hours south. They were discussing the tradition of Decoration Days, which are common throughout north Alabama but not held in the southern part of the state. Most churches in the Sand Mountain area seem to hold a Decoration Day, which serves to remember the dead and as a gathering for church and family members, but Liberty is (as far as I know) the only one to hold a Sacred Harp singing as part of the event.

The day combines regular singing and a family event, and the signs of this combination were evident from before the singing began. Bill and Reba Windom's large van pulled up holding not only Bill and Reba but their four grandchildren, and Reba's elderly uncle hurried over to meet the grandchildren for the first time in years, asking to be reminded how long ago he had last seen them.

The singing started shortly after nine thirty, with at least two rows of singers in each section but few nonsingers. David Ivey, as chair, opened with "Bound for Canaan," page 82 on the top, then asked for prayer from Joel Jenkins, a man in his early thirties who—though he had known singers all his life—did not start singing until shortly before he married a lifelong singer in 2002. Rod Ivey, as vice-chair, followed, and then his and David's aunt Norma Green, who was always the secretary of singings at Liberty. Shane Wootten, a second cousin who generally shared the vice-chairship with Rod, arrived late and before he got up to lead apologized for the air-conditioning being broken, his lateness a result of attempts to fix it.

After the officers led, Jackie Tanner (another second cousin) took over as the arranging committee. In its most highly developed form, arranging, as the practice of ordering and calling song leaders is called, reveals the priorities of a community in identifying particularly valued participants by having them lead at desirable or high-status times of day. (The choice of an inexperienced arranger can be a source of frustration to experienced singers in a community and can reveal that expertise in Sacred Harp practices is not widespread through the community.) Jackie is an experienced arranger with close ties to the family and church community of Liberty and knows not only all of the regular singers but also those people who only sing at Decoration Day. Given that this particular singing draws on these family and church communities as well as on Sacred Harp singers, that depth of knowledge is necessary so that everyone who wants to lead has a chance and does so at the time most beneficial to the singing.

The singing was full and vibrant from the beginning. When nineteen-year-old Aaron Wootten led "Consecration" in the first hour, a series of subtle signals were exchanged between leader and singers, and the class took the slow, intense repeating end section—"Serve with a single heart and eye, and to Thy glory live or die"—an extra time. Though Aaron ultimately signaled this repeat in his role as leader, many of the singers were ready for him to do so both because the quality of the singing called for it and because of the signals that had been passed around the room. Those signals, consisting mostly of eye contact and slight nods, would almost certainly have been invisible to an outsider. Similar signals might be used to ask for a cough drop or bottle of peppermint oil (which singers use to prolong their vocal stamina) from a friend across the square, or to establish that some adult knows where a young child is. This requires deep familiarity—a sense of when to look over to someone so that they can catch your eye, knowing the range of requests they might make, interpreting gestures, reading lips, remembering a shared joke. At Liberty, this familiarity exists between many people around the square, so several silent "conversations" might be going on at once. Yet while this silent communication produces intimacy, it can also produce a sense of exclusion for those sensitive enough to observe it but not be included in it.

One of the distinguishing features of the Decoration Day singing, unique as far as I have been able to determine, is that instead of having a memorial committee read lists of deceased and ill singers and speak in their memory, the memorial is held outside the church, in the cemetery. Nobody speaks as part of this and no lists are read. A few songs are sung, not only from *The Sacred Harp* but also from a small booklet of other shape-note songs compiled by the church. Unusually for a Sacred Harp singing, this is done for an audience composed of nonsingers who are attending Decoration Day to remember their dead and spend time with family and friends.

In 2005, this memorial took place under a hot sun, the morning haze having burned away. "Jackie, I hope you're not getting too hot in that suit," David teased as the strength of the sun began to sink in. "Part of it's fixing to leave," Jackie responded of his dark suit jacket.

With the singers standing in a rough horseshoe, unreliably divided into parts, a song from the 1991 revision of *The Sacred Harp* was followed by three from the 1992 (Cooper) edition, and the lesson closed with the song most commonly known as "Amazing Grace," though called "New

Britain" in *The Sacred Harp*. David then called for a relatively long break to allow for visiting between singers and others, and the cemetery filled with clusters of talking people. These included a large number of young people, even by the relatively young standards of Liberty singers. Many of the teenage girls and young women were wearing dancing dresses—bright colors, spaghetti straps and halters, and fluttery, uneven hemlines—and high-heeled sandals. More than a dozen children ran around the grounds.

During the hour of singing leading up to lunch, the church grew increasingly hot; cardboard fans were handed out and the room blossomed with their waving. Although some children remained outside the church (as did some adult singers who stayed to visit with family), many were inside, even on the front rows of sections. As is often done at Liberty, Jackie called a string of children to lead during this hour, beginning with another cousin, a small boy in a wheelchair whose devotion to Sacred Harp has become legendary among singers there. Rod Ivey kneeled next to him and they led together while his father took pictures from every available angle and Bill Windom, who videotapes every singing he attends, slipped into Rod's seat to film up close. When they finished, there was an unusual bit of applause. None of the other children drew applause, but their songs were given careful attention and the only response when one's hand was moving opposite the beat of the song was that the front row tenors began beating time with particularly defined gestures, both so other singers would be able to follow and to provide the hapless leader with a hint. By contrast, twelve-year-old Scott Ivey led "Sweet Union," a camp-meeting song that, at Liberty, has an oral tradition of the repeating section of the song speeding up the second time through, and Shane Wootten and Rod Ivey helped him drive the speed up through an extra repeat, as the singing intensified and a smile spread around the room. As the last child finished leading and an adult was called up, Shane Wootten said, "We sure are proud of all these young people. They did a good job."

By this point in the day, the church was nearly full, at least the first four rows of the center tenor section were singing, and four video cameras were filming from the back of the room. Bill Windom and Nate Green typically do this, but neither of the other two cameras was operated by a regular singer, again marking Decoration Day's blend of regular singing and family occasion. This singing has grown over the last several years, along with the growing strength of singing at Liberty, especially since the *Cold Mountain* recordings. Yet the only public reference to *Cold Mountain* came when one leader chose "Idumea," one of the songs included on that sound track, and the next leader called the other, "I'm Going Home."

Hearing the songs called, Rod said "back-to-back" loudly enough to be audible to the first rows of singers but probably not enough to carry back to the nonsingers several rows behind him.

When lunch was called, singers went out to join the nonsingers who were already setting out the food. The concrete table was filled before all the food was laid out, so two of the folding tables intended for eating were brought over to hold desserts. Another separate table held drinks. Rod Ivey and Eloise Wootten estimated that 350 people ate lunch, and unusually, the food was almost entirely eaten.[18] There were dozens of deviled eggs, fried chicken, barbecue, ham, multiple bowls of different versions of potato salad, coleslaw, creamed corn, green beans, okra, and baked beans; towering layer cakes, cobblers, pies, and every kind of gooey member of the trifle family; fifteen two-liter bottles of soda and several gallons each of ice tea and water; and throughout the lunch hour, the socializing continued.

This potluck dinner on the grounds, served at almost any all-day Sacred Harp singing—albeit with differences of organization and cuisine—is another occasion for bonding and another occasion for difference. For local singers, fixing and bringing food is an important act of hospitality; as Courtney Bender observes, to many people and in many ways, "food is love."[19] Not only is cooking for others an act of love, though. Eating together has resonance—people eat with their families and their communities of worship, often in honor and celebration of those bonds. As Daniel Sack writes in *White Bread Protestants*, his history of American Protestantism and food,

Church food is far more than a menu and a place. It is community. For many Americans, it's the closest thing we get to a communal experience any more. At its best, a church meal is a mixture of cuisines and qualities, served inelegantly alongside a virtual stranger—and all for free. It is far more than a meal; it is fellowship.[20]

The meals that singers bring and share, then, are not a trivial matter. Even the most casual onlooker at the lunch this Decoration Day would be impressed by the amount of work involved in producing the quantity (never mind the quality) of food laid out.[21] Singers and their families cook for days, with even nonsinging relatives often bringing multiple dishes; running out of food would be a disgrace for the singing as a whole and its hosts.

Food is also clearly an expression of love in the efforts of cooks to steer visitors to the dishes they are most proud of. There is pride of authorship involved, of course, but the question "have you tried my cake" also becomes an entry to conversation with a first-time visitor, an opportunity for the cook to act as host and say, indirectly, "I know you're here from far away; I notice you and I welcome you and I hope you feel well treated and want to come back."

Similarly, the differences between them speak not only to local culinary cultures—though they certainly do speak to that—but also to the kind of hospitality singers understand themselves to be offering and the fellowship they understand themselves to be entering into. Dinner on the grounds also becomes a point on which the authenticity (or commitment to authenticity) of a given singing is judged, with southern singings and the regional cuisines they offer standing, often very explicitly, as the standard to be met. The only way this Decoration Day meal was different from the ideal typical southern singing dinner on the grounds was in the relative lack of leftovers.

The singing resumed at one o'clock, with singers returning from lunch a little less promptly than usual so that the first song or two were slightly ragged, but the music was quickly back to full force. The heat and humidity were intense, and when the two great-grandnieces of the woman next to me came to sit on her lap, she began sweating so intensely that beads of sweat flew off her and landed on me as she fanned herself vigorously. She continued singing even as she juggled the two little girls, fanned herself, and sweated.

At one thirty, Coy Ivey and the Ivey first cousins were called to lead in one of the central traditions of the Decoration Day singing. All of the first cousins of Coy's generation who were at the singing filed into the square, with the nonsingers clustering at the back and the singers standing up front. The only living member of the previous generation in that family, "Aunt Bob," was wheeled into the square with them in her chair. Coy's voice was breaking as he spoke briefly about the tradition of the first cousins leading together, and Loyd Ivey asked the singers to remember a neighbor of the church who was ill. Everyone in the church who was kin to the Iveys was asked to stand, and many people did. The cousins sang three songs, none from the 1991 *Sacred Harp*, before regular singing resumed.

At two o'clock, Jackie Tanner announced that there were six or seven remaining leaders and asked David if he should continue calling leaders or if a break should be taken before finishing. Though Rod wanted a break, the general sentiment seemed to be that it was better to keep singing. The day ended with prayer and with thanks from David to everyone who attended, but without the formal resolutions of thanks delivered at some conventions.

West Georgia

I use west Georgia as a loose designation for an area that actually extends into east Alabama, all in the central part of the two states' north-south axis. Carroll County is at the western edge of the metro Atlanta area, and its population is clearly affected by proximity to Atlanta, while Haralson County, Georgia, and Cleburne County, Alabama, are demographically quite similar to Sand Mountain, with singers living in towns like Bremen, Georgia, and Oxford, Alabama, where the population is more than 87 percent white. In contrast to the more than 90 percent white populations of these five rural counties, Carroll County's population is only 80.5 percent white. Similarly, its education attainment rates are below those of the rural counties. Carroll County also has high residential mobility, while the rural counties have very low residential mobility.

The county seat of Carrollton has a population of only around 20,000 but is clearly a retail and entertainment center for the area, with many restaurants—including not just chain and barbecue restaurants or the (quite good) Mexican food that is common through much of the South, but Chinese and Japanese restaurants and, most strikingly, an upscale creative American bistro[22]—movie theaters, and stores, as well as being home to a state university. Outside of Carrollton, the area remains more rural; attending a Sacred Harp singing there is not unlikely to involve dirt roads and small crossroads towns similar to those on Sand Mountain, although greater proximity to a large city does produce subtle differences, and actual farmland is less common. A number of towns in the area also have old downtown districts that have been largely abandoned for Walmarts and strip malls; most towns on Sand Mountain have not had enough population for long enough to exhibit this pattern. Near these old town centers, there are also similarly aged neighborhoods of single-family houses on small lots, close enough together to call for sidewalks. Several towns even have neighborhoods of well-preserved Victorian homes of the sort found in so many New England towns.

Sacred Harp singing has a long history in this area, and its singers are perhaps most dedicated to a notion of the tradition defined entirely by the Denson revision of the songbook.[23] In fact, during the initial flush of Sacred Harp singing in the North during the 1980s, west Georgia was the iconic southern singing area, and its image among singers—its own as well as those elsewhere—continues to a large extent to be defined by a strong narrative about its place in the history of Sacred Harp singing, even as the actual practice of singing there declines due to an aging population of singers not being fully replaced.

The aging of the singers in west Georgia is such that almost all of them are retired. During their working lives, their occupations included working in the area's textile industry, teaching in grade school and high school, and farming. In recent years, some have been able to develop their former farmland into profitable ventures. Like Sand Mountain singers, they were and to some extent remain influential people in their communities; for instance, Lonnie Rogers was the mayor of Ephesus, Georgia, for years and was succeeded in that role by his son (who does not sing regularly), while Hugh McGraw is a high-degree Freemason. In the increasing exurban sprawl of the area, though, these forms of community influence are declining, and with the aging of area singers, new forms of influence are not being developed. Several of the most active singers have developed Alzheimer's disease, and death is taking a steady toll on the Sacred Harp singing community there.

West Georgia singers are drawn from denominations similar to those of Sand Mountain singers, but their small churches have suffered greater declines in membership and several of the churches in which they sing no longer have any members at all.[24] Most singers in the area are now members at more standard denominational churches, though a few attend services at Holly Springs despite not being members. This move away from the churches that sustained Sacred Harp for generations isolates Sacred Harp as a tradition separate from other parts of life, so that attending a singing at one of these churches may have a lifelong history and carry a sense of going home for existing singers, for their children and grandchildren Sacred Harp is a thing apart from regular religious observance and the churches in which it is carried out. For these children and grandchildren, gospel and contemporary Christian music are more commonly associated with worship, and Sacred Harp may seem unfashionably outdated.

West Georgia is significantly the home of Hugh McGraw, executive secretary of the Sacred Harp Publishing Company from 1959 to 2001 and the man rightly credited with shaping the practice of Sacred Harp among new singers outside the South. Since 1976, when he founded the New England Convention by co-opting a planned concert by the Word of Mouth Chorus, a Vermont performing group that included some Sacred

Harp songs in their repertoire, and turning the concert into a convention, McGraw has relentlessly worked to push new singers to follow the traditions of Sacred Harp. As Chicago singer Ted Johnson relates in folklorist John Bealle's *Public Worship, Private Faith: Sacred Harp and American Folksong*, when the first Illinois convention was being planned, for instance, "Hugh McGraw said, 'You *do* sing the notes?' And we said, on the phone, 'Why no, we don't.' And there was this silence, and he said, 'Well, you'll learn.'"[25] Singing the solfège associated with the shaped noteheads was a central part of Sacred Harp practice, and one McGraw and other southerners pushed and cajoled new northern singers into.

This process was repeated throughout the initial growth of singing outside the South: New singers who contacted Hugh McGraw found themselves amiably but implacably pushed to organize singing around participation rather than performance, to sing the notes, and to engage with the southern tradition directly. From the very first New England Convention, busloads of southern singers routinely traveled to northern conventions, stopping only with the 2003 death of Ruth Brown, a retired schoolteacher who had organized most of the bus trips. In this way, even new singers who did not travel south had some contact with representatives of the southern tradition.

At the time the push to organize new conventions outside the South began, singing in west Georgia was particularly strong. Sand Mountain singer Susan Harcrow says, "Back in the early 1980s, Holly Springs was *the* singing to go to. It was the biggest and the best." But at the same time that Hugh McGraw and other singers from his area were promoting Sacred Harp singing throughout the country, overseeing and supporting the founding of new conventions in the Northeast and Midwest, singing in their home area was declining. Time brought attrition in the population of existing singers, and they were not being replaced, both because the large families of earlier generations were less common, leaving fewer people in the traditional population of singers to take up Sacred Harp and because the members of these smaller families were not engaging in Sacred Harp at the same rate as earlier generations. As Shelbie Sheppard said in a 1998 memorial lesson, "Jeff and I used to be the young singers around here. The problem is, we are still the young singers." She was in her sixties at the time and could only point to a few regular local singers who were noticeably younger and almost none who would be considered young by ordinary standards.

As early as 1958, lifelong Georgia singer Earl Thurman wrote, in a letter to L. G. Denney, "Now Alabama is, no doubt, the bulwark of Sacred Harp singing. But there was a time in the early life of the Sacred Harp that

Georgia was the bulwark of Sacred Harp singing, and continued to be that for more than half a century."[26] Of course, the past of any tradition or group (or nation) is often idealized, and Sacred Harp is certainly not exempt from this tendency. Georgia is by no means the only place in which Sacred Harp is remembered as once better and stronger, but this mythology is particularly strong in Georgia.[27] Today the 1950s—by which time Georgia Sacred Harp had declined in Thurman's eyes—are presented as the glory days, with photographs of enormous singing classes proving the relative truth of this. Given the length of this decline, we can only speculate about its causes. It is clear, however, that the children of west Georgia singers did not take up Sacred Harp singing at the same rate that the children of Sand Mountain singers did. Perhaps the area's proximity to Atlanta made urban lifestyles more desirable and in turn made Sacred Harp seem old-fashioned,[28] perhaps the strict, purist Sacred Harp style that Teenie Moody describes being raised in—"We were not asked to sing, we were made to sing"—alienated some children of singers. Whatever the case, success breeds success and decline breeds decline, as it is easier to attract new singers to a strong singing that sounds good and provides plenty of attractive, age-appropriate role models and teachers for the beginner.

––––––

Holly Springs Primitive Baptist Church in Bremen, Georgia, hosts probably the largest singing in west Georgia. Although it is within two miles of I-20, the main artery running from Atlanta to Birmingham, and is off a state highway lined with fast-food restaurants and gas stations, the church is screened by enough trees that it feels secluded. Unlike many singings at out-of-the-way churches, there are no signs leading the way to Holly Springs. The church is a white wood-frame building with no real porch, just steps and in one place a wheelchair ramp leading up to entrances on three sides. There is no paved parking lot, and cars park on the grass on the three sides of the church not bounded by the cemetery.

In 1998, the first year I attended the singing at Holly Springs, I arrived at the published starting time and found that the singing was already underway and the alto section was completely full. In 2005, I arrived nearly forty minutes early, just before nine, and found that mine was only the third or fourth car there (though some of the organizers had been once and gone home briefly before this). The church never filled that day to the point where a late arrival would have had trouble finding a seat in any section, and the singing started a few minutes *after* its published starting

time. Hugh McGraw greeted me when I got inside the church and reminded me to register so that he, as arranging committee, would know
to call me to lead; written registration only took the place of the informal
system of relying on the arranging committee to know all attendees in
1998. The only other people in the church were Rod Ivey and Nate Green,
both from Sand Mountain.

Over the next forty minutes, the yard around the church filled with
cars, though the church was not full when the singing began a little after
nine thirty, nor did it ever fill completely that day. Charlene Wallace, the
chair of the singing, led the opening song and called on Henry Johnson,
also from Sand Mountain, to give the morning prayer; she had clearly
not planned in advance who to call on but scanned the front rows of
the tenor and bass sections before asking Henry. Hugh McGraw, assisted
on the arranging committee by a local woman, stood behind the pulpit
and, once the officers had led, called out the names of leaders through
the day.

A significant amount of money has been put into improving the church
in recent years. The first time I attended a singing there, as I waited in
line for the recently added bathrooms in the rear entryway, an elderly
woman turned to me and said, "I sure am proud we have these." Fluores-
cent lighting, air-conditioning, and padded fixed-location benches have
also been installed—the physical experience of singing there has changed
significantly since the first time I sang there, when the heat and humidity
stole my breath from me at one point such that my vision blurred and
I had to stop singing for a few moments—and the eponymous spring
restored and sheltered under a springhouse. Behind the church stands
a cemetery with the ubiquitous (in the South) long cement lunch table
covered with a corrugated metal canopy.

The interior walls, floor, and ceiling of Holly Springs are all broad
tongue-and-groove pine planks, and, as at Liberty, two boarded-up win-
dows can be seen on the wall now adjoining the bathrooms. Although
the church had no members, as of 2005 services were still held monthly
for visitors (some of whom attended regularly). To maintain the room's
suitability for preaching, the benches are fixed into place forming an
irregular square, with the trebles and basses overlapping with the altos
such that instead of singing into the center of the square, they sing into
and are muffled by the alto section, diminishing the resonant effect of
the wooden construction. The center of the square this forms is an extremely narrow rectangle, and leaders often stand directly in front of,
almost on the toes of, the alto section in order to obtain some distance
from the tenor section they face when they lead.

Despite all of this investment in the physical structure, though, the singing at Holly Springs is weakening, as the decline in class size during the years I have been attending reveals. On this Saturday, the length of the tenor benches meant that, while there were a number of strong tenor singers present, they were spread out so that their voices did not blend into a whole greater than the sum of its parts, but remained slightly ragged, with audible chinks in the sound. Likewise, compounding the fact that the trebles sing into the alto section rather than into the center of the square was a paucity of male treble singers. Although there were some very fine female trebles, men in treble and tenor sections lend body to the sound, allowing it to function as a counterweight to the rumble of the bass section.

Saturday's singing was solid but uninspired, workmanlike rather than soaring. With the exception of the hour after lunch, the music was pitched consistently low, so that while there was less opportunity for weaknesses in the tenor and treble sections to be revealed by high passages that some singers might have missed, there was also little opportunity for those sections to shine. Similarly, two or three singers on the front bench of the tenor section elected to set the pace of the singing, rather than allowing individual leaders to choose their song tempos. Since many of the seated singers cannot see the leader in the square, the tenors have significant power to take control; many front-bench tenors at least occasionally set a tempo for a particularly weak leader, but the tenors ought ideally to follow a competent leader. In this case, they simply did not meet the eyes of the leaders, who were left to either follow them, appear to be off the beat and therefore incompetent, or engage in a power struggle with a doubtful outcome.

Just as the low pitch of the songs may have prevented spectacularly off-key singing in some moments as people strained above their ranges, it also produced a muted quality to the singing overall, changing this day of singing from the typical course of a day of Sacred Harp singing, in which some leaders choose fast paces and others slow ones, to one in which there was little range in the tempo of the singing. Songs that leaders intended to go fast were slowed down and songs that they intended to go slow were sped up, so that much of the day's singing was at a steady, moderate pace. As with the pitch, this may have prevented a handful of noteworthy disasters brought on by inexperienced leaders making choices that did not suit their songs or were not sustainable by the class, but it also produced dull, uninspired singing, as devoid of high points as of identifiable low ones.

When a singing begins at nine thirty, the practice of taking a break

every hour becomes problematic, since lunch begins at noon. Some singings take two short breaks, while others take one long one, and on this
occasion, break was called at ten thirty. At noon, though, leaders were
still being called and, on the front bench of the tenors, Rod Ivey began
making faces and looking around at the officers and arranging committee, hinting broadly though silently that they should break for lunch.
Seeing this, Hugh McGraw said from the pulpit, "Rodney, I've been in-
structed by the food committee to sing until ten past twelve. You can go
if you need to."

Replying, "I need a drink—it's been an hour and a half," Rod got up
and walked out of the square, to chuckles from other singers. A singer less
confident of his status in the community would have simply left quietly,
or would not have been acknowledged when he began to express discomfort, but Rod is personally popular, a strong singer who often arrives with a
carload of passengers, and comes from a respected family and community
of singers, so the legitimacy of his complaint was quickly acknowledged
and turned into a source of camaraderie. When lunch was called, he was
already out by the table, helping the women who had been slipping one
by one out of the church for some time before to set out the food.

If there were bigger spaces between the dishes laid out on the long
concrete table than there had been the first time I attended Holly Springs,
there was still an amount of food that would have stunned a first-time
attendee of a southern Sacred Harp singing, and enough to thoroughly
and deliciously clog the arteries of all present.[29] A few benches line the
edges of the cement platform the table stands on, and some singers ate
on the (very) low brick wall edging part of the cemetery. Others laid out
blankets on the ground, and a few, particularly those who are unable to
stand for long, brought folding camp chairs. Singers mingled and talked
freely, those who didn't have seats regularly circulating between small
groups of friends.

After lunch, Richard DeLong took over the keying, and the music went
from being well on the low side to a bit on the high side, appropriate
for the after-lunch hour when singers are warmed up but rested and hy-
drated and not yet exhausted. Leaders spanned a range from the out-of-
state visitor inappropriately dressed in shorts, the sight of whom caused
the woman next to me to lean over and say, "I wish I had a camera so I
could get his legs," to elderly singers drawn from the area who have been
attending this singing all their lives.

The most public recognition I have seen of the deep ties some singers
have to Holly Springs Church came when Elder Homer Benefield stood up

to make a special presentation. Charlene Wallace is the perennial chair of the weekend's singing and one of its most prolific cooks; she also keeps up the church and grounds year round. As Elder Benefield presented her with a plaque and gift of money (which he exhorted her to spend on herself, rather than the church or singing) from the people who regularly attend his services there, he said, in his age-quavering voice, "On the coldest days of winter, she came up here and turned on the heater and called and told me she'd done it. I turned the key in the lock and warm air came out, and *Thank God!*" As he spoke and his intent became clear, Charlene's jaw dropped in shock, and she began to attempt to suppress sobs. Standing up to accept the gift, she said shakily, "I can't talk much, but this place means a lot to me. My parents, grandparents, are all buried up there." When she sat down, she took off her glasses and cried silently for several minutes, telling me quietly, "I didn't know they were going to do that" when she had regained a bit of composure.

After the day's singing, visitors are invited to a social fifteen miles away, in Carrollton at the Sacred Harp Headquarters and Museum (essentially a ranch house on land donated by a local singing family). The year I attended this, it was sparsely attended and stiff. Because of the advanced age of so many local singers, many are too tired after a day of singing and cooking to attend, and because it is held in an institutional space, rather than the home of a singer, the sense of responsibility for its success is less collectively held.

Saturday was the weekend's better day of singing at Holly Springs; on Sunday, faced with competition on Sand Mountain from Liberty Church's Decoration Day singing, the crowd dwindled severely. Had Hugh McGraw not turned the arranging over to his coarranger and sung treble, there would have been only one man in the section to lend ballast to the women's higher voices, and although there were several basses singing, many of them were prone to missing their entrances on fuguing tunes such that only Scott DePoy, of Atlanta, was audible on some songs. Jeff Sheppard, who had pitched the music for most of Saturday, was tired and turned the pitching over to two less-reliable men who shared the job, with one doing minor and the other major songs.

Although Holly Springs remains a relatively strong singing, its decline is visible even over the short time I have been attending. The number of singers has shrunk, and due to their aging, there is little energy available for things like putting up signs to lead newcomers to the singing or even pitching the music; the not inconsiderable work of hosting a large singing with many out-of-towners strains the local community as it is.

Two Southern Communities

The contrast between Liberty and Holly Springs, and between Sand Mountain and west Georgia more generally, highlights the degree to which, even in areas (and families) in which Sacred Harp has a long history, singing is a choice that must be actively made. Maintaining the size and vitality of singing communities in the South is more a matter of keeping young members of singing families in the Sacred Harp tradition than of recruiting new participants unfamiliar with the music. But although there is an existing pool of prospects, it is not a foregone conclusion that this pool will continue to yield enough new singers to keep the tradition viable everywhere it has flourished for the past century and more. In west Georgia, it has already all but petered out, with singers bringing their grandchildren rather than their children to conventions yet still unable to enforce frequent attendance on those grandchildren. Without a community of young people, the bar to entry for any individual becomes higher, as the singing is then not a social event.[30] On Sand Mountain, many singings, particularly those strongly associated with extended families, are social events for young people, creating a draw to Sacred Harp beyond the music, much as adults feel.

For most frequent singers in these areas (particularly in the more rural parts), Sacred Harp fits into established patterns of life: nonsingers know about it and understand it as a reasonable choice; many churches hold services only one or two weekends per month, leaving time to attend singings even as a churchgoer; it is an opportunity to see extended family and longtime friends, and in some cases serves more or less explicitly as a family reunion; its cuisine is familiar and comforting. All of these things apply to most occasional singers as well, but they have put Sacred Harp lower on their priority list, perhaps only singing on weekends their church does not meet, or at Sacred Harp events with which their family or church has a long history.

But many people from singing families simply drift away from the tradition. Through childhoods being brought to singings by their parents, they play outside rather than develop an attachment to the music. As teenagers they want to see their friends or earn money on sunny Saturdays. As adults, to the extent they still feel any commitment to Sacred Harp, it is low on a crowded list of priorities. In some cases their parents may be able to get them to a singing once or twice a year, where they sit in the back listening to the music. Others do not maintain even that level of connection. Through this process, west Georgia singing has suffered from having effectively lost a generation.

While the comparison between Liberty and Holly Springs shows clearly the degree to which singing is a choice, even in the South, and to which different southern communities today have widely varying vitality, they share certain structural resources. Liberty and Holly Springs *as churches* make room for Sacred Harp singing, and their physical resources are available for singing on the relevant days of the year. Singers do not have to seek out spaces to sing or give much thought to raising money to rent such spaces.

The culture of cooking massive amounts for conventions is another resource on which singers can draw. That is, it is a resource in the sense that while each singer cooks a significant—even huge—amount of food, they do so in the knowledge that the majority of members of their community are also doing so, and that there will be more than enough food to feed their guests. What foods are considered appropriate and appealing are also culturally agreed upon, and singers and visitors alike know what cuisine they will find.

Such cultural and structural resources may seem incidental to the success of a singing, and the ease with which it can be hosted, but as the examples of Chicago and Minneapolis-St. Paul will show, they are in fact central to the experience of hosting a singing and providing hospitality.

THREE

The North: Tradition, Complications, and Change

As the previous chapters showed, questions of authenticity and tradition are central to singers' understanding of what they are doing when they sing. But the tradition is not, after all, consistent even within the South, where differences are found not only between Sand Mountain and west Georgia but also between churches located ten miles apart on Sand Mountain and even between different singings at a single church. These differences are greatly amplified outside the South, even in singing communities that emphasize the importance of the southern tradition. Given differences within the South, nonsouthern singing communities may choose to emphasize one set of southern traditions over another; in other cases, the primacy of the southern tradition may be quietly set aside. Under what circumstances, then, do the Chicago and Minneapolis-St. Paul singers follow or disregard southern Sacred Harp singing practices, and which such practices do they emphasize? How are these understandings played out in their actual practice of singing? What do the practices followed imply about who is or should be included in the singing community in what ways? How are the relationships between singers enacted?

Many northern Sacred Harp groups emerged out of performing groups or folk music institutions, with Sacred Harp singing first appearing as part of a broader repertoire sung in the physical configuration and vocal style of the choir or folk group, and the shape notes either omitted or treated as a curiosity to be memorized for a handful of songs. Shorter singings were therefore much more the norm. Over time, groups' commitments to Sacred Harp as an independent tradition deepened and the shape notes, hollow square, and relative pitch, rather than reliance on a pitch pipe or piano, became central practices. All-day singings and conventions emerged as the groups continued to become more committed to Sacred Harp and began to enter into the broader tradition. In this way, by instituting the form of singing that dominates the southern singing year, new singing communities established themselves as participating in the Sacred Harp tradition, rather than being primarily folk singers who sang Sacred Harp on the side. The calendar therefore identifies a group's orientation to other Sacred Harp singers.

Whatever the distribution between short and all-day events, the frequency and rhythm with which they occur is one of the elements structuring the community that forms around Sacred Harp in a given area. As Zerubavel notes, "A temporal order that is commonly shared by a group of people and is unique to them functions both as a unifier and as a separator,"[1] unifying people within the group and separating them from others. In some places, most singers seldom meet except at singings, so that their relationships are founded on and carried out within the context of Sacred Harp; in others, they interact more frequently, but singing remains an important factor in their relationships. A recent singing provides a topic for conversation between two singers who bump into each other during the week, whether or not either of them attended it, while seeing each other at singings provides an opportunity to stay close.

In addition to structuring a set of opportunities for singers to interact with each other, the calendar of singings provides a commonly held structure for the year itself, producing a constant frame of reference for the passage of time. Though no individual attends every event, the set of possibilities reconfigures the calendar for its practitioners. Dates for singings are given in relation to which Sunday of the month they occur on or near, and many singers come to use this system for discussing dates more generally, first because they remember events in their lives as connected to singings, and then because this way of reckoning time simply takes over. Connecting singing dates to Sundays underlines the sacred nature of singing. Even when a singing is held on another day, the reference to

Sunday is a form of rhetorical, if not enacted, temporal segregation.[2] In adhering to a Sunday-based schedule, northern singings tie themselves in one more way to the southern practice of Sacred Harp.

Despite their growing adherence to southern practices, northern singings are necessarily differentiated by the organizational realities of the specific localities and also of singing in the urban North versus the rural South. Liberty and Holly Springs singings, for example, are always held at Liberty and Holly Springs churches. The locations are a fixed part of the singing. The same is not true of Chicago or Minnesota singings, which do frequently return to the same locations year after year but also often occur in two different locations during the same weekend.

This difference in the relationship between the singing community and the place in which the singing occurs has several ramifications.

Place attachments result from accumulated biographical experiences: we associate places with the fulfilling, terrifying, traumatic, triumphant, secret events that happened to us personally there. The longer people have lived in a place, the more rooted they feel, and the greater their attachment to it.[3]

Such attachment is firmly in place when a singing community has been rooted in a church for generations, when family members are buried in a cemetery on its grounds, when the individual singers have spent a lifetime attending both singings and church there. By contrast, when a singing's site changes year to year and singers do not go to the place for any reason but to sing, singers are less personally attached to it—it is less a repository of memory. As well, when the venue is a matter of choice (albeit severely constrained choice), the local singers' judgment may be questioned with regard to this choice, or the singing quality may be seen to vary from year to year as a result of location acoustics. Rather than being a beloved home, the location becomes an object to be assessed.

The proportion of the day spent actually singing versus that spent on other forms of convention business or on socializing also varies from place to place, with Chicago and Minnesota singing substantially fewer songs per day than the southern locations.[4]

Given the degree to which singers in both Chicago and Minnesota consciously emulate southern singing practices, this unacknowledged departure deserves attention. Singing fewer songs may provide other organizational and community benefits, but as these are unarticulated they tend to be obscure to visiting singers, and the use (and therefore the usefulness) of nonsinging time varies from place to place. If the stated purpose of a singing convention is to sing, then low numbers of songs require explanation—what are either the organizational constraints or perceived advantages of singing fewer songs?

Origins and Background: Chicago and Minnesota

Chicago singers are more difficult to characterize as a group than southern singers. They did not come to Sacred Harp through shared backgrounds, local ties, or kinship, and being drawn from different sources and existing in a larger ecosystem, they do not compose a recognizable class or community aside from their shared participation in Sacred Harp. It is simply not possible to replicate what I have done with regard to the Sand Mountain singers, that is, to talk about them as a group without reference to Sacred Harp.

Chicago singers today are dispersed through a number of the city's distinct neighborhoods, but in the 1980s, many were concentrated in the Wicker Park area on the north side. At the time, Wicker Park was heavily populated with artists and musicians lured by relatively affordable rents and real estate; since then, real estate values have risen as it has become a hip, trendy area filled with restaurants and boutiques. Some singers continue to live in Wicker Park; others are scattered through the middle-class neighborhoods of the city. A group of more recent singers oriented around the University of Chicago is concentrated in Hyde Park, a notably diverse middle-class neighborhood located around the university and in proximity to poorer areas on the south side. Despite this concentration in such a racially diverse area, singers remain almost exclusively white, as in other locations.[5]

These two loose residential groupings represent two distinct groups of Chicago singers, though they collaborate on large events such as the Midwest Convention. The north side singers are the original Chicago Sacred Harp singers. A group of friends who had been meeting to sing and play various folk music forms, they began singing Sacred Harp songs in 1983, moving to a public format at the Old Town School of Folk Music later in the same year, then helping to organize the first Illinois State Convention in 1985 and starting their own Midwest Convention in 1986. These early singers were firmly rooted in folk music revivals—as the involvement of the Old Town School in their genesis as a group suggests—though they rather quickly became engaged with the southern Sacred Harp tradition.[6]

Seen from the current vantage point, twenty years later, they appear to be a professionally successful group of people. Ted Johnson was a textbook editor until his retirement, while his wife Marcia ultimately became a traffic court judge; Ted Mercer has his own real estate business and does some developing; Connie Karduck worked in the insurance industry; and Judy Hauff went to work for IBM, where her sister Melanie, also an active Sacred Harp singer, had worked for years. North side singers who came to the tradition after the group was well established are similarly members of the professional/managerial class or, like sociologist Steve Warner or elementary school teacher Kris Richardson, work in education.

The Hyde Park/University of Chicago singers were started in the 1990s by students at the university. Student participation diminished after one of the group's founders and most energetic promoters, Kiri Miller, left to attend graduate school, but there continued to be singing in the area nearly every Thursday evening. In addition to students, librarians are heavily represented among these newer singers; another singer in this group is a legal secretary. Although this set of singers is generally well educated, and those who are not students have stable, salaried jobs, on average they are less affluent than the north side singers and less likely to own cars or be able to afford extensive travel to distant singings. The average age of the nonstudents is also somewhat younger than that of the north side singers.

Many of the men among both groups of Chicago singers are gay—in 2000, one local singer estimated it at one-third. This seems to be unique to Chicago, which suggests that at some point there was an avenue of recruitment of gay men in this area, although I have not seen evidence for any such avenue. At this point, relatively few people of any sort are becoming active singers. The gay population is generally acknowledged, occasionally joked about, and though it is more open and visible at local events, active closeting does not go on even at large singings attended by singers from elsewhere (the South being the relevant "elsewhere"). Overall, as Steve Warner observes, local singers are single, or partnered and childless, or have adult children not living at home. Though there are exceptions, few have children at home; a few of the North Side singers are beginning to have grandchildren whom they occasionally bring to singing conventions. Family involvement, when it occurs, is limited to close family; Sacred Harp in this area does not provide a gathering space for extended families.

Although there are similarities within each group of Chicago singers, there is no sense that they in any way (beyond being white, middle-class people) constitute or belong to a specific class, type, or community of people outside of their shared interest in Sacred Harp. This is in sharp contrast to singers on Sand Mountain and in west Georgia (Sand Mountain in particular) who share so many characteristics and points of contact that they do appear, at least from some angles, to form a class or community even separate from Sacred Harp. The only characteristic in which Chicago singers show less variation than Sand Mountain singers is age. Because Sacred Harp has only been sung in the area since 1983, there is an effective ceiling on age—elderly people are in no way barred from attending, but in practice the pathways in do not solicit them—and while some singers do bring their young grandchildren with them occasionally, there are rarely precollege age people present of their own volition. As a result, the Chicago singers cluster heavily in the forty to sixty range, which in itself might constitute a barrier to recruitment of younger people.

Singers are drawn from a variety of religious backgrounds—a number are active in mainline Protestant congregations, several are atheists, some are Jewish, some are Mennonites, and some were religiously committed earlier in life. Cathryn Baker is a Quaker who says that Sacred Harp "is the more joyful part of my religious experience because the Quakers are pretty darn solemn." All are drawn together by their love of the music and community of Sacred Harp. Occasionally a singer sets up a performance at their church, whether during the service or at another time, but otherwise their formal religious lives (if those exist) and Sacred Harp singing do not intersect, and no shared religious background is assumed at singing events.

In many ways, and certainly in its public image, Chicago singing remains a product of its original architects, sometimes referred to as the Old Guard. The two-day Midwest Convention, held in the spring, remains the defining event of Chicago Sacred Harp, followed in importance by the Anniversary Singing, held in January to commemorate the founding of Sacred Harp singing in the area. The Old Guard singers, however, seem to be suffering from some degree of organizational fatigue. After their period of truly remarkable activity in the late 1980s—which led to the formation of conventions in Missouri and elsewhere, the inclusion of songs by three Chicago singers in the 1991 edition of *The Sacred Harp*, and the only session of the United Convention ever held outside of the South being held in Chicago in 1990—they have pulled back. Many of them still travel south to sing at least once a year, but their average frequency of travel has diminished. A few now reliably attend only the Midwest or Anniversary singings and not local monthly ones. Few attend the weekly evening singings of the newer group in Hyde Park.

The Hyde Park singers are arguably more active in the local context, singing every Thursday evening and doing a substantial amount of the organizational work for events that predated them. This local organizational work is supported and enabled by their relatively close community feeling. Singing together every week provides a framework for this closeness, and they have built on that self-consciously. Cathryn Baker says, "Yes, I have friends who don't sing Sacred Harp, but my closest friends are the ones I sing with. How that came to be, I don't know. But they completely displaced everybody else that I used to be friends with."

Despite their success at forming a close-knit local community, however, the Hyde Park/University of Chicago singers have not successfully defined themselves as a distinct community of singers in the eyes of the broader Sacred Harp community. In fact, the population of the Chicago metro area should be more than large enough to support multiple independent singing communities, but the newer singers have not been very successful at establishing their own all-day singings and other institutions. Their own anniversary singing, variously called the Hyde Park Anniversary Singing or the University of Chicago Anniversary Singing, draws substantially fewer singers and almost none from significant distances.

Chicago is in some ways a diverse community of singers, with singers from several denominations and of differing levels of religiosity, as well as its gay population. Minneapolis-St. Paul, however, is perhaps the most ideologically diverse of my research sites, a partial, but not sole, cause of the relatively loose community structure there—one so loose I hesitate to call it a community at all. As in Chicago, there are two groups of singers: a longer-standing group composed of professionals in their forties and older, and a more recently formed group oriented to the University of Minnesota that is younger and populated largely but not entirely by students. The loose community structure, however, is not a product of the presence of two groups of singers. The original group, at the time I carried out my research, tended to show up to sing, then leave, while the University group worked to engage socially around singings more, despite the instability of a membership composed mostly of students. The original Twin Cities singers have their regular local singings on Sunday afternoons and, since the emergence of the University group, refer to themselves as the "Sunday singers," while calling the other group the "Tuesday singers." Unlike in Chicago, where the distinct subcommunities are separated by geography, in Minneapolis-St. Paul the two groups sing in the same room at the University Baptist Church, where the minister is a Sacred Harp singer.

In fact there is substantial overlap between the two groups of singers, but even most singers who attend both Sunday and Tuesday singings regularly become identified with one or the other. This distinction is in part related to how long people have been singing, since the Sunday singings predate the Tuesday ones by some years and some people who now attend as many Tuesdays as Sundays were already identified as part of the Sunday group, but it is also a matter of orientation. The Tuesday group is more dedicated to attracting and welcoming new singers, while the Sunday group in practice if not in theory is less interested in actively cultivating new singers. These orientations are shapers of group composition and the pathways into Sacred Harp in Minneapolis-St. Paul.

The Sunday group emerged in a scattered way out of a folk music performance group that morphed into a participatory model, including the characteristic hollow square, in the late 1980s a few years before their first convention was held in 1990. Strikingly, there does not seem to be a moment of group cohesion of the sort that the Chicago singers relate with regard to the first singing at the Old Town School, the first Illinois Convention, the first trip south, or the first Midwest Convention. This lack of collective memory or narrative of origins exemplifies the more compartmentalized role of Sacred Harp singing for Minnesota singers. Moments exist that could have created that feeling of a group coming together—the first Minnesota Convention, for instance—but while a lasting group did emerge, with some degree of continuity of membership and enough group identity to give rise to the Sunday versus Tuesday designations, they remain people who gather to engage in a particular activity, rather than feeling a sense of responsibility to or kinship with members of the group with whom they are not specifically friends outside of singings. Friendship groups exist among them, with the most significant one consisting of a number of singers who also participate in morris dancing[7] together. These singers see Sacred Harp as a site for some specific friendships, many friendly acquaintanceships, and periodic gatherings to which all singers are invited, but not necessarily as a site for the kind of community that breeds significant involvement in the lives of all participants.

In conjunction with each convention in the Twin Cities, several socials are held at the homes of singers. As a result, I've been to the homes of several of the Sunday singers; all were amply sized houses in quiet residential neighborhoods complete with the proverbial tree-lined streets. These comfortable upper-middle-class homes were consonant with the professions of these singers. Among the Sunday singers, Keith Willard is trained as a doctor but works in technology, while his wife Jenny does some music teaching; Jim Pfau is a lawyer; Steve Schmidgall is an architect; Bill Waddington owns a tea shop; Tom Mitchell is an executive at a large restaurant chain; Denise Kania is an occupational therapist; and Steve Levine is a technical writer. Several are teachers, with music teachers especially prevalent.

Traditional family structures are much more in evidence than among Chicago singers, though, as in Chicago, there are no extended families participating together. Minnesota singers are overwhelmingly married, and many have children at home. Having children at home may in part be due to a slightly lower average age than in Chicago, but it is also due to a higher proportion of people with children of any age. Though there are a few gay singers, they do not influence the culture of the group in the way that gay singers in Chicago do and are not understood to be a characteristic demographic of the Twin Cities singers. The greater proportion of singers living in nuclear families may be one explanation for the relatively low group cohesion: Singers may be less invested in having a community outside of their families, or be more oriented to their children's schools, activities, and friendships, leaving less time for participation in a Sacred Harp community.[8]

Singers in Minneapolis-St. Paul are religiously diverse in the sense of being drawn from many denominations and levels of religiosity, but the level of religiosity is slightly higher than in Chicago. Tim Eriksen suggests that "people don't really care *where* you go to church, but everybody goes to some church." In fact, at least a few local singers are not church-goers, but in this context even some of them come to understand Sacred Harp as a religious observance or expression. Steve Schmidgall says Sacred Harp has "sort of become my religion," while Martha Henderson says that church services she had attended "just felt alien to me, so Sacred Harp became my church in a way that no church has become my church." More traditional religiously observant singers include Seventh Day Adventists, Lutherans, Methodists, Catholics, Jews, and Baptists, falling at the extreme conservative and liberal ends of the religious and political spectrum.

Sacred Harp singers outside the South tend to be politically liberal, many having come to Sacred Harp directly out of the folk revivals of the 1960s and 1970s, the leftist inclinations of which have been well documented by many scholars,[9] and many Twin Cities singers do fit this image. But the area also notably contains a few of the most politically conservative singers I have encountered outside the South, and though one of those singers, Jenny Willard, expresses a sense of being outnumbered—she refers to herself and her husband as having made a decision to "come out" as conservatives after years of the mainly liberal singers in the area assuming the Willards to also be liberal—she and her husband, and to a lesser degree Tom Mitchell, another conservative, loom large among local singers, commanding special notice. Cordiality is generally maintained, but there is a definite sense that politics is one more thing dividing Twin Cities singers.

The Tuesday group grew out of classes taught by Mirjana (Minja) Lausevic, Tim Eriksen's wife and an ethnomusicology professor at the University of Minnesota.[10] In her large introductory course, Minja included a session on Sacred Harp, timed immediately before the Minnesota Convention, and invited her husband to be a guest lecturer. She also gave her students the option of doing their final research projects on Sacred Harp, an option which entailed attending more singings. The Tuesday singing was begun by two students who had followed this path.

Minja and Tim came from the East Coast, where they had been central in the development of the Western Massachusetts Sacred Harp singing community, probably the fastest growing in the country at the time (and possibly since). Although they sought to act as community members not leaders, the couple, in their midthirties when they moved to Minneapolis, to a great extent set the initial tone of the group. Some students who came to Sacred Harp were likely drawn in by the young professor and her rock-musician husband,[11] while others were drawn in by friends who had started singing Sacred Harp earlier. A few other new singers had been introduced to Sacred Harp through Tim's performances with various bands; some had first attended Sunday singings but found the atmosphere unwelcoming and only became regular singers when the Tuesday group gave them another option. The group's identity is shaped by its university affiliation and by the central role of students in organizing it, and even the nonstudents are slightly younger than the original Sunday singers and tend to work in less elite occupations.

At some points, members of the Tuesday group have engaged in strenuous outreach, including putting up flyers and posters around campus. In line with their greater emphasis on outreach to recruit new singers, this group is more likely than the Sunday group to pause to welcome a newcomer entering the singing late, or one experienced singer may get up to welcome the newcomer during the middle of a song and offer a loaner copy of *The Sacred Harp* and a little preliminary instruction. At certain points, especially at the beginning of the life of the Tuesday singing, people went to a nearby restaurant for malts after the singing was done; this practice was hard to maintain given the busy schedules of many involved, but it remained a reference point in the sociability of the group.

Minnesota State Convention

Unlike most southern singings, which are held in the same church buildings year after year and are hosted by the singers of those churches, most
northern singings move around, dependent on the availability of publicly available spaces for which they must compete with weddings, par-
ties, church services, and performances and which can entail substantial
rental fees. The choice of such locations can become a source of significant effort and frustration and almost always entails some form of compromise. In 2004, the Minnesota State Convention was held in a different
location each day, with each of the locations representing a different set
of compromises.

Saturday's singing was held at a centrally located church to enable
easy access, which might make it more likely that people unfamiliar
with Sacred Harp will attend; this church also had an easily accessible
lunchroom and restrooms. The singing was in a fellowship hall rather
than the sanctuary of the church, a large open room with a high ceiling
that contributed to the many complaints voiced over the weekend about
the acoustics of the room. In contrast, Sunday's location was well out of
town. Here the restrooms and lunch space required a walk over rough
ground and were not climate controlled, but the singing space, a town hall
building in a living history village, was architecturally and acoustically
similar to the southern churches in which Sacred Harp has historically
been sung and was, therefore, considered acoustically ideal.

On Saturday, a lengthy opening prayer was offered by a woman minister—prayers at southern singings are never offered by women, and very
rarely by seminary-trained ministers, so this immediately establishes
Minnesota singing as existing within the local cultural milieu as much
as it also seeks to emulate and enact southern Sacred Harp tradition.
The lunchtime blessing similarly revealed how a convention can be religiously orthodox, by having prayers at all appropriate times, yet reflect
the inclusiveness of its local context rather than adhering to a strictly
southern model: This blessing invoked Jesus and "others we worship."

The convention had drawn a handful of lifelong southern singers (five
who sang and led and two nonsinging spouses who attended the singing), as well as many singers from throughout the Midwest and two or
three from the Northeast. The southern singers were given pride of place
throughout the weekend, consistently offered front-row seats and called
to lead during the prime after-lunch hour of singing. On Saturday in
Minnesota, the only southern singer *not* called in the after-lunch hour

was the teenage granddaughter of Georgia's Louis Hughes. Visitors from other areas were called, and on Saturday at least, these choices seemed calculated to include one representative of each community from which singers had come.

Minnesota and Chicago singings are similar, and distinctive, in the amount of talking that goes on between songs (a common character-istic I was not aware of when I chose them as research sites, and one not generalizable to all new singing communities). In most places, it is rare for a leader to address the class before beginning their song, but in Minnesota not only do many leaders speak at least briefly, but remarks by seated singers are also made loudly enough to be widely heard and perhaps commented on rather than remaining private conversations be-tween two or three people seated adjacent to each other. (This is true in Chicago to an only slightly lesser extent; in both places, local singers are the most likely to speak, often to welcome visitors or acknowledge some local tradition.)[12] Once during the first hour of singing and once in the hour after lunch, a leader prefaced her choice of a quick-tempo song perceived as being somewhat challenging by referring to the class's readi-ness to sing the song. In one case, this was framed as a question, "Are we ready for 411?"[13] while in the other it was a statement, "All right, we've got warmed up enough, 269"—both statements served to draw attention to the perceived difficulty of the song (and therefore the leader's implied skill at feeling confident in leading it). The framing of such a statement as a question is purely rhetorical; if the song is unpopular or the leader perceived as incapable of leading it, any statement that draws attention to a song choice may draw quiet joking or complaints by seated singers (as will be discussed below), but the choice will never be publicly chal-lenged unless the song has already been sung that the day.

Other leaders during the two days of the singing commented on the correct pronunciation of words in song lyrics or the presence of a song's composer at the convention, claimed particular songs as their own sig-nature pieces,[14] or identified their choice of song as being connected to their family in some way (though not necessarily because anyone else in their families sing Sacred Harp). As Wuthnow writes of religious seekers, "Faith is no longer something people inherit but something for which they strive,"[15] and new singers often experience an analogous striving—reaching for a connection they can observe southern singers to have inherited.

The business meeting, at which officers are elected, is another occa-sion for jokes, or at least for one annual joke. Compared with Chicago (discussed below), Minnesota's business meeting is brief and restrained.

The incoming chairs and the chair for Minnesota's annual Cooper Book singing, held in February, have already been selected by local singers, but the selection is publicly ratified at the convention. This process may entail humorous moments, but the most consistent joke associated with the business meeting is the handover of the clipboard used by the convention chair, which is labeled (and the label ceremoniously read aloud) "Official Minnesota State Sacred Harp Convention Chairperson's Clipboard (conveys the mantle, but not the substance, of authority)." This statement makes explicit something more generally true of Sacred Harp convention chairs but assigns it to a physical object and insists that it be publicly acknowledged. Once again, something that is silent at southern singings is spoken, indeed embodied, at a northern one, with the combined effect of providing an explanation of the convention's hierarchy to newcomers and providing a year-to-year in-joke for experienced singers.

During the singing, the pitching, or keying,[16] of the songs was another subject for occasional remarks or delays. Sacred Harp singing does not use a pitch pipe or other instrument to determine the correct pitch of a song; rather, a particularly experienced singer determines the pitch based not only on the official notation of the song but also on the abilities of the class and the time of day at which it is being sung. The person pitching the music almost always sits in the middle of the front row of the tenors, since the tenors carry the melody of the song. The 2004 Minnesota Convention was a rare exception to this rule; instead, this role switched for every hour-long session of singing, and at least two of the people designated to key did so from the treble section. At most southern singings, no more than two people (almost always men) pitch in a day of singing, and at all-day singings and conventions, this role is usually restricted to people who are very experienced and skilled at it.[17]

The wider sharing of the role in Minnesota meant that the singing was pitched inconsistently from hour to hour, and some of the people pitching it were somewhat inexperienced (at least at dealing with the pressure of doing it in front of a large convention class rather than a small local singing). As a result of this lack of experience, not only were some sessions pitched noticeably high, but at several points there was a minor delay as the pitcher struggled to find an appropriate note. At one point, the woman pitching asked for help on a song she anticipated having trouble with. When, after a brief wait, no one responded with a suggested note, she struggled through finding a note and did ultimately succeed. But such moments, as well as those when a leader wanted to key their own song and had to communicate this to the person keying the session as a whole, contributed to the time taken between songs.

This talkiness most unambiguously means that fewer songs can be sung in a weekend—an effect that is less relevant in Minnesota, where all attendees who wish will be able to lead twice during the convention, than it is in Chicago, as I discuss below.[18] Talk can have two contradictory effects. On the one hand, it can be used to express and affirm a shared experience—the power of a song well done, a leader's skill, the humor of a misunderstood page number. For this reason, it can bring some members of the class together and help develop and make public a sense of community. On the other hand, by disrupting the flow of the singing, by introducing a significant amount of content besides leaders and songs, it divides the class, creating more different ways of experiencing the day of singing. Everyone, of course, experiences the singing itself in personal ways not fully shared by their neighbors, but talk, however seemingly inconsequential, can further divide the experience.

First, it divides the square geographically. Although seats are not assigned and anyone who sees an open front-row seat can take it, the front two rows of most singings (in all locations) are overwhelmingly occupied by "insiders," by valued guests, and by particularly active local singers. More marginal participants tend to sit in the back rows, toward the edges of the square, where comments addressed ostensibly to the room as a whole are much less likely to be audible. People in these positions are therefore left out of these rhetorical questions, jokes, and emotional references to family. Particularly when some of the comments already refer to information that may be available to the insiders who can hear it most clearly, talking reinforces existing but perhaps unacknowledged hierarchies or divisions.

Additionally, talking lessens focus on the singing itself, interjecting personality and individuality into the experience. For some people, this is a welcome reminder and exercise of their close relationships with other singers, making it a valued part of the sense of community. It is particularly important at singings where little nonverbal communication goes on, and it seeks to replace that nonverbal communication by rendering it out loud. For others, though, even those for whom it is not a reminder of their marginal status, it can be an unwelcome distraction from singing and a personal irritant if the jokes are found to be unfunny or other comments to be attention seeking.

The provision of food is, of course, another component of Sacred Harp tradition and community building. Minnesota singers take pride in the quality of their dinner on the grounds, and, as for many northern communities trying to recreate a southern singing experience, their assessments of quality are often based in part on the recognizability of the food, including the presence of southern staples like barbecue and deviled eggs. Considering the food at this singing, one Minnesota singer said, "Having enough food of the kind that people want to eat is important. It took us a while and we still have some things to work through. I kind of felt Saturday there was a lot of weird kinds of food. There was a lot of food, but there was some food that was kind of, you know, strange and scary."

Here, as elsewhere (including Chicago), singers who travel South to sing frequently make southern specialties, both marking their community as respectful of the tradition and hospitable to southern guests and themselves as personally knowing what constitutes traditional food and how to make it—perhaps having gotten recipes from southern singers particularly known for them. As I noted in the previous chapter's discussion of food, dinner on the grounds is not merely an occasion for ingesting food, it is deeply symbolic of community, fellowship, and love.[19] But the ability to provide a recognizably southern spread may also operate as a form of cultural capital that northern singers deploy in their pursuit of authenticity as "an idealized representation of reality . . . a set of expectations regarding how such a thing ought to look, sound, and feel" (or in this case, taste).[20]

Murphy's Landing, a historical village where Sunday's singing was held, is about thirty minutes outside Minneapolis and is the location to which this convention most often returns. Once again, the issue of trade-offs faced by northern singings becomes apparent. As I mentioned previously, the building in which the singing is held is structurally very similar to singing churches in the South and, as such, has similar acoustics, which are considered ideal for Sacred Harp. Unlike the vast majority of those southern churches, though, this building has been preserved to be historically accurate; this means there are no bathrooms attached to the singing space. Instead, the rather primitive bathroom facilities are located elsewhere on the Murphy's Landing grounds—the walk, down a dirt road, is negligible for an agile person but presents something of a challenge for less fit people. To help compensate for this, the singers rent a portable toilet, which sits beside the building. Lunch is held a similar distance away from the singing building, under a wooden canopy similar to (though larger than) the ones found beside so many southern singing churches.

In a careful allocation of roles between local and visitor, northern and southern, the memorial lesson was given by Kim Bahmer, a young Minnesota singer who had started singing four years earlier after taking a course from Minja Lausevic, and by Cheryl Foreman, a singer from Texas. Kim spoke about her growing sense of connection to Sacred Harp and the way that "the songs take on a new and rich meaning every time you sing them," building new memories and sets of associations around specific songs. This was a quiet, restrained memorial, due in large part to the personalities of the committee members—Cheryl was not eager to engage in extensive public speaking, and Kim's approach was thoughtful, reflecting on the operation of Sacred Harp in the lives of singers rather than eulogizing specific singers.

As is much more often the case at northern than southern singings, I recognized few of the names on the lists of deceased and sick and shut-in, as they were composed more of friends and relatives of local singers than of singers. In addition, northern singers sometimes add references to more remote and collective experiences. The Minnesota list, as recorded in the minutes, included "the victims of hurricanes in the southeastern United States; the victims of war; and the people killed in the school seizure at Beslan, Russia."[21] These departures from or additions to southern tradition may in part be due to the relative youth of northern singers, fewer of whom die in a given year than do southern singers, but I believe that it also represents an attempt to add weight to the memorial lesson—the memorial gains its power not just from who is on the list read that day but from the associations singers have, remembering loved ones whom they have sung for in the past. By adding names to the list, singers become more involved in this part of the Sacred Harp tradition. Moreover the people making such additions to the memorial list are surely moved by their thoughts of the deceased, as well as seeking to connect their everyday lives with their Sacred Harp lives. At the same time, these altered practices can shift the function of the memorial away from delineating the bounds of the Sacred Harp world to addressing the world at large, or providing the individual singer who listed a nonsinger with a sense of connection to the memorial lesson as a tradition, without building as much cohesion between singers.

At the end of the day, committee reports were held. The list of thanks from the resolutions revealed the extent to which the Minnesota Convention is bureaucratized: it included food, refreshment, child-care, and housing committees in addition to the standard arranging and memorial committees, plus the hosts of the various socials, people who had worked at the registration table, brought loaner books, knitted an afghan for raffle to help with convention expenses, and others. The majority of these thanks were followed by general applause, lengthening the report still more. The secretary's report then included information about how many states were represented, and the names of states were called out with the expectation that their residents would stand to be recognized.

Finally, announcements of upcoming singings were made. Northern singers in general tend to make lengthy announcements, attempting to use the opportunity to "sell" their singings by touting the acoustics of the singing space or the anticipated beauty of the weather and scenery. A singer from Missouri pointed out that their convention was one of the few places you could sing from the new *Missouri Harmony* book; one from Chicago acknowledged that the Midwest Convention would conflict with a Texas Cooper Book singing but hoped that Minnesotans would attend nonetheless. Once again, these lengthier statements may reflect a cultural emphasis on individual expression as well as an understanding of Sacred Harp as an activity that needs to be actively promoted in order to secure its survival and expansion in the North.[22]

Midwest Convention

As in Minnesota, location was a major issue for the 2005 Midwest Convention. The convention was planned for Ida Noyes Hall, a space at the University of Chicago obtainable for a reduced price because the Hyde Park area singers have managed to maintain their status as a student group despite having no regular student singers. In recent years, a student with tangential connections to the group had agreed to serve as the student contact to enable continued student group status.

Like most singing locations in northern and urban areas, Ida Noyes Hall represents a series of trade-offs—there are no nearby hotels, it can be difficult to find, and it is up several flights of stairs, but the acoustics are acceptable and there is another room in the same building that can be used for lunch. The Wednesday afternoon before the convention was to begin, one of the previous year's cochairs, Ted Mercer (who would remain cochair until a business session was held Saturday morning and new chairs were officially elected, though in fact the incoming chairs had already been decided), called the University of Chicago to check that everything was in order with the location and was told that the singers had not reregistered as a student organization that year and after several attempts had been made to contact the (nonsinging) student who had served as a contact for the group the previous years, the singers had lost their booking, leaving the Chicago area's major annual Sacred Harp singing event with no singing space just two days before it was to begin.[23]

Ted Mercer sent out an e-mail to the Chicago area singing e-mail list, titled "EMERGENCY re UC for Midwest Convention," explaining the situation and asking for suggestions of replacement locations close to

Ida Noyes Hall so that singers who had not heard about the last-minute location change could easily be redirected to the new location. Exhibiting the organizational skills that had made Chicago's Old Guard singers so instrumental in the development of Sacred Harp singing throughout the Midwest, the 2004 and 2005 cochairs followed up on some twenty locations suggested by singers who received this appeal for help and found and announced replacements just 24 hours after Mercer's initial e-mail.

There was therefore a palpable sense of relief at the beginning of Saturday's singing, which was held just three blocks from Ida Noyes at the University Church. Normally, many singers (northern and southern alike) would have complained bitterly about the large stone church, with its acoustically problematic high, vaulted ceilings and general surfeit of space around the hollow square, which allowed the sound to dissipate somewhat. On this day, though, the realization that the convention might not have happened at all was strong enough to mute complaints, at least about acoustics.

The morning's singing was arranged by Leah,[24] a young woman who had recently moved away from Chicago. Although she is an experienced *singer*, her arranging suggested less experience. According to the fairly standard arranging practice, particularly accomplished leaders should be called in the hours before or after lunch, when the class has warmed up, and people who have traveled great distances to attend a singing should likewise be called at "good" times of the day; the former practice is for the benefit of the class as a whole as good leaders produce good singing, while the latter practice is to recognize the effort made by visitors (and thereby benefit the singing by making it more likely visitors will return). Leah's arranging choices suggested that she was putting thought into the job, not just calling names in random order or in the order registration cards had been filled out, but nonetheless led one southern visitor to turn to a family member sitting next to her and say, "They've been doing this for twenty years and they still don't know how."

For example, Leah called three particularly good leaders from Alabama to lead within the first hour of singing—simultaneously violating the imperatives to save both the best leaders and the farthest-traveling visitors for the prime hours of singing. Since in most years, a substantial number of people at the Midwest Convention are only called to lead once in the weekend, rather than once each day, due to time constraints, Leah may have intended to ensure that these valued leaders would be called again on Sunday but did so in an inappropriate way.

Interspersed with leaders too good to be appropriately called early in the morning were a number of the weak leaders permitted by the Sacred

Harp practice of allowing anyone who wishes to lead a song to do so. That morning, noteworthy among the leaders was the man who had been understood as the group leader when Sacred Harp singing first started in Chicago. As Chicago singers started traveling South and pressing for more traditional organization of singing at home, he became alienated from the group. In 2005, he attended for the twentieth convention, and when he led, his past contributions were specially noted.[25] He would have drawn attention even without this introduction, though, due to being dressed much like a caricature of an aging hippie, in a purple shirt under a vest, with a matching purple headband, but still more because he led in a flowery choral style unlike the simpler conducting motions typical of Sacred Harp. A longtime Chicago singer who had known him before he all but stopped singing said of this leading style, "If he doesn't do it *just* to piss us off, he does it in full knowledge that it pisses us off."

In locales like Liberty, where singers' connections to one another are denser, more longstanding, and more elaborated, a particularly bad leader will often cause a current of silent hilarity to pass around the square, as people catch their friends' eyes, winking or smiling around the words they are singing. Some similar interactions happened at this Midwest Convention, but such silent communication relies on established friendship—on knowing what your friend will find funny such that a wink or nod will tip them over from private amusement into outright laughter, on that friend knowing to look back at you at that moment, on having a shared history such that you can trust that you will not be rebuked for mocking a singer and such that your response to silent communication draws on past moments of laughing together—and because at the Midwest the friendship networks are not very dense (though there are several clusters of very tight friendship groups, no single one comprises a large enough part of the convention class as a whole), these moments of levity tended to happen between two or three people rather than becoming general occurrences shared throughout the room.[26] So for instance, one man waited until the first break of the morning to share his amusement with two of his friends who were seated together. During the singing he had been watching them but without a direct line of sight had been unable to catch their eyes, and at the break he found one of them and, shaking his head in amusement, told her he had been watching her "sitting over there, laughing at people . . . and you *should*."

Chicago singers frequently refer to the fact that many singers at the Midwest Convention only get to lead once over the two days of the singing as a product of the size of the convention, implying or saying directly that there are simply too many people in attendance to allow more. However, the inability to get through the leader list twice is actually a product of a lower number of songs sung per hour as much as it is of the size of the list.

There are several reasons fewer songs are sung per hour in Chicago than in many other places. Chicago exhibits much of the same talkiness described above in the discussion of Minnesota. Other factors, such as differences in norms governing attention and inattention, contribute as well. At one point on Saturday of the 2005 Midwest Convention, first one person, then another was called to lead only to have someone else reply that the person called had left the room or the singing for a while, unnoticed by an arranging committee seated in a location without a complete view of the crowded room. In each case, this information took moments to emerge, and when the third person called was present, he took an extra moment to choose a song, having been denied the usual one-song warning period. In this case, collective expectations, such as the assumption of attentiveness to one's place in the order of leading, have less ability to regulate individuals' behavior, as some individuals feel themselves less answerable to the community. The most practical/visible consequence is a reduction in the number of songs sung in a day, while the cost to the larger dynamic of the event and collective spirit of the group may be less discernible but no less significant.

The times at which singing stops for convention business to be conducted are also notably longer in Chicago (and my observation is that they are generally longer at conventions run by singers who came to Sacred Harp as adults than at those run by lifelong singers). Ironically, although Chicago business meetings may be longer than is typical, they have also in recent years gained something of a reputation for irreverence, with some local singers choosing to do tongue-in-cheek send-ups of the Robert's Rules of Order approach of the standard Sacred Harp business session. In 2005, for example, despite the efforts of outgoing cochair Ted Mercer to counter this trend, the business session again both lasted longer than average, and its function was made light of by the incoming cochairs, who were dubbed "cochair critters" in an elaborate, mocking nomination process. When nominated and elected by acclamation, new cochair Marcia Johnson declared, "I'm shocked" in stagy tones. Cathryn Baker was already acting as secretary and when she was asked, "Cathryn, you volunteered to be secretary again?" she replied in a dramatically resigned tone, "I was volunteered." Such an event is an excellent example of the division produced by added talk in a day of singing. For some singers, such a business session is an occasion for levity and bonding; a more basic business session is rarely of real interest to anyone and laying bare that "the fix is in" or that the secretary had been pressed into duty can be an enjoyable break that lets the community publicly acknowledge its inner workings. On the other hand, for some singers this is a mark of disrespect.

The collection of donations after lunch to support the convention was also a lengthy process at the Midwest Convention (as it has been at most if not all Chicago all-day singings I have attended). In part, money collection may take longer in Chicago and other northern locations because the expenses involved in putting on a convention are greater than for rural southern churches; however, singings held at expensive locations in the Atlanta area do not have equivalently long collections. Where at southern singings, the statement accompanying collection is often limited to a simple "we're going to pass some baskets for expenses" before the singing resumes,[27] at new northern singings this occasion is often taken as an extra opportunity to publicly recognize the work that has gone into a convention (especially before a broader audience of new singers who may not realize the amount of work involved in putting on a convention) or simply as a chance for an individual to talk publicly.

In this case, a member of the finance committee noted that although hosting a convention is not free, this was "a free-will offering. All are free to come here; all are free to sing; all are free to participate." He went on to jokingly suggest that if all went well with the collection, there was a vacant lot at 61st Street that could be a building site for a permanent location for the Midwest Convention. More seriously, he noted that the twentieth session of the convention was a time to "start building, not necessarily bricks and mortar, but the relationships we need if we're to get to the fortieth session." He specifically singled out the building of relationships between people from the Midwest and people from the South, prompting an Alabama woman seated beside me to mutter, "You need to *go* South, then," commenting on the mismatch between his rhetoric and his actions.

Indeed, although the Chicago singers' collective narrative celebrates the distance they have traveled from their early, nontraditional singing practices to being important followers and promoters of traditional singing practices throughout the Midwest, this convention, and several interviews I have done with area singers, reveal the fragility of those claims. Ted Mercer, who spent several years working hard to create a culture among Chicago singers that would emphasize traveling to sing, expresses disappointment that when he stopped working actively toward that end, the level of travel declined dramatically. Chicago singers do still go in substantial numbers to Midwestern singings within several hours driving distance, several travel greater distances at least once a year, and a handful travel five or more times per year, but this represents a significant drop-off from the late 1980s and early 1990s when a dozen or more Chicago singers would travel together to southern singings on a regular basis. In an interview with Anne Heider, Ted Mercer noted, "To some extent, the Midwest is still the beneficiary of that activity from way back," but a corollary of that, and one that seems increasingly to concern some Chicago singers, is that this benefit will fade if Chicago singers do not continue traveling and incurring reciprocity.

The food at this singing was a mixed bag if judged by the typical Sacred Harp standard of identifiability, as invoked by the Minnesota singer above and by many southern singers in discussing their experiences at northern singings. Quantities seemed a bit scant, possibly because several active singers had spent the previous days hunting for a new space and had been unable to devote their usual time to cooking. Someone had ordered large pans of chicken skewers and potatoes from a restaurant, which added substantial amounts of recognizable food. Several longtime singers brought dishes common at southern singings—Melanie Hauff had made a towering, gleaming white coconut cake, while Karen Freund and Jerry Enright brought sweet potato casserole, corn pudding, and the punch-bowl cake they had learned to make from Coy Ivey on Sand Mountain, as well as his daughter-in-law Karen's sticky bun recipe. Cathryn Baker, a newer singer but one who also travels to sing regularly, similarly told me in an interview, "I usually make an entrée, but for the Midwest I make deviled eggs, because southerners are coming up and they like them." In contrast to these efforts to focus on "traditional" singing food, that is, dishes with southern roots, some food was not readily identifiable even to a northerner with some familiarity with northern potluck cuisine.

As in Minnesota, the after-lunch hour included many of the visiting southerners as leaders, as well as other people who had traveled significant distances. Unlike in Minnesota, priority was not given to leading local singers (though this was also due to the greater number of travelers in Chicago, such that the entire hour could much more easily be filled by skilled leaders from significant distances); the only local singer who led during this hour was the man on the finance committee who gave the speech described above. In fact, since he had already led that morning and was not supposed to lead again, his assumption that he would lead concomitant with the collection took the arranging committee by surprise, causing some reshuffling of the leader list.

During the final hour of the day, in a significant departure from the traditionalist rhetoric of the Chicago singers, one of the founders of the first Chicago singing passed out photocopies and led one of his own compositions. Although the organizers of this convention work to prevent the singing of songs not in the 1991 revision of *The Sacred Harp* (a Minnesota singer who called a song from the 1992 Cooper revision several years ago, for instance, was chastised for doing so), this founding singer routinely leads his own compositions, an exception that makes it harder to curtail other diversions from *The Sacred Harp*. As with many other departures from standard or "authentic" Sacred Harp practice, this is one that draws mixed reviews. For some singers, the presence of accomplished composers in the community is a point of pride, and their songs are especially appreciated. For others, it is a breach of etiquette or a tangible distraction or both.

Sunday's singing was held toward the north side of Chicago, in an Irish American heritage center at which Chicago singings have often been held over the years, so while it was not close to the originally scheduled location, it was a familiar destination for many convention attendees. Almost immediately upon my entry, cochair Marcia Johnson asked me to serve as secretary, so I spent a significant part of the day seated at a table at the back of the room with the arranging committee, noting who had led what songs.

The day proceeded very much as had Saturday, but before lunch an unusually long memorial service was held. In recognition of the twentieth session of the Midwest Convention, a memorial was given for all of the people who had supported the convention at any point during its life. Ted Mercer, whose part of this tribute was recorded in the convention's official minutes,

The Midwest Convention might not have happened at all, or kept going for these twenty years, except for all the assistance we had from so many people. It could very easily have been an ethno-musicology [*sic*] statement, or maybe had a piano in the square. But that was changed because of some very patient people who were eager to teach the Chicagoans the traditional methods of singing Sacred Harp. Without them, we would not be here today. Part of that learning and sharing community has passed away in the last twelve months. They are from all over the country, but especially the South.[28]

In addition to Ted, the memorial was given by Mary Rose O'Leary, one of the early Chicago singers who left the area and has lived in California for many years, who spoke for the sick and shut-in; Linda Thomas, an Alabamian, who spoke about the impact on her of Ruth Brown's bus trips to singings; Georgia's Richard DeLong, who made concrete the year's loss by asking the front benches of the alto and bass sections to stand, then pointing out that this was the number of people on the list of those who had died in the previous year; and Chicago's Jerry Enright, who spoke for lifelong Texas singer Kelly Beard, who had, some time before his death, requested that Jerry give a memorial for him when he was gone. Finally, cochair Marcia Johnson moved that a donation be made to plant a grove of trees near Jerusalem in honor of the convention, "to symbolize growth and renewal."

Late in the day Sunday, with singers tired and those who had not yet led a second time wondering if they would have a chance to do so, a young man who had recently moved away from Chicago was called to lead. He first chose page 217, a song that had already been led that day, and when informed of this, chose "Rose of Sharon," a long anthem that would take significant time and is particularly and vocally disliked by some singers. At hearing that this was his choice, several people groaned and one said, loudly enough to be heard by people within several seats of her, "Can we go back to 217?"

The leader did not acknowledge hearing this, but, referring to a bad experience he had the previous year while attempting to lead a different anthem without holding his book open and making several mistakes, he said, "I have learned my lesson from last year; I'm using my book." He then turned to face the alto section in preparation for the beginning of the song, only to be told by the trebles "it's us" who begin that song. My neighbor in the alto section quietly said, "*Look* at your book, don't just hold it." Where etiquette calls for seated singers to sing songs they may personally dislike without complaining, leading a long, demanding anthem too early in the morning or late in the afternoon is enough of a breach that, while the choice will not be publicly or formally challenged, individual singers may feel free to make their complaints loud enough to be heard by the leader and the front row or two of singers. Leaders who too often lead anthems, particularly at inappropriate times, may also find themselves called to lead at less-desirable times of day, or only called once in a two-day convention.[29]

This particular leader may have been leading at the end of the day Sunday precisely because of his errors the previous year in leading without a book. In any case, he was soon followed by announcements of upcoming singings and reports from the convention committees and officers. As in Minnesota, the announcements dragged on, but they were substantially outdone by the report of the resolutions committee. After many minutes of elaboration of people to be thanked and more general thoughts on Sacred Harp singing and the Midwest Convention, cochair Marcia Johnson began nudging Henry Johnson, an Alabama man not related to her, and directing him to move that the resolutions be adopted; that is, urging him to interrupt and end the by-now outrageously long resolutions. He ultimately did so during a pause, producing audible sighs of relief from many of the people seated around me.[30]

Finally, the officers led page 62, "Parting Hand," while singers milled around the room taking the parting hand by shaking hands and hugging. After a prayer, the convention was at an end. Sunday's lengthy memorial lesson had asserted an explicit identification of the Midwest Convention with larger Sacred Harp tradition, particularly that of the southern singers who had encouraged and fostered the Chicagoans' commitment to that tradition. Yet aspects of the Convention suggested departures from that tradition. What is not clear is how these departures are to be interpreted: did they reflect selective understandings, based in local consensus, of the tradition the Chicago singers had so long prized, or did they indicate a lessening ability to hold individuals accountable to its conception of community?

Tradition and Adaptation

The majority of singers in Minnesota and Chicago would point to southern tradition as their model, and in many ways—from the hollow square, to allowing anyone to lead, to including prayer, to serving a potluck dinner on the grounds—they faithfully uphold this model. But in subtle ways they also adapt to and reflect their broader regional and cultural contexts.

Some of these adaptations are encouraged by structural differences: The necessity of finding and renting public spaces for northern singings creates pressure for, though does not require, more bureaucratized organizational practices than the typical southern practice of holding a singing in the same church year after year, with the singing built into the church's schedule and no negotiation or formal payment required (though most singings make a donation to the church). In the urban South, however, the competing pressures of the necessity to rent a public space and the informal organizational norms of southern singers create a slightly hybrid form, in which one or more singers actively negotiate with venue managers, but which rhetorically bears more similarity to the informal traditional norm, lacking the public discussion Minnesota and Chicago singers tend to have about the work of finding a singing space. In Minnesota and Chicago, the process is more bureaucratized both in practice, with meetings to discuss venues and relatively carefully kept paper trails, and rhetorically, with the language of committees and coordinators much more employed.[31]

These differences reflect the structural pressures of more urban settings, the cultural orientation of northern singers toward professionalized language, and the lack of a longstanding shared community among northern singers that would enable them to take each other's continuing participation and knowledge of necessary tasks for granted (as demonstrated most dramatically in the string of organizational breakdowns and miscommunications that led to the loss of the location for the Midwest Convention in 2005). Locating a space is not the only requirement of planning a convention that shows these pressures and responses. As I mentioned above, the resolutions offered at the Minnesota Convention included thanks to the food, refreshment, child-care, and housing committees. At a southern singing, thanks would almost certainly be extended in the abstract to anyone who had brought food or helped set it out, but there would be no formal committee constituted around those tasks; likewise, someone might be thanked for having brought coffee, but snacks and drinks served at times other than lunch would not be emphasized to the extent of giving them a separate designation of "refreshments," let alone having a committee responsible for them.

Child care and housing, too, are additions to the list of committees involved in a Sacred Harp convention. Though their status as committees reflects the tendency toward at least the trappings of bureaucracy, the focus on these two services emerges from a desire to offer the fullest possible hospitality. Northern conventions tend not only to offer special block rates at local motels, but as much housing with local singers as possible. Southern singers have long invited their singing friends to stay during multiday conventions, but this was done informally among friends. However, friendships in the Midwest are of a more recent vintage; therefore, singers in Minneapolis-St. Paul and Chicago have formalized this process, so that in theory any visitor can easily locate free housing, regardless of whether or not they have established friendships in the area. This does not necessarily indicate a greater desire to extend hospitality than southern singers show, but it is highly responsive to the looser networks of northern singers and to the realities of travel for them and expresses again the northern ethic of going beyond welcoming everyone to actively facilitating participation more broadly.

The existence of a child-care committee (which often consists of hiring the teenage child of a local singer to care for younger children during the singing) reflects a careful adaptation of the tradition of southern singing hospitality, not just to local structures, but also to ideological differences. Southern singers typically embrace more conservative gen-der roles, with women expected to care for their children during sing-ings, even if this means giving up significant singing time themselves. Although most male southern singers I know are loving, involved fathers, few of those who are married consider their children to be their primary or equal responsibility during a singing. As one Alabama woman said to me, her husband "loves those kids and he's there for all of us, but the fact is, *I* raised our children."

Northern singers, by contrast, are somewhat more likely to see caring for children as the responsibility of both parents, as well as a responsibil-ity that can be handed over to an organized child-care committee for the duration of a singing. This enables both parents to sing, which can be a novel experience for southern parents of young children attending a northern singing: At one year's Garden State Convention, a Mississippi woman took a moment before leading her song to thank the convention for providing child care, noting that it was the most time she'd had to sing uninterrupted since the birth of her young son. Having a child-care committee therefore accords with the ideological positions of some northern singers, but it can also serve as an incentive to some singers who otherwise might not find it worth the trip to attend a singing at which they would actually get to sing very little.

Southern and northern practices around the public prayers that begin and end singings and bless the dinner table are also conspicuously gen-dered. As I mentioned in my discussion of the Minnesota Convention, a woman minister gave the opening prayer at that singing. Women also routinely are selected to deliver prayers in Chicago (and other northern singing communities I have visited), whereas I can think of no occasion on which I have heard a woman give a public prayer at a southern singing, many southern singers being drawn from denominations in which women are not allowed to become ministers or take on ministerial roles. Even many northern singers who are themselves not Christian or not religious in any way would argue for the importance of prayer as part of respect for southern singing traditions, but within that broad framework, singings in Chicago and Minnesota and other places engage in specific practices that draw much more on their own relatively liberal cultural locations than on the ones in which southern Sacred Harp singing takes place.

In Minnesota, the mention in a prayer of Jesus and "others we wor-ship" opened the prayer not just to Jews and members of other non-Christian religions, but also to singers who are uncomfortable with a notion of God as unequivocally male. In some locations, particularly in New England in the 1980s, singers routinely changed the words of songs to make them gender neutral ("He sends His showers of blessings down," for instance, became "God sends God's showers of blessings down"). Though I do not believe that changing the words of songs ever gained widespread use outside New England, where it was abandoned after a few years, prayers have been somewhat more elastic, sometimes referring to an ungendered creator, or offering a list of possibilities including both father and mother. Such prayers rarely draw explicit attention to their departure from Christian orthodoxy and never reject Christianity, but they do broaden the definition of appropriate Sacred Harp religiosity. This is often done in the name of religious pluralism, with a recognition that people of several faiths or of no faith may be present, but it also taps into the language of negotiation with which spiritual seekers are familiar.[32]

A final difference in prayer practices, not having to do with gender, lies in the amount of preparation devoted to the prayers given. Several of the denominations common among southern singers believe that no prayer or sermon should be prepared in advance of its delivery, that the speaker should open himself to God's influence and deliver an inspired message. These denominations also eschew seminary education for their preachers. The men called to pray at singings like Holly Springs and Liberty are not all preachers, but none would bring a prepared message; rather, they speak extemporaneously if often hewing to certain formulaic phrases. By contrast, prayers in Minnesota and Chicago are often prepared in advance and read out loud, and in cases where a minister is asked to pray, he or she is almost always seminary educated.

Preparation and effortfulness, the degree to which every aspect of a singing is self-consciously choreographed and that choreography is explicitly explained and recognized publicly, is the major thread tying together the differences between singings in west Georgia and on Sand Mountain and those in Chicago and Minnesota. Singers, both southern and northern, embrace the same schedule for a day of singing, the same ethic of hospitality and open participation. But Sand Mountain and west Georgia singers draw on much-richer and longer-standing repertoires of cooperation with each other, on deeper knowledge of the habits and traditions of the other individuals they sing with and of their singing communities as entities that existed before and will exist after them. This enables them to be more relaxed about many of the aspects of hosting a singing—the church will be available when they need it, there will be several men on the front rows of the different sections appropriate to call on for prayer and ready to pray without advance notice, there will be enough food. None of these things is effortless, but long habit can make them appear so, even at times to the singers engaged in the effort.

By contrast, the effort involved in hosting a singing in Chicago and Minnesota is always readily visible on the surface. In part, this is because of structural factors that require more work, as well as because singers are not only working to host a singing but also to construct around it a community out of people who may never see each other except at the singing. It is also because the very appearance of effort has been raised to a principle among many singers, not just in Chicago and Minnesota, but at other newer singings outside the South. The visibility of effort serves several purposes. It seeks to show visitors how very much their presence is valued, that they are worth the work of hosting them to the utmost. It also gives the host singers a way to identify their centrality in their local singing community—one is not just a Sacred Harp singer but a member of the housing or food committee, identifiably a contributor to what is being built. This provides them recognition in the singing community, a personal sense of contributing and being valued, and a way to explain the intensity of their involvement to nonsinging friends.

Similarly, the talking between songs that is common in Minnesota and Chicago serves a concrete purpose in replacing the nonverbal communication that takes place in the more densely networked communities of Sand Mountain and west Georgia, expressing out loud many of the reactions and observations that at Liberty are expressed through a wink and a nod; it also publicly proclaims the existence of a community, with in-jokes and longstanding relationships. At the same time, though, the anxiety it sometimes conveys can highlight the relative fragility of that community, the degree to which it is held together through constant effort rather than easy familiarity.

Singing in each area is therefore simultaneously a product of local factors, of current Sacred Harp practice, and of a narrative of a little-changing historic Sacred Harp tradition. Enough commonality exists between locations to allow a singer from any Sacred Harp community to attend a singing in any other and know how to conduct themselves and what is going on at any given moment; enough difference exists for well-traveled singers to refer with confidence to "typical" Chicago or Sand Mountain singers and singing practices.

———

Sand Mountain, west Georgia, Chicago, and Minneapolis-St. Paul therefore encompass four distinct bodies of people, histories of Sacred Harp singing, and sets of pathways available for new singers to enter and which existing singers themselves travel along and keep cleared. These, along with the interpretive frameworks discussed in the next chapter, are the bases for the regular practices and community norms established when the singers in a particular area come together to sing.

Sand Mountain exhibits the greatest integration of kinship, church, Sacred Harp, and other forms of community, with singers also sharing local town concerns, political affiliations, and in some cases, professional involvement. The strength of the family tradition leads to age and generational diversity; otherwise, singers constitute a type to a remarkable extent. Although, as we shall see, subgroups of singers in the area have different ways of organizing their participation, and in particular their interaction with outsiders, in the local context the extent of the shared background and understanding leads to a particularly tight-knit foundational singing community.

The west Georgia singing community is driven largely by a narrative about its past. Although singers here share many characteristics with those on Sand Mountain, their population has shrunk drastically, with singers aging and not being replaced by a new generation. Faced with these dwindling numbers, west Georgia singers define themselves through a story about their past, pointing to the historical significance of the region to Sacred Harp singing and, in some cases, extending that narrative into the present despite evidence to the contrary. Although the success of Sacred Harp communities is often cyclical (twenty years ago Liberty was a relatively weak singing) and it is not impossible that west Georgia singing could be turned around, at present it appears that the area faces a dispiriting present and ever-diminishing future. In response to that, singers in the area have turned ever more to the past, with their greatest organizational energy going toward memorializing—often in concrete physical form—the historical significance and strength of the local tradition rather than finding a new generation of singers.

Chicago Sacred Harp singers have partial success at two distinct types of community function but have not managed to fully unite the two. The Old Guard has been successful at organizing and presenting a highly visible, respected public face for Chicago Sacred Harp and over the years has formed many close friendships among themselves and with singers from other areas. At this point, though, they are not a fully active group, but one somewhat like west Georgia, oriented to the past, albeit to a more recent past and not in as extreme a fashion. The newer Hyde Park/University of Chicago singers have formed a close-knit, supportive local community but have not been as able to extend their ties and influence outward.

In contrast to Chicago, where a successful public face overlies two reasonably distinct but generally cordial subcommunities, in Minneapolis-St. Paul the two subgroups are at once less distinct and less cordial. Strikingly, although the origins of Sacred Harp singing in the area are relatively recent, singers there seem to lack even a coherent, shared origin story. Similarly, they lack a strong community ethic, residing instead in more atomized friendship groupings. Their political and religious diversity is higher than in other groups, and this in combination with their weak community cohesion seems to create difficulty both in reaching out to new singers and in managing conflict among themselves.

Both communities, though, share a cultural milieu to a significant extent and share structural challenges posed by being new, urban singing communities. The comparison between a day of singing in each of the four locations discussed in this chapter and the previous one lay bare many of these differences; in the next chapter, I consider more deeply how cultural milieu, existing beliefs, and structural considerations shape the communities constructed around Sacred Harp in different areas.

FOUR

Belief into Organization

In his study of the homeschooling movement, Mitchell L. Stevens finds that "people really do attempt to turn their ideals into organizational reality,"[1] with Christian home-schoolers not only making curricular decisions based on their religious beliefs but also forming associations and advocacy groups on the same basis, while other homeschoolers focus more on establishing groups that reflect their values of consensus and individual freedom. Like the homeschoolers Stevens studied, Sacred Harp singers come from differing backgrounds and have differing belief systems. But in contrast to the homeschoolers, who run along parallel but separate tracks, singers do frequently interact and expect in those interactions to find that they are engaged in the same activity, with the same practices upheld. Yet, in a delicate balance, they still try to shape local practices according to their ideals.

The differing ideals singers bring to Sacred Harp organize every community in which Sacred Harp is sung. The act of singing is primary, acting, in DeNora's words, as a "constitutive medium of social life,"[2] and the ways that Sacred Harp singing is almost universally structured—the hollow square, the opportunity for each person to have their choice of song—shape people's understandings not only of how Sacred Harp is *done* but also of what it *means*. People who come to singing as adults often find their preconceptions reshaped as they engage with the music, community, and tradition. At the same time, though, the religious, musical, and organizational ideals that people bring with them to the practice of Sacred Harp also powerfully structure the localized ways Sacred Harp is done. To understand the final product of the combination of these different groups of people, their group style, and the meaningful and often spiritual experience of group singing, we must first understand the tool kits that shape local practices and communities.

I identify five major categories for thinking about Sacred Harp and organizing its practice: religion, musical genre, authenticity and tradition, authority, and history. Individual singers arrive at Sacred Harp with a set of beliefs about these categories and how they relate to Sacred Harp. Local singing practices are then shaped by those beliefs.

Each category at times overlaps with others, the moments of overlap themselves providing important evidence of how thinking about the tradition is organized. Additionally, while the content of what people think about each of these areas varies, so too does the importance—or lack thereof—they place on a given category. For instance, *everyone* has to engage with religion when it comes to Sacred Harp, but they do so in different ways. For Christians it is self-evidently Christian music and the lyrics have great significance, while others have to find ways *around* the lyrics, ways to say that this is not merely or most importantly Christian. Other categories operate more implicitly, such as authority, which I find to be a pervasive shaping force, but which many singers would not understand as an important force shaping their understandings of or engagement in Sacred Harp.

Religion

Work in the sociology of religion suggests that one way to typologize religious orientations is between individualist spiritualities and tight, sometimes repressive, community, as Bellah and his coauthors suggest in *Habits of the Heart,* or between a spirituality of dwelling and a spirituality of seeking, as Wuthnow suggests in *After Heaven.*[3] In both Chicago and Minnesota (and elsewhere), most of the singers who have come to Sacred Harp as adults are baby boomers, a generation that Wade Clark Roof has characterized as one of seekers, and many reflect his conclusion that the 1980s and especially the 1990s saw new patterns of deepening and specializing spirituality, pluralism, "multilayered belief and practice," and "transformed selves."[4] Many of these new singers came to Sacred Harp in part through seeking identities, and those values inform their practice of it.

Even among singers who identify themselves as Christian and who connect Sacred Harp with their Christianity, the religious meanings people look for in and seek to extract from the music and the practice of Sacred Harp vary. The relationships understood to exist between Sacred Harp and formal worship also differ. The question of the relationship between Sacred Harp and formal worship is not only a question of the meanings singers attribute to the two activities but also a structural one, dependent on the time demands placed on churchgoers and on whether a given church is familiar with Sacred Harp.

Churches on Sand Mountain have greater involvement with Sacred Harp than churches in west Georgia, Chicago, or Minneapolis-St. Paul, with *The Sacred Harp* used in services at Liberty and Shady Grove. These churches also make time to hold all-day singings, and such singings are often attended by church members who do not go to other churches for the purpose of singing Sacred Harp. The creation of such space for Sacred Harp within the church context is a product not only of the histories of these churches—Ebenezer Primitive Baptist Church in Dunwoody, Georgia, has a long history of Sacred Harp singing and singers and their families have long been stalwart members there, but this has not prevented Sacred Harp from being made unwelcome there—but also of the broader local context in which Sacred Harp (or "four-note" singing as it is called by many in this area to distinguish it from the more gospelized seven-shape "New Book" singing) is widely known and understood as a family, in addition to a church, tradition. This interplay, bolstered by the continuing rural nature of the area, supports the continuation of Sacred Harp as a strong local tradition. This is where singers live in the strongest spirituality of dwelling, in very concrete ways. Sacred Harp is grounded in the family and church contexts in ways that shape its practice.

The Ivey family has a long connection with Liberty Baptist Church. Several generations of Iveys are buried in the cemetery there, and the preacher there in recent years is Tony Ivey, while Loyd Ivey is a deacon. Importantly, these ties have not devolved into a commuter relationship; Tony and Sandy, Hobert and Sylvia, Loyd and Louise, Coy and Marie, Rodney, Loyd's married daughters, Teresa, Marian, and Martha, and other extended family all live within a few miles of the church. This physical proximity facilitates relationships between these family members and between their roles as kin, as church members or attendees, and as Sacred Harp singers. Also, though a significant number of family members live at greater distances, the core of people remaining close by the church means that, for them, the journey back to Sand Mountain and Liberty is not an homage to a distant memory but a visit to loved ones and to an ongoing way of life.

Before the annual fifth Sunday singing at Liberty in March 2001, for instance, Coy, Rodney, Loyd, Hobert, Tony, Marian Biddle, Teresa Bethune, and Eloise and Marlon Wootten (Loyd and Hobert's sister and her husband) gathered to prepare the church and grounds for the singing. In contrast to the khakis and button-down shirts they usually wear to singings, most of the men wore overalls and drove their work pickup trucks rather than the cars or newer pickups most drive to singings. Hobert rode a four-wheeler with a small trailer behind it to haul brush away. The work was for the most part gender segregated, with the women cleaning the interior of the church—vacuuming, polishing the pews, cleaning and restocking the bathrooms—and the men outdoors, clearing branches that had fallen during the winter from the ground and the roof over the table and hosing off the table. No one was visibly in charge or issuing instructions; the work was carried out with no time pressure felt and coordination of activities taking place in brief conversations. Otherwise, conversation was relaxed and social, revolving mostly around anticipation of the singing to come. This cleaning was done with the immediate purpose of preparing for the singing but would have been necessary at some point for the general upkeep of the church. Of the people participating in the cleaning, some, like Coy and Rod, are most active as Sacred Harp singers and attend church less regularly, while others attend church much more regularly than singing (although of the people gathered on this day, all attend at least a handful of singings at churches other than Liberty).

Such cooperation between Sacred Harp–identified people and church-identified people is routine at Liberty, as at Antioch and, to a lesser extent, other churches in the area. Singings are also family events at these churches. In particular, as discussed in chapter 2, Liberty's Decoration Day singing melds a singing with the family reunion qualities of the Decoration Day tradition in the area. Most of the small country churches in that area of Sand Mountain[5] have a day in advance of the singing during which the graves in their cemeteries are cleaned and decorated with flowers, and on which family members gather and visit with each other, bringing food to share. Liberty is one of the few churches that adds a Sacred Harp singing to these traditions, adjusting the typical organization of a singing in several ways to accommodate nonsingers and to allow for visiting between singers and nonsingers.

At Liberty's Decoration Day singings, the inclusion of songs from books other than the 1991 revision of *The Sacred Harp* also signals an orientation to family and church, as the other songs chosen are familiar from church services and have been particular favorites over the years. Although *The Sacred Harp* is central in the body of music sung at Liberty, in particular moments these other favorite songs form a distinct grouping, invoking family sentiment and history. Sacred Harp singers not from the area who attend many singings at Liberty may learn these songs, but the moments they are sung are palpably about the local community rather than the broader Sacred Harp community.

This intense interweaving of church, family, and Sacred Harp does not exist in any of my other research sites. By many accounts, something similar could have been found in west Georgia twenty or thirty years ago, but today most singers there belong to churches where few, if any, other members are familiar with Sacred Harp. They do continue to have singings that draw nonsinging family members, but in smaller numbers and with less intense participation. I have never, for instance, been to a west Georgia singing where you could find, as at Liberty's Decoration Day, a dozen or more teenage girls who had clearly dressed for a social event. Absent such involvement between church and singing and family, west Georgia singers who attend church regularly, therefore, face church-singing relationships similar to those of religious singers in Chicago and the Twin Cities.

Singers in these areas who attend church regularly can face time conflicts between church participation and singing. For instance, Jenny and Keith Willard live in St. Paul, Minnesota, and have long been mainstays of the singing there, having been instrumental in the founding of the Minnesota Sacred Harp Convention. They are active in their Seventh-Day Adventist church, where, Jenny says, "No, we don't sing Sacred Harp in our church. They do try to sing but it's a paltry thing. Keith and I don't even sing in our full Sacred Harp voices, but even so, they're still like 'there's someone singing back there!'" For Jenny, therefore, though she considers Sacred Harp singing to be worship and finds the religious lyrics to be "kind of sweet and comforting," when it comes to time and energy, church and singing obligations are in competition with each other, with work done to sustain one not crossing over to support the other.

As this case reveals, there are at least two axes to consider in the relationship between religious worship and Sacred Harp singing. Belief is an important question, and the religious beliefs of singers, even Christian ones, are diverse, but structural and community issues are also crucial. Coy, Rodney, Hobert, or Loyd Ivey—any of the people who met to prepare Liberty for its fifth Sunday singing in 2001—and Jenny Willard are all Christians (albeit from different denominations) who assert that they understand singing as worship, but when one of the Iveys spends an afternoon moving benches, chairs, and tables for a singing, he is understood as having contributed to his church community, while the same is not true for Jenny.

The Willards are far from alone in this. For many Sacred Harp singers who started to sing as adults and who belong to churches where Sacred Harp is, at most, a once-a-year novelty during a Sunday service, singing and church can in effect be two activities and communities struggling to fit into spaces in the week intended to fit only one such activity. Singers with children also struggle to juggle school and sports obligations.[6] Organized religion and Sacred Harp are in competition with each other more commonly than they are complementary, as is the case for so many singers on Sand Mountain.

People from families that have participated in Sacred Harp for generations, and especially those who continue to live in the broad context into which Sacred Harp was originally scheduled, therefore live a spirituality of dwelling (though the most dedicated singers among them also step outside that by traveling regularly to sing, visiting with people from other traditions). By contrast, among newer singers, even those committed to and grounded in a particular faith tradition, Sacred Harp necessarily partakes of what Wuthnow describes as the emphasis on negotiation in a spirituality of seeking; not only do they experience different forms of spirituality in church and at singings, but they also must literally negotiate between the demands on their time, energy, and ability to join in community.[7]

Singers who are not Christian or not religious at all do not have such time conflicts (at least between Sacred Harp and organized religion; other activities may, of course, compete for free time), but many experience difficulty with singing explicitly Christian words or participating in an activity that is religious for many participants. First, nonreligious singers work to explain why they enjoy singing Christian lyrics, or why the Christianity of the lyrics is not relevant. Such singers include the New York woman I overheard telling a Georgia singer, "My friends say, 'You're Jewish and a Buddhist, how can you sing this stuff about Jesus?' and I tell them, 'I know a metaphor when I hear one.'" Her blithe tone signaling that such a dismissal of the overtly Christian poetry would be a comfortable sentiment for many of the people she regularly sings with.

Others struggle more with this issue. When National Public Radio's *All Things Considered* ran a story on Sacred Harp, Western Massachusetts singer Kshama Ananthapura was quoted saying:

I fell in love with the music first, you know. I didn't much care for the words at all in the beginning, but when you sing it over and over again, you know, it takes on a meaning of its own, and if you can get past the fact that it's religious music—I sing with Jewish girls, I sing with people that don't really have a faith, and I'm a Hindu from India. All of us sing this with equal joy.

Her statement reflects a struggle with the words of the songs but also a sense that she has come to terms with and found meaning in them. In the end, though, what matters most in this account is the joy with which people sing, which may entail "get[ting] past the fact that it's religious music," a thing with "a meaning of its own" separate from religion. "Joy," then, becomes a universalized emotion, tied to spirituality for some and separated from it for others, but a measure of genuine participation for all, and the words take on a meaning detachable from their explicit Christian content. Similarly, one Chicago singer says,

I can believe that other people are understanding this stuff in a way that I could describe in theologically neutral terms. They believe that there's a real Jesus person that's going to do this stuff for them, and I don't believe that, but I can understand some of this as personally useful for them or socially useful in ways that I can let it not bother me because I don't have to believe it and I don't have to be bothered that they believe it.

In his words, too, ascribing Christian sentiment to the songs becomes a choice rather than a requirement of the lyrics. At least a few Christian singers would take issue with these characterizations, arguing fiercely that they miss the central point of the music; others willingly enter into discussions of Sacred Harp in which loose, open language is used to broaden the grounds of agreement and shared experience—the term "spirit" is often used in such conversations, capitalized as "Spirit," an incarnation of God, in some people's minds and uncapitalized as a vigorous emotional state, an incarnation of group spirit, or of a non-Christian deity in the minds of others.[8]

For other non-Christian singers, the struggle to come to terms with Sacred Harp as a Christian tradition comes less with the words than with the degree to which Sacred Harp is actively constructed as a Christian, or at least a religious, practice. One woman, noting that she was uncomfortable being identified by name because of how other singers might perceive her, said, "I'm not sure that the people I spend time with at southern singings are aware . . . a large number of them probably are aware that I'm not a Christian. I doubt any of them is aware that I am not a believer in anything religious . . . in any sort of God. . . . I'm afraid of them finding this out, to be honest." Not being religious makes this woman feel herself to be an outsider among southern singers, concealing a fundamental part of her identity and beliefs from them. Yet she goes on to acknowledge the power of the religiosity of Sacred Harp and to affirm her commitment to singing with people for whom Sacred Harp is importantly Christian, saying,

I think Sacred Harp without religion would be empty in a way. This again ties me in knots because I stand there watching the people who are obviously emotionally caught up in the religious experience that they are having and I'm uncomfortable as hell. At the same time if it wasn't there, if everyone at a Sacred Harp singing was like me, I'd probably be miserable.

For this woman, religion *is* an important part of the Sacred Harp experience, even though she herself does not participate in it. Something that she understands religious singers to bring to the hollow square both makes her uncomfortable and enriches her experience there. The avoidance of public statements makes her participation in Sacred Harp possible, since she is never called upon to lay out the extent of her nonparticipation in the religious aspects of the tradition. At the same time, because the potential reactions of Christian singers to her atheism remain a mystery, she may be holding herself at a greater-than-necessary distance from some singers who might, as she acknowledges, think "well, we didn't expect you to [be Christian] because we know who you are . . . and we'd like you to come to our singings anyway and you're a Sacred Harp singer so in that capacity we love you because you're part of a family of Sacred Harp singers."

Finally, some singers come to understand Sacred Harp *as* their church or their most meaningful connection to religion. Minnesota singer Martha Henderson expresses such a sentiment, noting, "I wasn't religious when I started singing. I kept thinking how can I sing this stuff about Jesus, well alright I like the tune." Over time, she found that, due to a combination of the music and exposure to other singers, in particular southern singers, "it started to mean something to me." Although she continues to attribute a primary importance to the community she finds in Sacred Harp and the people she sings with, she says that ultimately, "Sacred Harp became my church in a way that no church has become my church," because the many church services she had attended in her life "just felt alien to me."

Musical Genre

What broader musical genre people consider Sacred Harp to be a part of is more closely tied to issues of religious belief than might be expected. Many southern singers would answer a question about musical genre by saying, as Alabama singer Shelbie Sheppard does whenever the chance presents itself, "This is not folk music, it is sacred."[9] Such a statement is not intended to say "this isn't folk, it's more like Handel's Messiah," but represents an attempt to switch the topic from music to religion, asserting the primacy of the latter. Such beliefs about what musical genre Sacred Harp belongs to can structure aspects of participation, such as how people dress to attend a singing or what venues are considered appropriate to sing in.

Nonetheless, Sacred Harp *is* music, so the recurrence of the characterization of it as folk music specifically is not the only reason to consider its place among musical genres. Folk is the genre to which Sacred Harp is most frequently assigned[10], and many new singers come to Sacred Harp through folk revival channels, such as folk festivals or recordings. The genesis of the Chicago group was in a search for something that fit within the folk rubric but was new and different to sing. As Judy Hauff describes it, she and Ted and Marcia Johnson had been playing guitars and singing "Tom Paxton songs, 'Blowing in the Wind,' all the stuff we'd been singing fifteen years before—even in the early '80s it's kind of passé—and I'm like, 'Marcia, I can't stand to sing this stuff anymore.'" In response to this fatigue, Marcia found some photocopies of Sacred Harp songs that had been given to her by a folklorist friend, and they pieced out how to sing the music, although without singing the shape notes before the words. The Minneapolis-St. Paul singers similarly emerged in part out of a performing choir called Almond Tree, which sang some songs from *The Sacred Harp*. Although singers in both locations have moved toward serious identification with the southern Sacred Harp tradition, including singing the notes, engaging more fully with the religious content of the music, and holding participatory conventions, these folk-music roots continue to be felt and are observable in the other musics practiced by local singers and in the annual demonstration singings that are held at folk festivals in both areas.

Minnesota singers in particular seem connected to various forms of folk music and dance. The extent of this became clear to me on a visit there in 2002, during which I attended a concert by British folk singer

Louis Killen. In the small audience at the show (which was held in the basement of a private home) were approximately one-third of the people who had attended the Sacred Harp singing earlier in the day. The next day, at that same singing, a woman who did not attend the Killen concert mentioned to me that she had been contra dancing the night before (with her husband, also a Sacred Harp singer), focusing on the band that had played at the dance. Two days later, three singers (who had been at the Killen concert) stopped in at another local singing for a short time before proceeding to their morris dance practice. In all, at least fourteen local singers were involved in at least three different kinds of folk music or dance (or combined music and dance) *besides* Sacred Harp in that four-day period.

Despite this intense involvement in explicitly recognized folk forms, though, the public discourse around Sacred Harp in Minneapolis-St. Paul is very much focused on the southern Sacred Harp tradition. Singers here frequently invoke particular southern singers between songs, with leaders dedicating their songs to southerners or self-deprecatingly noting that they won't lead a song as well as a southern singer who often leads that same song, and seated singers similarly, if more quietly, making such associations. In doing so, they draw attention to their knowledge of authentic Sacred Harp (as embodied by southern singers), associating themselves with this authenticity while recognizing that they cannot claim to embody it in any straightforward fashion; in this, they engage in identity construction similar to that of the white blues musicians studied by Grazian, for whom enacting black forms of blues authenticity might appear as racist mimicry, but not engaging in blues conventions would appear as inauthentic. Grazian writes that, to escape this dilemma, white musicians "construct authenticated roles for themselves based on a different set of criteria than those governing the credibility of black blues musicians." Where these blues musicians draw on "*white* stock characters . . . such as rock stars and folklorists,"[11] northern Sacred Harp singers emphasize their allegiance not only to southern styles but also to individual southern singers, highlighting that their knowledge is gained through experience and personal relationships, not academic or abstract learning. In this way they also negotiate the distinctive limits that the southern Sacred Harp community has placed on northerners' enactments of the tradition.

Emphasizing status relationships and meanings that derive from an organization of Sacred Harp that predated their involvement in it—rather than in the process William Roy describes in which "because folk music was a music of the 'other' it could easily be appropriated by anyone who wanted to claim it"[12]—serves to distance Sacred Harp from the folk genres in which these singers participate. Although the Minnesota singers, and new northern (and urban southern) singers more generally, often do treat southern singers in many ways as "other," appropriation is never easy and must always be accomplished through reference to the desires of this other.

This attribution of authority to lifelong singers is unusual in genres defined as "folk." As the historian Benjamin Filene details, from the late-eighteenth-century beginnings of the popularization of the concept of "the folk" and the music, dance, and art associated with them, "the pursuit of folk culture involved a complex series of ideological distinctions. First of all, not just anyone counted as 'folk.'"[13] Rather, constructions of who and what were "folk" involved projections of how the academics and elites considering the question desired to understand their country's heritage. In the early twentieth-century United States, where song collectors were "mostly white Anglo-Saxon Protestants," they "asserted that mountain culture was America's authentic folk inheritance and at the same time stressed that the mountaineers were British. In effect, therefore, the collectors established *their* heritage as the true American culture."[14] In different political moments, different groups of "folk" are valorized, but in every time, they are exoticized; as Roy, a sociologist, notes, "the past of folk music is typically set against the present, and usually with a message."[15]

Roy identifies folk music as "especially challenging to our sociological endeavor of probing the relationship of artistic genres and social boundaries,"[16] because it at least partially ruptures the principle of homology, "the notion that the boundaries between cultural forms align with the boundaries between groups," with, for instance, country music associated with whites and rap associated with blacks.[17] Sacred Harp presents a particularly potent case of boundary crossing, though not one that involves the crossing of racial boundaries, because of the emphasis on participation, which has had the (not inevitable) effect of repeatedly bringing together the people from the different groups that sing it. This complicates the process of "othering" so common in folk revivals, with lifelong southern singers insisting that they are not merely, or perhaps at all, "the folk," and new singers divided between the impulse to imagine those lifelong singers as an other and the understanding they gain of those singers as complex, real, and modern people like themselves. Given this pushback, conceptions of authenticity are more complicated and contested than in most folk genres.

Lifelong southern singers, for their part, rarely draw connections between Sacred Harp and other kinds of music and often explicitly

disclaim knowledge about music or music theory. Even in teaching singing schools, accomplished singers and teachers such as David Ivey, Jeff
Sheppard, or Richard DeLong will point to what they do not know about
music theory and its operation in other forms of music in the process
of explaining what singers need to know about music theory in Sacred
Harp. This strategy could function to define Sacred Harp as a classic folk
music, in which knowledge is supposedly instinctual rather than learned.
However, the emphasis within Sacred Harp on the written tradition of
the songbook and the singing school tradition separates Sacred Harp
from other musics, establishing it as a distinct body of knowledge, such
that—especially in the context of the singing school—an expert on other
forms of music should not assume him or herself to be an automatic expert on Sacred Harp and may even have to "unlearn" previous musical
training.[18]

Although they tend to draw a line between Sacred Harp and other
music, many southern singers are participants in or fans of other kinds
of music. A few sing in church choirs, although because of the overlapping time commitments, it is impossible to be in a church choir and be a
very dedicated Sacred Harp singer. Nonetheless, some people do restrict
their Sacred Harp singing mainly to Saturdays and spend Sundays playing
piano in church or singing in church choirs.

A number of singers on Sand Mountain are involved in bluegrass music. This involvement may be largely as fans, attending bluegrass festivals and concerts; as musicians who occasionally perform; or as social
musicians. Many social gatherings associated with Sacred Harp singings
on Sand Mountain, such as the social held for the last several years at
Coy and Marie Ivey's house the Saturday evening of the July convention at Liberty or a dinner held at Betty Shepherd's house before a local
Fort Payne singing, feature picking sessions by singers with banjos, guitars, harmonicas, and other instruments. Because the musicians at these
events do not play together regularly, they must determine what body of
songs they know in common, negotiating between songs, with one musician sometimes playing a few measures of a song to determine if the song
being discussed is one they know. The success of the *O Brother, Where Art
Thou?* sound track provided a core group of songs that singers from different places knew and could play together. At the July social at Coy and
Marie's house in 2001, several songs from *O Brother* were played more
than once by a group of musicians that included singers from Alabama,
Tennessee, Chicago, and Minnesota. The pervasiveness of commercial
culture therefore facilitated this noncommercial activity by giving people

from different places and backgrounds a common reference point and suggests the multidirectionality of appropriation.

Authenticity and Tradition

"Authentic," and functional synonyms such as "genuine," "true," or "real," and invocations of "tradition" are enormously vexed concepts when applied to culture. A substantial body of work has shown how practices often labeled as "traditional" are in fact of recent vintage, with the idea of the tradition as age-old having been invented "to inculcate certain values and norms of behaviour by repetition."[19] In *Creating Country Music: Fabricating Authenticity*, sociologist Richard Peterson argues that the appearance of authenticity is manufactured and mobilized in the marketing of commercial cultural products; similarly, David Grazian shows how ideas of authenticity are deployed in Chicago blues clubs to provide heightened appeal to patrons interested not only in hearing music but also in having a particular experience of Chicago blues.[20]

Discussions of authenticity are, therefore, always complicated by the often-invented character of authenticity and by a multiplicity of possible grounds for claiming authenticity. This slipperiness has led a number of scholars to attempt greater specificity for the concept, considering what features are required for a form to be labeled authentic, or breaking it apart into types based on the question under consideration.[21] Peterson lays out six requirements for the perception of authenticity, that a performer or performance must be "1. Authenticated, not pretense. . . . 2. Original, not fake. . . . 3. Relic, not changed. . . . 4. Authentic reproduction, not Kitsch. . . . 5. Credible in current context. . . . [and] 6. Real, not imitative."[22] These requirements apply to commercial products, which must offer proof that they are not solely intended for profit but from some deeper—more "authentic"—impulse. The question of from what area their authenticity derives, however, is left open in Peterson's framework.

In *Sounding Indigenous: Authenticity in Bolivian Music Performance*, Michelle Bigenho elaborates on the concept of authenticity by identifying three distinct forms it may take, while cautioning that "these different ideologies of authenticity should be seen as mutually inextricable"[23]— pointing again to the difficulty of dealing with the term at all. In Bigenho's typology, "*experiential authenticity* refers to the entire sensory experience of music performances," not just sound but the desire to dance, the emotions raised by listening to or making music; it is "the groove" and the discourses that surround "the groove," raising it up to an ideal.[24] Next, "*cultural-historical authenticity* . . . purports a continuity with an imagined point of origin, situated in a historical or mythical past"[25]; taken to an extreme, this is the invention of tradition, but shades of it are found in discourses surrounding almost any folk music or art form. Finally, "*unique authenticity*" is used to "refer to the idea that something is authentic because it is singular, new, innovative, and usually perceived to emerge from the depths of the composing musician's soul."[26]

While experiential and cultural-historical authenticity are central to discourses about and within Sacred Harp, unique authenticity is rarely, if ever, invoked. Composers are credited in *The Sacred Harp* and are frequently discussed, but, particularly in the case of recent composers, uniqueness is something to be avoided, with compositional authenticity derived from *similarity* to older songs that are already established as "real" Sacred Harp and from the experiential authenticity singers report in singing the new songs. Another form of authenticity, however, is frequently invoked: *spiritual authenticity* can be a component of experiential authenticity, as when singers refer to a singing being "filled with Spirit [or spirit]." It can also stand as a means of assessing the intent or the respect for Sacred Harp felt by another singer.

The many forms of authenticity are typically discussed in multiple ways by Sacred Harp singers and used selectively to endorse ritual repetition or to call for changes framed as true to the authentic spirit of Sacred Harp. Attempting to isolate a form of authenticity, to find a debate in which one and only one form is found, is fruitless. However, in many such debates over the proper practice of Sacred Harp, one type of authenticity is most salient.

Cultural Authenticity [27]

Although this form of authenticity generally refers back to an imagined past, among Sacred Harp singers discourses of the past are often largely detachable from those of authentic Sacred Harp culture, understood as the culture of lifelong southern singers. Lifelong singers themselves often leave the question of authenticity unaddressed, at least with regard to southern singings populated by other lifelong singers, taking for granted that they, their singings, and their churches are and will be accepted as unproblematically "real." Because they presume their authenticity, they feel little need to assert or document it. Thus their descriptions of different singings tend to revolve not around authenticity but around quality, around good and bad singing, food, or behavior. Asked about a day of singing, for instance, one Sand Mountain singer said,

Well, the crowd was a little off, but we had a good bass section and the tenors and altos were solid. Then Bobby and Mac got in there on the front bench of the treble and Lord! You know how off-key they are and can't nobody do a thing about it. I was sitting next to Bobby and he was right in my pitching ear and Crystal was behind me, bless her heart, and between them it was all I could do to get my note. We had plenty of good treble singers, but they were all stuck in the back where you couldn't hear them. And you know how that drags a singing down.

These evaluations of a singing frequently include reports of the amount and quality of the food ("they don't usually have barbecue or anything big like that, but I think it's one of the best singings for little-old-lady casseroles and cobblers"), of the memorial lesson ("she didn't talk about the singers who'd passed hardly at all, she just preached a sermon and that's not what the memorial lesson is supposed to be"), and of songs that went particularly well or badly. Criticisms of singers for whom the speaker has affection are liberally sprinkled with the phrase "bless his/her heart" to indicate this affection and that the criticism is of a specific trait or behavior and not the person overall, but these criticisms are made, from the standpoint of singers who feel entitled, by their location in the tradition and the region, to make them. Among newer singers, these kinds of evaluations of specific events or people are much less employed; rather, discussions about Sacred Harp tend to focus on the tradition as a whole and to articulate judgments about authenticity, rather than about specifics.

Newer northern singers, therefore, tend to emphasize the pilgrimage South, to authentic singings and to relationships with authentic singers. Knowledge gained through these channels is elevated, with "Shelbie said" or "in his singing schools, David Ivey/Jeff Sheppard/Richard DeLong/Hugh McGraw teaches that" acting as verifiers not simply of the piece of information being conveyed but of the speaker's license to instruct or debate with others as to the correct way to do Sacred Harp.

As much as they explicitly discuss cultural authenticity, though, newer singers try to enact it, to provide visible evidence that they have immersed themselves in authentic Sacred Harp culture. This often includes buying clothes similar to those of southern singers, which are usually understood as church clothes; preparing common southern foods, such as deviled eggs, barbecue, or coconut cake—foods that in the daily lives of most northern singers would be considered appallingly unhealthful—

for nonsouthern conventions; or adopting song-leading styles of specific, respected southern singers. Such actions are delicate and must be performed carefully lest they appear to be mimicry rather than developed knowledge. For instance, a new singer who leads difficult songs beautifully and in a traditional southern style is likely to be praised for this ability—unless it becomes apparent that she can only lead one or two songs in this style as a product of extensive rehearsal and that overall her leading is unpracticed and weak, in which case the praise may turn to criticism.

Spiritual Authenticity

In contrast to cultural-historical authenticity, which tends to be discussed in factual, tangible terms (albeit ones up for debate), experiential and, often, spiritual authenticity are understood as difficult to assess. As with sincerity, there is no reliable external evidence of experiential authenticity or of a particular type of spiritual authenticity. Spiritual authenticity is discussed in two ways, one more akin to the fact-based understanding of cultural-historical authenticity and one the unquantifiable experiential authenticity.

The former approach to spiritual authenticity often involves a challenge to orthodoxy, as happened in Minneapolis-St. Paul in April 2002. After Doug Donley, a local singer and the pastor of the University Baptist Church (an American Baptist Church where many local singings are held), invited singers to "Sacred Harp Sunday," in which the music for the ten o'clock service would be largely drawn from *The Sacred Harp*, another local singer responded by writing to the group's e-mail list providing links to "three sermons that give you an idea of the disastrous teaching you might hear from the pulpit on 4/7 if you are considering this singing opportunity." One sermon explored the possibility that, rather than being the product of a virgin birth, Jesus was the product of Mary having been raped; the second described going to Lynchburg, Virginia, to convince Jerry Falwell that "calling homosexuality a sin is a form of spiritual violence"; and the third included the argument that "the theology of the Koran is not all that different from the Old and New Testaments." The e-mail also pointed to a fourth sermon, from Easter Sunday, based on the teachings of Mahatma Gandhi—this last sermon was not explicitly identified as an example of "disastrous teaching" but was clearly implied to have been inappropriate.

This brief e-mail was readable both as a warning to the collection of individuals who had been invited to sing at the service and as a statement that those sermons were insufficiently orthodox Christianity to be linked to Sacred Harp more generally. Another singer quickly responded, taking on the latter reading by saying, "I had been assuming (up to now anyway) that our Sacred Harp singing community, because of its diversity, was built on a sense of a certain respectful forbearance and gentle tolerance of other people's religious beliefs and opinions. . . . Attacking the church that is kind enough to be hosting our singing feels to me like the worst kind of self-righteous ingratitude." To this singer, the true spirituality of Sacred Harp involved respect and tolerance and gratitude for hospitality—positions he identified firmly with Christianity by citing Matthew 7:1–5—rather than adherence to a highly specified theological orthodoxy.

This debate continued through one reply from the singer objecting to connecting Sacred Harp with the positions of the University Baptist Church and a final message from another singer arguing that true Sacred Harp spirituality involved fellowship and precluded attack. Other singers voted with their feet, with apparently heightened participation in the church service and with the church's pastor officiating at the wedding of two singers, held the following September at the annual Minnesota Sacred Harp Convention. It represented an unusual moment in which a singer asserted that appropriate Sacred Harp spirituality comes not from what singers *do* while they sing, but from things external to the act of singing, from the location to the beliefs of the sponsors.[28]

More commonly, singers consider each other's spirituality as it is manifested in the hollow square. The appearance of passionate engagement, of singing Christian lyrics enthusiastically, may allow others to assume a singer to be Christian, or at least as coming to a spiritual understanding of the music. As Sand Mountain singer Terry Wootten says of non-Christian singers, "I'm not one to tell them what they can do and what they can't do. That would be their own little thing but if they really participate in the way that I do in it, if they was looking to get out of it what I do, they would have to change their mind." The appearance of participating in it "the way that I do," then, can suggest that the singer's mind is in fact changing, that they understand whatever the observer feels to be most important in Sacred Harp—be it Christianity or community fellowship. Particularly good singing can be used as evidence that this is the case. As Shane Wootten said, when asked about a particularly good singing we had both attended,

I look at singings like that as a service, a religious type service, and every time you go to church or to a religious service it's got to do with the mood people are in when they get there and what's happened during the week before, and every church service or every singing is not going to be as moving or as enjoyable because of the different situations. Sometimes, some few times, you can have a setting to where everybody's in the right state of mind and everybody's in harmony with each other and it comes out in the singing.

In his thinking, the reasons a singing might be especially good are the same as the reasons a church service might be, with the frame of mind of the participants a crucial factor in enabling a powerful, spiritually moving result. In some cases, an elision takes place in which it may be said of a person who is not Christian that they "don't know it" but they are in fact moving toward an acceptance of Jesus—because if they were not, they couldn't sing the way they do. Thus, even for a conservative Christian, the expression of a vaguely defined but deeply felt spirituality seems to trump doctrinal religious standards.[29]

Chicago singer Cathryn Baker expresses a similar sentiment, characterizing the best singings she has attended as

like being in a gathered meeting. That's what the Quakers call a meeting where you can feel that everyone's spirit is joined and it's almost—because I'm a Christian I've got to put it in Christian perspective—the power of the Holy Spirit is palpable, you can feel it. It's like having Jesus standing right beside you and there is . . . it's too powerful.

Such a sentiment is common among singers with a range of religious beliefs and is often expressed in shorthands, such as "the Spirit came" or "we sing for the Holy Ghost to come in."

Spiritual authenticity is therefore often evaluated with regard to one's own experience, which may then be extended onto the other singers present—if I am having an unusually spiritual experience of singing today, and you are contributing to it, then you must be in a spiritually similar place to me, whether or not you profess Christianity. These are the moments in which there is a near-total overlap between spiritual and experiential authenticity.

Experiential Authenticity

Experiential authenticity can be incredibly difficult to talk about with regard to individuals—it is the form of spiritual authenticity discussed immediately above, but without spirituality as a means of assessment. In these cases, most of all, it becomes a question of how one judges the sincerity of a singer's love of and engagement in Sacred Harp. Without a widely agreed-upon language—other than the spiritual language discussed above—for what exactly the "groove" of Sacred Harp singing is or what produces it, a number of concrete factors are mentioned with some frequency.

————

The *physical* aspects of singing are occasionally used to explain its emotional effects: Singing Sacred Harp from nine thirty to three thirty, pausing only for short breaks every hour and one hour for lunch, is physically taxing. Especially at the end of a hot day, singers can come away drenched with sweat, sometimes heavy enough to lift wood stain off of the benches they are sitting on. Boston Sacred Harp singer and Wellesley College Christian Studies professor Stephen Marini argues,

> Sustained singing is an ancient technique for creating altered states of consciousness through hyperventilation, elevated blood oxygen, and cranial and somatic vibration. Sacred Harp singers sing at full volume and extreme range for hours at a time, accruing all of those effects in abundance.[30]

Minnesota singer Christine Stephens, in a posting to the MNfasola mailing list, echoes the attribution of physical effects of singing that in turn influence the psyche, arguing that singing "is healing, even physically. Very good for the pancreas, which means it supports blood sugar balance which causes a peaceful feeling."[31] Confronted with another similar claim about the physical effects of singing, one Primitive Baptist singer from Georgia quickly asserted that "it's a lot more than that," suggesting that it's the working of God in and through the singing that is responsible for the transformative effects of singing Sacred Harp, rather than simple anatomy.

Many singers turn to the acoustics of singing spaces to explain the varying experience of singing. In the South, almost all singings are held at small country churches with longstanding historical associations with Sacred Harp. In most cases the church and singing are inextricably linked, so when the quality of the singing from year to year is assessed, the acoustics are a constant. There are a few exceptions, though. A few conventions, such as the United and the Young People's, move from year to year. In these cases, the *building* they go to in any given year is not the focus of the locating decision; rather, a singing *community* asks for the singing.

The singing sound afforded by small southern country churches is generally understood among singers to be ideal for Sacred Harp singing— presumably had the tradition been sustained in buildings with different acoustics, that sound would have been considered ideal—and it is reverberant but not echoing, most intense at the center of the square, where some overtones amplify the sound and can create the impression that even more people are singing than actually are. There is variation among these churches, of course, which are architecturally similar for both historical and theological reasons but whose construction was not coordinated in any way. Small differences in size, proportion, and building material produce differences in sound; naturally, most southern singers believe *their* home church to sound the best.

As discussed in the previous chapter, however, in areas where particular singings do not have longstanding ties to particular buildings room acoustics become an important means of assessing a singing. Rather than being a given, with the acoustics remaining the same for all singings at Holly Springs, the acoustics for the Midwest Convention may vary from year to year. Singings in Chicago and Minneapolis-St. Paul are held at many denominations of churches with many styles of architecture, in college buildings, a living history museum, and an Irish-American heritage center. With no standard style of space, differences can be endlessly debated. Moreover, because the same singing and same singers inhabit different spaces from year to year and even day to day of a two-day convention, the experience of singing in the room is somewhat detached from the experience of the singing as a whole, and the room can be critiqued without insult to the hosts. The hosts themselves, without sentimental attachment to a space, can spend months debating the merits of possible locations and can be, as Chicago's Ted Mercer describes himself, "acoustical determinists." Singing space, therefore, becomes a central site for debate over what is authentically Sacred Harp.

Finding a singing site that *looks* like or has a similar history to a southern singing church can be a source of cultural-historical authenticity, "prioritize[ing] narrative forms and what can be visually represented and perceived." While a site that *sounds* and in which singing *feels* like a southern singing can be a source of experiential authenticity, "root[ing] people to places through bodily movement and the achievement of a performative 'oneness' with sonorous events and other people."[32] In some discussions, though, the look and the feel of a room are collapsed into one another, with a strong presumption being made that a building that looks right will also feel and sound right.

Even for singers who rarely travel south to sing, and who have experience with other kinds of music in which other acoustics are considered desirable, the small one-room southern church remains the meaningful standard, the route to a real and good Sacred Harp singing experience, with the room as much as the singers providing the possibility for the "groove" of experiential authenticity. Obtaining cultural-historical authenticity thereby becomes seen as the most secure route to experiential authenticity, and this prophecy is often self-fulfilling.

As described in the previous chapter, one site frequently used for the Minnesota Convention is Murphy's Landing. The site is inconvenient in a number of ways, yet the excitement of many local singers at the prospect of singing there each year is palpable. As Martha Henderson wrote to the MNfasola mailing list during a discussion of the merits of different singing spaces, "That time we have at Murphy's is so wonderful, like magic almost, that it would be a shame to sacrifice that. . . . We ought to please ourselves and go where the singing is best and the site is prettiest, if more inconvenient in other ways."

Weak days of singing held in other Minnesota locations are often blamed on the room acoustics, while weak days of singing held at Murphy's Landing are unlikely to be acknowledged as such. A similar process occurs in Chicago, where Ida Noyes Hall, a room at the University of Chicago, is widely held by local singers to be acoustically exceptional and is procured whenever possible, despite a lived reality that is more complex. As local singer Ted Mercer says,

That's a great room if you have a very powerful class. It magnifies the experience. If the ratio of experienced to inexperienced is low it makes it very hard to sing fast songs because people are waiting for the echo before they start the next note so it gets slower and slower. "Africa" [a slow song] sounds wonderful and "Morning Prayer" [a fast song] sounds hideous. If you have a good ratio of experienced singers that are just going to keep plowing ahead then it works really well.

Mercer is thoughtful about the interaction between room and people; others are less so, and the search for good singing is sometimes presented less as a question of number, skill, and talent of singers than as one of varnished floors, ceiling height, and even bulletin boards hung on walls. This discussion does not reach nearly the same level of detail among lifelong southern singers, who, though they are attentive to acoustics and have in recent years been removing carpet from their churches in part to improve acoustics, see spaces as being less variable than classes and so give more critical attention to the latter.

Ultimately, singing quality receives the most descriptive and explanatory attention when it is judged to have been lacking. The language most often applied to an especially good singing is a language of inadequacy on the speaker's part to describe their experience of the ineffable. These are the moments when spiritual descriptions are often used, but as often, the speaker expresses an inability to describe or even fully comprehend what happened. As Susan Harcrow says of the singing at Fuller Cemetery on the evening of July 28, 2001,

I don't know what happened that night; I truly don't know what that was. . . . I know that something happened there that night that is a once in a lifetime thing. I don't think we've gotten that feeling since. . . . I knew we couldn't ever recreate that. I think it was just a combination of everything, and I'm just glad I was there to be a part of it, because it's just one of those things you can't explain to somebody. You just can't figure out what it is, and probably if you talked to every person that was there that night they would give you a different interpretation of what it was.

Asked about the same singing, Betty Shepherd groped for words, then simply began to cry, as overcome by the power of her memory as she had been visibly overcome by the power of the singing on the night in question, when a steady stream of tears and an expression of absolute joy were mixed on her face from early in the evening when she led "New Jerusalem," one of her late mother's favorite songs, with her cousin Eloise, until the end of the singing nearly two hours later. Within certain Christian frameworks, this might be understood as the reception or bestowal of God's grace.

Authority

In his study of the homeschooling movement, Stevens's observation that "people really do attempt to turn their ideals into organizational reality,"[33] pertains particularly to ideas about authority, which he argues have significant implications for group organization. Among homeschoolers, those that Stevens refers to as "believers" held strong views of the appropriateness of vertical authority structures for the family and for society as a whole. The education and lobbying groups they have formed reflect these views, producing "an organizational model [that] can only work in a social universe in which people are willing to work in hierarchical relationships with one another."[34] By contrast, other homeschoolers idealize personal autonomy and consensus, producing an organizational model that reflects these beliefs at a cost of efficiency.

Similarly, in her study of free schools, Ann Swidler finds that "the aspect of ideology most relevant for collective control is the one that determines the publicly legitimate language of debate about individual behavior and group direction."[35] Both free schools and homeschoolers seek to establish nontraditional forms of educational organization; in both, questions of authority and how participation will be regulated and maintained become central. Authority may be vested in an individual who asserts it over the group, in each individual's right to go their own way or in a notion of the collective itself. Because the new form of organization has been chosen actively as an alternative to traditional schooling, exit—whether from the specific alternative organization or the overall form of the free school or homeschooling—is a viable strategy and organizations must guard against loss of membership. Looking at studies of communes and other collective groups, Swidler notes that "few organizations overcome these difficulties."[36]

Sacred Harp singing communities face similar challenges. There is no official structure of authority, no formal hierarchy that persists from place to place or year to year,[37] yet there are strong norms, some local and some pervading throughout most if not all singings. Singing is not a widely known and accepted form of worship such as church, yet it places many of the same demands as some churches. Because it is wholly voluntary, with exit a structurally easier option than staying, it must provide continued incentive to stay. For most singers, the music provides this incentive, and for many the community fellowship is an additional motive. The exercise of authority within such loosely structured organizations (indeed, singings are not truly organizations, though they share traits) is a delicate issue.

Ultimately, each singing community deals with—or fails to deal with—the question of authority by drawing on and maneuvering around singers' more general beliefs on the subject. Hierarchy and direct authority are more accepted in some places than others, creating very different ways of organizing singings. On Sand Mountain and in west Georgia, this translates to collective controls based on traditional church and social organization, with a few people in each community, most often men at least in their thirties and generally older, looked to for and actively exercising leadership. Such leadership may be exercised softly, as David Ivey does at Liberty. In fact, David lives outside the immediate area of the church and is rarely present to help prepare for a singing; on the day of a singing, he privately defers to his brother, father, and other relatives on questions such as when to start singing and how long to sing. Despite this, though, he was always during the years of this study named as the chair of singings held at Liberty and provides the public face of authority. He is the person most likely to be approached by visitors who have questions or wish to thank someone for hospitality received, and he is the person who publicly offers welcome from the community to visitors and recognizes the work done by others. Meanwhile, behind the scenes, in preparing for a singing, authority falls along the lines of the church, with the preacher and deacons (who are also singers) determining how the church and grounds will be maintained through the year or altered for the singing. At other times of the year at Liberty, during regular services and other events, these people, rather than David, would hold authority, because Sacred Harp singing is understood as his specific field of expertise while the church and congregation are theirs.

Because both sources of authority are widely understood as legitimate by singers in this area, the exercise of authority as a constraining or creative force rarely occurs. Instead, singers know their roles within an accepted authority structure (which is an adaptation of one found outside the singing) and act accordingly. By contrast, this issue is less settled in Chicago and Minnesota, where singers do not draw on such uniform church backgrounds, do not share other forms of community that guide them in their interactions, and do not possess well-established organizational bases to host all-day singings or conventions.

The lack of a center of authority in these places is at some times the result of an intentional dispersal, with official roles, such as convention officerships, rotating annually so that as many singers as possible can have an experience of responsibility and leadership and do so in a way that garners some public recognition. At other times, though, the lack of a central authority seems less intentional than a product of unresolved rivalries, with multiple people feeling entitled to claim authority and vying for control or attention. For instance, in January 2004, Tim Eriksen taught a workshop on Sacred Harp singing and related styles at the Old Town School of Folk Music in Chicago. The workshop was done in Tim's guise as a professional musician—at such events, his intent is always to bring new singers to Sacred Harp, but he teaches them in a self-consciously different way than he teaches singing schools for people already committed to Sacred Harp. Further, this event was also a part of his livelihood and an opportunity to develop a relationship with an important and well-known folk music institution.

Chicago singers, however, were very much aware of the event, particularly as it happened shortly after the release of *Cold Mountain* and as Tim's visit produced more coverage in local newspapers than Sacred Harp singing usually receives in that area. Their annual Anniversary Singing was the day after the workshop, which therefore represented a valuable opportunity for them to publicize Sacred Harp and draw in new singers. The range of ways that they sought to achieve this goal reveals the open field of authority and how each singer understands their own role, the role of the local singing community, and the ultimate goal differently.

Before the workshop, one local singer with ties to the Old Town School took it upon herself to negotiate a special lowered fee for experienced Sacred Harp singers, thus depriving Tim of income from a workshop primarily intended for people entirely new to this music. Another arrived early and began directing the staff at the school on the appropriate formation in which to set up chairs. A third tried to answer questions addressed to Tim by people in the class who had never sung Sacred Harp before, while a fourth got ahold of a reporter in attendance and explained to her why *he* was more knowledgeable about Sacred Harp—and therefore a better interview subject—than Tim. Any or all of these people may have sincerely intended to be helpful, but each was in effect appropriating some form of institutional or public authority for themselves in a situation in which they felt that Chicago Sacred Harp singers *should* have some input but in which none of them were necessarily or officially involved. Each was attempting to publicly represent Sacred Harp or affect how it was presented and to whom by the Old Town School, but they did so as individuals rather than as a community acting in consensus about who its leaders were and who should be publicly acknowledged by Tim as an authoritative source.[38]

This process was essentially repeated the next day at the Anniversary Singing, where, though Tim was no longer an alternate center of authority against which local singers had to define themselves and though there were convention officers from the local community who did provide a public center of authority, the presence of a crowd of newcomers drawn by the newspaper coverage and the previous day's workshop spurred a number of experienced singers to publicly figure themselves as experts. Several prefaced their song choices by giving brief explanations of aspects of the tradition, encouraging newcomers to take a turn leading a song, or by inviting newcomers to join them in the center of the square. These tactics certainly served to help welcome and orient people who had never been to a singing before, but they also publicly identified the speaker as an insider, as a source of knowledge, and as someone with the authority to disrupt (however slightly) the usual course of the singing by making a public pronouncement. The emphasis was therefore not on the *community* as offering welcome as a whole through one public representative but on *individuals* offering their own welcomes in individualized ways.

Pitching or keying the music is another case in which local practices reflect local conceptions of authority. On Sand Mountain and in west Georgia, the front tenor row is anchored by one of a fairly stable group of men who key; in most cases, the same one or two such men handle this duty for singings at a particular church. At Muscadine and State Line, close to the Georgia-Alabama state line, for instance, Jeff Sheppard serves in this role. At Antioch, on Sand Mountain, Terry Wootten generally does. At Liberty, David Ivey or Shane Wootten do so. This system is restrictive, with no women routinely keying music at long-running southern singings[39] and with entry into the group of men allowed to do so strictly, if informally, controlled. Similarly, seats on the front row of the tenor section in particular are controlled at least loosely.[40] The skills required are more widespread and many more people can sit on a front row at one time, but it is considered a privileged position and the host singers are seen to have at least some right to issue invitations.[41]

Singers in Chicago and Minnesota conform to these practices in varying degrees. Most new singers rapidly come to understand the responsibilities associated with sitting at the front of a section, singing consistently, watching the leader, and helping when necessary. At the same time, the status issues associated with sitting on the front row of a section (and especially of the tenor section) are more individually contested than is the case among lifelong southern singers. The 2004 Minnesota State Convention reveals the benefits of southern restrictions on who will key the music (if not the benefits of gender restrictions). At that convention, nearly every hour of singing saw a different singer responsible for pitching, not all of whom were entirely qualified to take this job at a large convention (as opposed to a smaller, more relaxed local singing at which they are familiar with the vocal ranges of most or all in attendance), despite the presence of more qualified people who could have done the job for longer periods, introducing greater consistency as well as greater skill. Some of those keying at this convention did so while remaining in sections other than the tenor, which as the melody or lead part is, practically speaking, the best place to situate the pitch in relation to. Allowing keying to be done from other sections also represents a selective disregard for southern tradition.

The proliferation of keyers is part of a broader lack of community agreement on status. More people pitch in Minnesota because more people believe themselves to be qualified, and in the absence of a long-standing tradition of informal apprenticeship, community pressure, and agreed-upon if never formalized authority hierarchies such as exist in many southern locations, individuals believing themselves to be qualified can press their own cases with no system in place to check those who are not effective at the job. Similarly, seating on the front rows becomes a question of who is willing to assert their fitness for that status rather than something influenced by a small number of people who the host community has acknowledged as its leaders.

Authority as a guiding concept is rarely mentioned by Sacred Harp singers, who focus much more on the democracy of allowing every voice to be heard and every singer to lead a song. Yet embedded ideas of authority are lived out in the ways that singings in different locations are organized. Sand Mountain and west Georgia singers work hard to be good hosts and to strengthen their singings, but during the singing itself, they do not seek to stand out as individuals. As Wuthnow describes the freedom found in a spirituality of dwelling, it "can provide healing, even levity, because of the opportunity to share responsibility with other inhabitants. . . . Each occupant is, in a sense, inconsequential and thus able to relax, relieved of taking oneself too seriously or of striving too hard to be outstanding."[42] In direct contrast, precisely because singers in Chicago and Minneapolis-St. Paul are invested in individual autonomy rather than hierarchy (however informal), active displays of several forms of authority (keying ability, knowledge, leading ability, the right to speak in the square and to offer welcome) become ubiquitous.[43]

History

Although I discussed some approaches to Sacred Harp history above in the larger discussion of authenticity, and although the two concepts are often linked, two distinct ways of thinking and talking about Sacred Harp as history emerge in discussions with singers. I refer to these two understandings as "emotional history" and "fact-based history." Neither style is unique to singers from a particular location, though access to an emotional history of Sacred Harp only comes with experience singing it and the associations that accumulate. Fact-based history is, on the other hand, something that many people who come to Sacred Harp as adults are interested in. To the significant extent that the length of time a person has been singing correlates to the region in which they live, then, concepts of Sacred Harp history are related to region, but there are numerous exceptions, and some singers draw on both concepts at different moments.

What I refer to as "fact-based history" includes the use of reference to academic or journalistic work on US history or musical history, and to popular (if not always accurate) notions thereof, to place Sacred Harp. Fact-based history is often used in the public presentation to indicate that this is a unique and historically important musical form, one that has ties to well-known historical figures and events, or is of interest as a piece of living social history. This view is probably most prevalent among New England singers, many of whom began singing Sacred Harp through the early music movement and who therefore, at least initially, took a similar approach to Sacred Harp as they did to Renaissance or medieval music, musics with which many of them still compare it in discussing what it is and how it sounds. Midwestern singers, especially in Chicago but also in Minnesota, routinely deride New England singers for the ways this approach manifests itself—in the emphasis of groups of singers in Boston and Vermont on rehearsal and performance rather than participatory singing, on a period in the 1980s of making song lyrics gender neutral, and most of all the treatment of Sacred Harp as a reconstructed tradition based on textual scholarship, rather than a living one based in a strong culture of travel South to connect with lifelong southern singers. These practices are frowned on in the Midwest, although the Minnesota singers did originate at least partially in a performing group. However, even in Chicago and the Twin Cities, with their singing cultures so firmly oriented toward the southern Sacred Harp tradition, some expressions of this approach emerge.

Nick Pasqual, who is a regular attendee of the Hyde Park weekly singing in Chicago, is by far the strongest exponent of fact-based history I have encountered outside of New England, saying, "To me the oral part of it is no more, at best, than 50 percent of it." In an interview, he connected Sacred Harp with Lowell Mason and the better music movement of nineteenth-century New England, as well as with the Campbellite and Stonite religious movements of the nineteenth-century Midwest and South. For this singer, the place of Sacred Harp and associated musics in such histories amplifies its appeal today, situating him in a broad web of intersecting historical meanings.

The Missouri Sacred Harp singers have recently engaged in a concrete fact-based history practice most common in New England—they have released a songbook, *The Missouri Harmony*. In fact, their *Missouri Harmony* is intended as a revision of an 1820 book of the same name, following the

Sacred Harp practice of including some newly composed songs. As with New England revival publications, such as *The Northern Harmony* and *Norumbega Harmony*, the early American history of many of the songs is emphasized: the description of the new *Missouri Harmony*, for instance, includes the information that "Abraham Lincoln and his sweetheart, Ann Rutledge, are said to have sung from *The Missouri Harmony* at her father's tavern in New Salem, Illinois."[44] *Norumbega Harmony* is billed as including songs by "America's earliest composers, the itinerant New England singing masters whose schools were the principal form of music education in the Early Republic."[45] In publishing and marketing such books, singers lay claim to the particular musical histories of their areas, implicitly pointing out that, while they may not have been born into families that have been singing Sacred Harp for generations, they are not without a distinct regional heritage.

More commonly, though, Midwestern singers use fact-based history to validate Sacred Harp to outsiders, defining it as important through its age and association with important historical figures and events and, above all, stressing its Americanness. They are not alone in this usage, either; west Georgia singer and longtime executive secretary of the Sacred Harp Publishing Company, Hugh McGraw, often does the same, stressing the music's early roots in England and lengthy history in America, citing for instance a reference to fa-sol-la solfège in a Shakespeare play.

People who draw on what I call emotional history situate Sacred Harp rather differently. Although many of these people are also adept at using fact-based history to explain Sacred Harp as important in non-Sacred Harp contexts, they use emotional history to explain its importance in their lives and the way Sacred Harp connects them to a community and to particular beloved individuals. Many people who have come to Sacred Harp as adults wholeheartedly embrace emotional history as the most meaningful, though singers in Chicago and Minnesota doing so tend to refer briefly to fact-based history in order to dismiss it as being less significant than emotional history. Chicago singer Karen Freund, for instance, thinks of Sacred Harp history "as families. That's pretty much the only way I think of it. The New England singing schools . . . I don't care."

Perhaps the most common trope in the discourse of emotional history is that a particular song calls to mind a deceased singer who often led it, and that, upon hearing the song, the speaker can envision that singer in a characteristic location or pose. This is often mentioned in memorial lessons, privately, and in interviews; a related way of drawing such an association happens when a leader dedicates their song choice to a deceased singer. Such a moment is captured on a recording of the

1999 United Convention, *In Sweetest Union Join*, during Richard DeLong's brief remarks before he led his song. Telling about the first time he sang at Liberty, at the 1979 United Convention, he pointed around the room: "Irene and Bob sat right over here, and Mac and Leonard and Noah and D. T. White was the arranging committee, and I sat right back over here on the aisle with a tape recorder under my chair."

Asked about Sacred Harp history, Sand Mountain singer Susan Harcrow immediately drew on emotional history, saying,

I can think of so many people who were the core of Sacred Harp for me, Leonard [Lacy], Andrew Ivey, Eulas Ivey, Noah Lacy. I thought of them as the older singers and now I look and Ricky and Terry and David and me, we're those older singers; we're the ones that younger singers are looking at like we looked at all those that are gone. I can't help . . . there's not a singing I go to, not a song sung but that brings one of those people to mind.

Her formulation includes the central point that songs become memory, that singing a song raises echoes of past experiences of singing it, and she elaborates on the point by framing herself and her contemporaries in this context, highlighting both the constant change of Sacred Harp community and its endurance.

She then turned the question on me, calling on me to engage with this emotional history: "When you sing a particular song does it not bring someone to mind? At some point in time that's going to be a historical memory for you." In this, she was obliquely calling on me to remember Karen House. By the time Karen died, I had heard so many singers refer to their memories of the deceased while singing that I knew to expect to "see" Karen across the square in certain buildings and during certain songs. The fact that I had been primed to expect it, though, does not mean that I do so less sincerely. Similarly, when Tim Eriksen taught a singing school at the Garden State Convention in May 2003, in talking about the emotional ties that singers form, he began to tell the class how difficult it was for him to be in a room where he had always before sung with Karen, before breaking off in the middle of a sentence, unable to continue speaking through tears as he gestured at the place Karen would have been sitting. After repeated attempts to communicate his emotion, he said simply, "Let's sing" and called a page number.

One of the effects of the widespread emphasis on emotional history is that singing Sacred Harp is supposed to become entwined with the life of even a new singer, who may not remember Leonard or Noah Lacy but can know and, ultimately, remember their successors. Being part of the history of Sacred Harp is, therefore, theoretically made available to anyone who participates in the music and loves and is loved by their fellow singers, not solely to those who are raised in the tradition. The responsibility for history then also devolves on all singers, with those who came to Sacred Harp as adults encouraged to create family traditions by bringing their children to singings. At the same time, the importance of having been there, having known singers who are now gone, can become a barrier, a way for someone who has been singing for ten years to assert their insider status over someone who has been singing for five, simply by naming a singer and saying, "Oh, you never knew Check, did you?"

Such moments can be genuine or strategic, and given the lack of reliable measures of sincerity, singers have to assess these interactions on a case-by-case basis. For most people, the loss of a friend is cause for sincere, unalloyed grief, so it is a perverse fate to find that losing a singing friend can become a sign of one's full inclusion in Sacred Harp community and history. This can extend to entire communities; the ethnomusicologist and singer Kiri Miller writes of the Western Massachusetts singing community that "the loss of such a young and well-known singer [as Karen House] seemed to bring a binding gravity and maturity to this very young convention."[46] Having witnessed what appeared to be strategic grief from certain singers before her sister's death, at the same time as she acknowledged the transformative effect of her and their loss, Kelly House cautioned Karen's friends against insincerity in the memorial lesson at the 2000 Young People's Singing in Western Massachusetts, saying that losing a friend was "not something to be *proud* of."

Sacred Harp singers, therefore, speak in many voices about history, at times mobilizing fact-based history to market the music to outsiders or to claim regional heritage through the reclamation of locally written or published songs from earlier centuries, with some people expressing intense interest in such long-ago histories. For many singers, though, the meaningful history is the emotional one they live, see their loved ones within, and expect to take place within as they age and die. Emotional history becomes a measure of belonging in Sacred Harp. As such, it is sometimes used strategically, though far more often it is an expression of sincere (if loosely scripted) love and memory.

FIVE

Creating National Community

Chapters 2 and 3 showed how a major convention runs in each location; chapter 4 attempted to disentangle some of the strands of meaning that go into local Sacred Harp communities, focusing on how those meanings are inscribed in practice. In what follows, I examine the way these local practices are adapted to create a nationwide Sacred Harp community.[1] Local communities are of varying sizes and levels of coherence but can be relatively easily defined geographically. By national community I refer to something more transient, occurring when singers from different local communities come into contact with each other, whether in person at a large singing or in online discussions; all such meetings require the production of a shared practice and culture out of the distinct local ones.

Despite the abstract character of a national community that is constantly coalescing and dissolving, many singers cite this national community as an important facet of their Sacred Harp experience and of their lives, as ongoing relationships form across geographic and cultural distance.[2] The most important sites, certainly the most purposeful sites, for the development of national community, though, are the singing conventions, specifically the larger ones that draw visitors from significant distances. Such a convention may simultaneously be local—for those singers who sing entirely (or almost so) in that area and are not attentive to the presence of visitors—and national, as visitors interact with those of their host singers who themselves travel frequently. Of the conventions discussed in chapters 2 and 3, the Midwest and Minnesota Conventions are most self-consciously national in character, sites in which an overarching Sacred Harp community identity is stitched together, with travel providing the binding thread.

The Necessity of Travel

There are two main meanings attached to traveling to sing; one is specific to new singers and the other is shared by new and lifelong singers. The nationwide community of Sacred Harp singers is founded upon travel, with some singers traveling three or more hours to sing as many as a dozen times a year. Those same singers, and others, will drive two hours each way more frequently, but three hours seems to be the tipping point, a commitment of time and energy that feels significantly greater, since it automatically entails leaving the house around six o'clock in the morning and being gone for a full twelve hours. The meanings of travel depend on the journey and the singer making it, with reciprocity and pilgrimage the most common ways it is understood.[3]

"Because they always come to our convention."

Reciprocity is the most universal value attached to travel. Few local communities have so many singers that they do not benefit by having more at their conventions, and given a relatively strong reciprocity norm, attending other people's singings is the most direct way to bring in travelers.[4] Being at a distant singing provides the opportunity to stand during the announcements and publicly advertise your singing, but perhaps more significantly, it affords more opportunities to issue personal invitations and engage in diplomatic pressure on people, reminding them that you have attended their singings.[5] Northern and southern singers alike engage in this practice, both within and across regions—a Chicago singer might travel to either Sand Mountain or to St. Louis hoping to draw residents of those places to the Midwest Convention, just as a Sand Mountain singer might go to either Chicago or west Alabama on behalf of their own singing.

I turn here from referring to other communities' singings to referring to other people's singings, because this development of reciprocity is often highly personalized. In cases where a group of singers from one location attend a convention in another en masse, the debt is spoken of as between locations. For instance, several Ballingers, from Mt. Lebanon

Church in west Alabama, usually attend all-day singings at Liberty, and people from Liberty reciprocate by attending the singing at Mt. Lebanon. But more typically, reciprocity is incurred by one or two emissaries.

As is often the case, in Sacred Harp and elsewhere, strength breeds strength; a singing community with many possible emissaries has the best chance of incurring a sufficient sense of obligation from people in other areas, and a strong singer, or one with significant personal status, is the one whose favor is most likely to be sought through attendance at his or her singing. There are, though, ways for one or two singers—even if they are not musically outstanding—to create this sense of obligation.

First, one or two singers trying to support a weak singing may do so through consistent attendance at a large number of singings within the same region during a given year. This strategy is most possible in the South, where there are enough singings to attend one in a different church nearly every weekend through the year. For instance, after the singing at their church, Chestnut Grove, grew weak enough that there was talk of canceling it, sisters Amy and Loretta Smith moved to promote it. In the late 1990s, Chestnut Grove had been the only singing either woman is recorded as attending. From 2001 on, though, one or both of them attended the majority of Sand Mountain–area singings, so that Chestnut Grove was represented at seven or more singings each year, including ones at Liberty, Pine Grove, Shady Grove, and in Huntsville. Neither woman is known as a particularly strong singer or leader, and they typically sit several rows back in the tenor section and lead one song together, but their faithful presence—and the commitment to preserving their own singing that it represented—was noted by active singers in the area. The Chestnut Grove singing has increased in size, from the late 1990s when almost every leader led two songs and the singing ended early, to 2003 and 2004 when, during the after-lunch session, leaders only led one song. It is still a relatively small singing, but no longer appears in danger of being discontinued.

The same strategy was employed more dramatically by Wilton and Ivalene Donaldson, an elderly couple from northwest Alabama. Miss Ivalene appears in the minutes of the late 1990s as attending up to seventeen singings per year.[6] But in 1999, their participation jumped, with Wilton appearing in the minutes twenty-four times and Miss Ivalene thirty-seven. In 2001, their recorded attendance jumped again, to fifty-five for Wilton and fifty-five for his wife. This faithful attendance was made more dramatic and touching by Miss Ivalene's failing health. She passed away in April 2005, after several years of visibly struggling for breath as she sang and led despite congestive heart failure. And again, during this time, the strength of the singing she traveled to promote increased.[7]

Another strategy one or two singers can employ to incur reciprocity drawing travelers to their singing involves developing an ongoing relationship with a particular convention elsewhere. Georgia's Richard DeLong has employed this tactic. In addition to attending many singings through Georgia and Alabama, he very regularly attends not just the Midwest Convention but also Chicago's one-day Anniversary Singing, as well as singings in California, Western Massachusetts, and Indiana. In his travels, he solicits people to attend his family's singing, the DeLong and Roberts Memorial. Due to the declining singing population in Georgia generally, and in the DeLong family's home area of north Atlanta specifically, this singing has had weak years. But Richard's strategy of being at the same distant singings year after year has paid off to some small extent. In recent years, there are usually at least two or three long-distance travelers in attendance, because when they were making their decisions about which southern singing to attend, they remembered that Richard was the southern singer who had faithfully been at their singing, and who had personally invited them to his singing. There are rarely a large number of such travelers, but even two or three enthusiastic singers can make a difference to either the sound of the singing or the sense of vitality in the room. Most strikingly, when the DeLong and Roberts Memorial was threatened with the loss of its historic home in 2005, a larger number of travelers—four from the Chicago area, two from California, two from Oregon, one from North Carolina, four from Massachusetts—turned out to provide moral support to Richard.[8]

It is somewhat more difficult for newer singers to incur the kind of moral obligation for reciprocity that a lifelong southern singer can, but it is possible. Chicago's Ted Mercer uses his travel to promote Chicago singings and encourages others to do the same. While the travel of Chicago singers has dropped off from its high levels (both in terms of widespread participation and frequent travel by some individuals) of the late 1980s and early 1990s, almost every Midwestern all-day singing draws one or two carloads of Chicago singers, and several continue to go South at least once a year, and in four or five cases, four or more times each year.

The presence of Chicago singers in general, if not of individual Chicago singers, is therefore enough to produce at least some reciprocal attendance. This is hard to gauge given the Midwest Convention's status as the largest convention in the Midwest, such that most dedicated singers in the region would choose to attend it as a large and accessible convention regardless of moral obligation. But it clearly serves to draw more southern singers than would otherwise attend. For instance, Minnesota singers are less ubiquitous throughout the Midwest and direct more of their southern travel to the Cooper Book tradition of the Lee family in south Georgia, such that the pool of singers from whom they might receive reciprocal visits is smaller; this is reflected in the lesser attendance of southern singers at the Minnesota Convention and Midwinter Cooper Book Singing. A few southern singers attend one or both of those events very regularly, but the overall number of southern singers who have attended a Minnesota singing in recent years is much lower than is true of Chicago singings.

"If [he] would only travel, he might learn a few things."

Although northern singers do travel to incur reciprocity or reciprocate the visits of others, their travel South is most commonly framed in a wholly different way. There is a strong discourse of the South as the root and source of knowledge about Sacred Harp, and traveling there as a sign of commitment to the tradition. Among northern singers, having traveled South extensively or being friendly with lifelong southern singers often stands as an authenticator, a sign that their claims to knowledge are not merely from books but from experience with the genuine tradition.

The dominant narrative about the emergence and growth of Chicago Sacred Harp is heavily focused on the importance of southern travel and the subsequent absorption of lessons learned there. The first Illinois State Convention, held between Chicago and Charleston, Illinois, during Memorial Day weekend in 1985, was attended by Hugh McGraw and several other Georgians, including Richard DeLong. As he had done in New England in 1976, Hugh pushed the Illinois singers to hold a traditionally organized convention, though several of the Chicago singers who were there are very clear in retrospect that they had not yet learned what this entailed.[9] They first began singing the notes when Hugh informed them that he would be coming to their convention; they only knew a small number of songs in the book; the convention included performance segments by the Chicago and Charleston singers; and, as Judy Hauff relates, "We made them sing from nine or nine thirty until noon. We gave them no break, didn't realize that recess was part of this routine. Then gave 'em Jewel pop and chicken and made 'em sing again."[10] Here Hauff highlights the inadequacy of the food served—"Jewel pop and chicken" rather than a full dinner on the grounds—as a deviation from tradition almost as great as their failure to sing the notes to that point. The Chicago singers had yet to learn the forms of fellowship and community building so central to Sacred Harp, and learning these, and especially coming to appreciate the importance of the shared meal, was a significant part of their initiation process.[11]

At this convention, though, connections were formed that were to be very important, and the foundations for Chicagoans traveling South were laid. A large group decided to go to Alabama for the National Convention in mid-June, but even before then, Ted Mercer and Judy Hauff decided to go to Holly Springs the first weekend in June, and as Judy describes it, tongue partially in cheek, "We were never the same after that. We came back washed in the blood and raving to the group about what we had seen and heard."[12] The belief that Sacred Harp *must* be learned from southerners and through travel South quickly developed. According to Judy, "We realized that in a battle of means and methods, we were unarmed. What they had was absolutely superior. They had everything in place; it worked beautifully. We didn't understand why they did anything, but it was working."[13] Authenticity, then, was not merely an ideological standpoint but a practical one—"it was working."

In addition to these practical reasons for adopting southern practices, there were also more overtly ideological ones, as Ted Johnson expresses,

We were out here in the middle of the prairie, we didn't have traditions or roots to go back to, we figured the fount of this is still living, down there in Georgia and Alabama, that's where it's happening, that's where the creative impulse was coming from. We fell into wanting to go South as much as we could, wanting to do things the way they do.[14]

His wife Marcia echoes this, saying, "Chicago doesn't have a tradition, we're not old enough. . . . What we do is celebrate and try to adhere to the southern traditions, including the democracy of a southern convention."[15] Or, according to Ted Mercer, "We sort of uncritically began enjoying the traditional ways of doing things, adopted them whole hog."[16]

Chicago exported this emphasis on adherence to southern practice throughout the Midwest, but it is important to note that some people who were singing prior to the encounter with Hugh McGraw drifted away from Sacred Harp due to disagreement with this path. In Chicago, the man who had been the group's initial leader, "felt that Hugh right away was kind of a take-over man . . . he came in and told us that what we were doing was absolutely wrong, we weren't singing the shapes, you don't [perform] for one another, blah blah blah." In fact, he said, "The breach was never quite healed" and "my participation became less and less."[17] Something similar happened in Minneapolis-St. Paul, with a man who had been an early leader drifting away from the group because of disagreements over the orientation of local practice to Sacred Harp vs. choral practice. According to another local singer, "They didn't want to sing the way he liked to sing, with dynamics and things, and I think there was some friction and one point at which he was asked not to pitch at a convention because they were afraid he was going to do it wrong or something"—and in this case, "wrong" would mean not according to southern tradition.

Where the people who today still form the cores of the Chicago and Twin Cities Sacred Harp communities, and who established the forms those communities still take, felt that southern singing practices both worked better than anything they could come up with and were ideologically preferable as authentic, these people who drifted away placed Sacred Harp more within the context of other folk music they participated in and did not want to adjust their folk-revivalist practices and understandings. This represented an early conflict over whether and which authenticity *should* be valued. Within the Sacred Harp world, the conflict was resolved quickly and decisively, but there remain people who sing Sacred Harp songs occasionally in folk festival settings; this could be seen as another segment of Sacred Harp practice in which the understandings are radically different.

In addition to those individuals in places like Chicago and the Twin Cities who drifted away from Sacred Harp when the allegiance to the southern tradition began, some entire communities of singers may be criticized by tradition-adherent singers for insufficient interest. As Ted Mercer notes, singing the notes is "definitely the Sacred Harp shibboleth,"[18] with groups that do not do so definitively outside of the Sacred Harp world. But finer distinctions of traditionalism—and therefore authenticity—continue to be made and are often predicated on an individual's or community's relation to travel South. The Old Guard Chicago singers, for instance, define themselves most actively against singers in New England, which was the major other northern community during their formative years and where no equivalent culture of travel existed. Judy Hauff says, with regard to travel, that the "absolute oblivious holdouts were the northeastern people."[19]

Ted Johnson, who attributes part of the Chicagoans taking up the southern tradition with such enthusiasm to their not "hav[ing] traditions or roots to go back to," continues this logic in considering New England.

In New England they had discovered this stuff in the '60s and feeling 'This is going back to our New England roots,' kind of insular or parochial. They're very nice people. . . . I think they just weren't that interested. . . . occasionally they'd make a foray into the South, but mostly they were doing their own thing.[20]

"Their own thing" involved performances and lack of travel, and as a result, Johnson admits, "some of us look down our noses at the New England approach."

But this attitude is not limited to Chicago's Old Guard singers nor to being directed against New England singers. Minnesota's Jenny Willard, who in recent years has sung nearly as much in the South as in her home state, says, "Especially us northerners, we have so much to learn. I get frustrated with people who feel like they don't have to, and we get these northerners who feel that way. . . . They feel like they don't have any more to learn." Similarly, Chicago's Jerry Enright says of people, wherever they are, "who like Sacred Harp and they like to sing it and they put on a convention but they do not travel south" that "they're not part of that sort of commitment to try to learn the tradition to the humble extent that the people like us can to help support it and carry it on." He goes on to say that he sees in such people a "we don't need to learn no Sacred Harp from anybody" attitude, such that "I lose interest. I don't care to be part of that." His wife, Karen Freund, suggests that she too does not so much condemn such people as simply feel unconnected to them: "They're using the same book but that's the only thing we have in common." For these people, singing from *The Sacred Harp* without attention to the ongoing southern tradition—without travel South and acknowledgement of the authority and authenticity of lifelong southern singers—is simply not equivalent to what they do.

This attitude is most often and most explicitly expressed among new northern singers, but it represents an absorption of the lessons communicated by Hugh McGraw when he participated in the establishment of northern conventions, such as the Illinois State, the Midwest, and the New England, and, often more subtly, by other southern singers. In public statements and formal interviews, southern singers are typically slow to condemn others' Sacred Harp practices, saying things like "They're just starting their singing life and they don't have the extended traditions that some of us have that grew up in it, but most of them seem to enjoy it just as well or maybe more than some of us that grew up in it."

Privately, though, many southern singers also evaluate northern ones by their commitment to travel. In part this is a product of which northern

singers they know personally—more likely to be those who travel frequently—but it is also a value judgment centered on the importance of
engagement with the southern tradition.

Crossing Cultural Distance

The fact that northern singers value travel, and northern and southern
singers alike agree that northerners benefit from exposure to the southern
tradition and should therefore seek it out and study it, does not mean
that singers from different places, even ones who share this general belief, automatically mesh. The idealized relationship blends instruction
and learning with the Sacred Harp ideal of democracy and equality, a
difficult balance to achieve, particularly as it is supposed to happen ef-
fortlessly—or at least with no visible effort. In fact, this relationship is
created and maintained both through the efforts of individuals to modify
their own behaviors and through community efforts to host singings that
will be congenial to locals and visitors alike. This is where the promotion
of silence as a norm becomes crucial to the creation and maintenance of
community.[21]

One standard way to avoid controversy in any group of people is to
prohibit discussion of religion and politics, but in Sacred Harp singing,
religion's centrality is welcome for some, regrettable for others, and unavoidable for all. This could make the avoidance of controversy that
comes with a ban on religious topics more difficult to achieve, or could
effectively prevent some people from participating.[22]

As I discussed in chapter 4, singers handle the relationship between
Sacred Harp and more formal types of worship in very different ways and
privately negotiate their knowledge that they are singing with people
who believe differently from themselves. The religious practices of local
communities emerge from rather general consensus on the community's
religious makeup and responsibility to the religious aspects of the southern Sacred Harp tradition. So, for instance, with a shared church background, singers at Liberty have prayer not only at all-day singings but at
their local night singings, dress for singings as they would for church,
and understand singing as linked to if not identical with their church
lives. In Chicago, by contrast, singers understand their local community
as being most characterized by religious diversity, and so downplay religion and assume that everyone will bring their own degree of faith to
their singing, while at the same time their commitment to the southern

Sacred Harp tradition means that they would never omit prayer from an all-day singing.

There is a broad national consensus that Sacred Harp's religious aspect means that all-day singings should begin and end with prayer and have a blessing before lunch; however, for some singers, these prayers can be bracketed as part of the southern tradition rather than a meaningful religious observance for themselves. Moreover, beyond this, the consensus—as it is verbalized but more significantly as it is lived day to day—becomes more tenuous, with subtle behaviors often revealing the religious framework within which one views Sacred Harp.

The clothing singers wear to a convention or all-day singing is perhaps the most visible marker of this kind of difference. With few exceptions,[23] lifelong southern singers dress for singings as they would for church, out of respect for the churches they sing in and the Christian lyrics they sing. As Alabama's Shelbie Sheppard says,

This is sacred, it is not folk music. Every singing is sacred. When I was growing up, you wore your best clothes whatever they were. They might be threadbare, but whatever was your best. Until a few years ago no woman would wear anything but a dress, I don't care if it was a Tuesday night, a Wednesday night, whatever, and there are still places a woman would dare *not* wear pants. They might not say anything about it but it will have been an unpardonable sin.

Her account points to some recent change in dress—"*Until a few years ago no woman would wear anything but a dress*"—but even as she acknowledges this change, she points to still-existing standards in some places against women wearing pants, which, along with wearing shorts for either women or men, remains probably the strongest taboo.

Elder Ricky Harcrow similarly points to changing standards, saying that, in his youth,

All the men wore a white shirt and a tie, women wore hats, and that's completely changed. You wore a white shirt and a tie and sat up there all day, and the sweat, Lord have mercy! But we did it, we thought that's what we were supposed to do; the influence of more modern culture has brought us down off of that, I guess.

Though this degree of formality no longer applies, the idea that the occasion should be marked by special dress remains evident. The prevailing styles of dress among women in west Georgia and on Sand Mountain are somewhat different due to the different age distributions in those places, but women overwhelmingly wear dresses or skirts, and many men wear ties on Sunday. The degree to which dressing with less formality is actively frowned on differs from church to church, depending both on the theological conservatism of the church and the degree to which its members and pastor understand singing as a separate activity with its own rules.

Northern singers, particularly those coming from folk-revivalist and left-wing backgrounds, tend to be less prone to dressing formally in their everyday lives; ironing clothes, for instance, is a less common practice, as is the wearing of makeup for women. Men are more likely to wear sandals, and to consider shorts and T-shirts appropriate for activities other than manual labor.[24] Additionally, since many northern singers do not understand Sacred Harp as religious practice, they do not apply church-dress standards to singings, or they do understand it in a religious context but themselves attend churches at which informal dress is accepted and women wear pants without controversy.[25]

In Chicago and Minnesota, a number of experienced singers who have traveled to sing and who work to observe southern practices are careful to emulate southern formality standards (although the styles of clothing they choose are often different), but as many or more local singers treat events casually, wearing T-shirts and jeans or even shorts. Visiting southern singers may privately raise their eyebrows or frown at such clothing but as guests would not say anything. However, when northern singers go South and dress in this way to sing in churches, the possibility for tension or even conflict is greater.

One such moment occurred the fifth weekend in July 2001 on Sand Mountain.[26] On Saturday, Zion Hill Primitive Baptist Church hosted the Young People's Singing, at which all officers and committee members are "young people"—under thirty-five years of age. On Sunday, not far from Zion Hill, the annual singing in honor of the Lacy family was held at Lacy's Chapel, a small Baptist church originally built by the fathers of two women present at the day's singing.

The weekend, due to little competition from other events, drew a substantial number of out-of-town singers, including most visibly two vanloads of young singers from Western Massachusetts, which had hosted the previous year's Young People's. In keeping with the valuing of young singers by a community concerned about the survival of Sacred Harp, the Western Massachusetts singers were received enthusiastically. In particular, in the evening after the Young People's Singing, a two-hour singing was held at Fuller Cemetery in Ider. This singing—the one of which Susan Harcrow says, "I don't know what happened that night, I truly don't know what that was. . . . I know that something happened there that night that is a once in a lifetime thing"—proved, as Susan's words suggest, to be one of those explosively good ones that becomes a reference point for its attendees and provides a standard for comparison for other good singings. Goodwill between the singers from different areas had existed before that evening's singing, but the shared experience of transcendence cemented a new level of relationship between them, which was tested the next day.

Before the Massachusetts singers had begun their trip, one of the more experienced singers in the group had discussed appropriate dress with the other travelers, stressing that women (who comprised the majority of the group) should not only wear skirts but choose ones reaching at least to their knees, and they should avoid sleeveless tops, particularly if their underarms were unshaven. On Saturday, all of the women did wear skirts and dresses, but on Sunday, two women wore pants. One was in wide-legged pants of lightweight pale blue cotton with a matching top, while the other was in a rather "butch" ensemble of a man's shirt with heavy, oversized workpants and a wide leather belt. Tim Eriksen, traveling from Minnesota but generally considered to be with the same group, was similarly obtrusive—though he wore slacks, dress shoes, and a shirt and tie, his shaved head and earring set him apart.

Lacy's Chapel was small and poorly ventilated, and with the crowd filling even most of the standing room, it quickly turned into a sauna. Many of the men had brown spots covering their backs where they had sweated through their shirts and lifted some of the wood stain off the benches. Shortly before lunchtime, a storm moved in, and because the church had no covered space for lunch to be held under, lunch was postponed and the singing continued while local singers called around looking for an indoor space. Ultimately, having sung straight through the usual lunch hour, they decided to finish the singing early and go to Liberty, which is nearby, to eat at its covered table and in its roomier building.

The two churches are both located in Henagar, perhaps two miles apart, and though the Lacys built Lacy's Chapel, many of them are buried in Liberty's cemetery. The two churches have significant ties and broadly similar beliefs and practices, therefore. However, Lacy's Chapel had only a bare handful of church members, and the singing was in large part supported by people whose home singing is at Liberty—indeed, David and Rod Ivey were that year's chair and vice-chair of the Lacy's Chapel singing. In contrast to the vitality of Liberty's congregation and the church's great involvement with Sacred Harp and with singers from distances, Lacy's Chapel hosted singers only once a year, did not draw many singers from outside the region in most years, and its members did not attend many other singings.

At the end of the singing, chairman David Ivey asked the pastor of Lacy's Chapel to offer a prayer, as was customary and polite. The pastor opened with thanks for the good day of singing but quickly moved on to inveigh against the dress of the two visiting women who wore pants and the man who wore an earring, saying, "God I pray you will help these men, Lord, that's not dressed in manly apparel, that you'll help them Father, that they might look to you. Help them God to realize they need to learn how to protect their vessels."[27] He continued on to ask the Lord to speak to the hearts of the "ladies that's dressed in manly apparel"[28] and to say, "It's time that men and women, if they're going to sing our precious word of God and praises unto you, God they ought to know what they're singing about, and God if they get right, Lord, they'll be dressed right." In the prayer itself, he acknowledged that people would be angry with his words, but said that he felt obliged to speak. He did not go to lunch with the singers.

Although for a woman to wear pants to church on Sunday is, in fact, widely frowned on by southern singers, the response of local singers to this prayer was swift and was made both publicly and privately. The pastor of Lacy, acknowledging in his prayer itself that people would be angry with him, said, "Our Father just shut this mouth" (with the implication being that if God did *not* shut the preacher's mouth, it was a sign of God's approval). In immediate response to this, Betty Lacy Shepherd, daughter of one of the men who had built the original Lacy's Chapel, the woman who more than a year later still began to cry when I asked her about the singing at Fuller Cemetery the previous night, angrily said, "AMEN!" (i.e., calling on God to, in fact, shut the preacher's mouth and end the prayer) and began to make her way out of the church. Rod Ivey, too, simply walked out. These were immediate, individual responses, but a broader response was made as well. David and Rod rushed to Liberty and spoke to its pastor, Tony Ivey, who is also their cousin, about what had just been said. Before he offered a blessing for lunch, Tony addressed the gathered singers, eloquently acknowledging that hurtful words had been spoken and saying that it was necessary to remember that people came from different backgrounds and had different styles of dress, but that as singers, they were a family and were all welcome at Liberty.

Following this, throughout the lunch period, a number of local singers made an effort to approach the visitors individually and tell them (vehemently and with many bitter characterizations of the preacher's intelligence, emotional stability, and moral uprightness) that the pastor of the first church did not speak for them, that he was bitter because his preaching drew few people to the church while the singing had filled it to overflowing, and that they hoped the visitors would not hold his words against all the singers on Sand Mountain and would return to sing there again. Indeed, his prayer, and singers' anger at him, was the subject of discussion for weeks; Betty Shepherd characterized his words as being "of Satan" and the visiting singers as having been "a blessing."

Although the man who offered the offensive prayer was a member of the broader Sand Mountain community (several of the singers had known him all their lives and others had worked with him for decades) and although he invoked the norms with which singers in that locale had been raised—that women should not wear pants in church—he was not a regular singer. When he violated the hospitality norms of *that* community, the local singers, people who shared two possible communities with him, moved quickly to assert that the singing community was the more important one to them and that hospitality to visitors was, at least in this moment, more important. This was not simply rhetoric for the visitors: despite the family ties with Lacy's Chapel, the singing was relocated and is now held at Fuller Cemetery, which had been the site of that weekend's exceptional Saturday evening singing. This decision followed announcements by several local singers, including Betty Shepherd, that they would not go back to that church while it had the same pastor. Rod Ivey made his anger with the preacher widely known in their town and refused to speak to him for over a year whenever they crossed paths.

At the same time, such defense of visitors violating behavioral norms would not extend indefinitely. The Western Massachusetts singers were given the benefit of the doubt because of their youth and enthusiasm, because many of them were skilled singers and leaders, and because they did show respect for other traditions and behavioral norms. If they had returned repeatedly without showing that they were learning and respecting southern practices, they would have worn out their welcome—never to the point of being asked not to return, but facing declining enthusiasm. Instead, each year since, a group of Western Massachusetts singers has attended the Young People's and the moved and renamed Lacy Memorial, which have become the primary southern singings attended by people from this community, and a few Western Mass singers have also attended other singings in the area or the South more generally. Moreover, several of the women from Western Mass have made a little ritual of shaving their legs and underarms together before a southern singing, and none have again worn pants, despite the degree to which local singers had come to their defense against the Lacy's Chapel preacher.

This was an unusual moment of open conflict, and the explicit statements of goodwill it provoked perhaps suggest the issues contained within to be less important than I believe they in fact are on a regular basis. Each summer at Camp Fasola, a weeklong camp that draws lifelong and new singers alike, Shelbie Sheppard emphasizes the importance of proper attire in classes she teaches for a reason: She and, she believes, other singers understand it to be a meaningful part of Sacred Harp tradition and do assess visitors on that ground. Similarly, Rod Ivey half-jokingly explains his decision to always wear a tie to Sunday singings as being intended to "set an example for all these Yankees who don't know how to dress."

Both Shelbie and Rod have found ways stress the importance of proper attire at singings—Shelbie through her teaching and Rod by example—that do not directly confront any individual with an accusation of behaving inappropriately, and it is unlikely that either would directly confront an individual with whom they were not already good friends. This silence despite strong feelings on a subject is due to the Sacred Harp tradition of avoiding controversial subjects.

Controversial subjects avoided include politics and sex, as the saying "you can talk about anything but religion, sex, or politics" indicates, but religion becomes more complicated given the religious nature of Sacred Harp music itself, and politics and sex are far from the only subjects avoided. Indeed, many topics having to do directly with Sacred Harp itself can prove dangerous, given that singers from different areas may have allegiances to more than one, or different, revisions of *The Sacred Harp*, or may have distinct localized singing practices. Then, the question of where politics begins and ends can be a difficult one, touching on religion when issues related to the relationship between church and state are raised, or on personal lives where singers have differing sexual politics—some gay or living with partners they are not married to, others disapproving of those identities or practices. The prohibition on controversial speech is therefore much broader than the simplest interpretation of "religion, sex, or politics," but it is also far more public spirited than the avoidance of politics Eliasoph describes among activists and recreation club members. Instead, silence opens up possibilities; as Courtney Bender suggests of God's Love We Deliver volunteers, "The apparent absence of conversation about meaning allowed volunteers to practice cooking in ways that often continued, or reinterpreted, work they had done for others in other times and places."[29]

Where Eliasoph found that among members of a country-and-western club, racist and sexual jokes were the accepted front-stage behavior but caused some people unadmitted discomfort, the silence of Sacred Harp

singers is for the most part exquisitely sensitive to the probability of difference. Controversial topics are discouraged because they may make
someone feel excluded from the community. However, this prohibition
coupled with the existence of strong informal behavioral norms produces
a tension. How are behavioral norms conveyed when one of the strongest
ones prohibits open discussion of the subject in most settings?

Here what is required is not simply politeness but, in Goffman's term,
the "more pervasive ecologically" requirement of decorum, "the way in
which the performer comports himself while in visual or aural range of
the audience but not necessarily engaged in talk with them."[30] In the presence of strategic silence, singers are also expected to pick up on forms of
decorum that extend to dress and physical movement. Although initially
these norms are not conveyed to new singers with great efficiency, there
are a number of avenues through which teaching and learning take place.
Most bluntly, singing schools such as the Camp Fasola ones at which
Shelbie Sheppard emphasizes clothing, as well as shorter singing schools
that precede the singing at a handful of northern conventions and free-
standing events put on by local communities, provide their established
and respected teachers with an opportunity to speak more directly than
usual. Because these events are explicitly intended to teach, information
about things like appropriate dress, the importance of prayer, and appropriate demeanor while leading and singing can be conveyed.

If similar remarks were made at a regular singing, they would almost
certainly be interpreted as intending to berate or single out a particular
singer or group of singers. The case of the Lacy's Chapel prayer is an extreme example of what might happen, but on the rare occasions I have
seen a lifelong singer take a moment before leading to say something
about appropriate leading or behavior, this has always occasioned discussion of who they were upset with and whether the public statement was
appropriate. Such a statement also disrupts the democracy of a regular
singing, with one singer asserting their right to instruct others. That right
may in fact be unquestioned in the case of very respected singers, but it
is not to be exercised in that setting.

Instruction is also commonly transmitted individually or in small
groups. For instance, as I mentioned above, before Western Massachusetts singers went to the Young People's and Lacy's Chapel singings, one
of their more experienced members discussed appropriate dress with
the group of travelers. Similarly, when an individual singer is preparing
to make their first trip South, other local singers who have experience
traveling are likely to explain how expectations there differ from the
home community. These explanations are given not only out of concern

for the individual singer's popularity at the convention they attend but also because their behavior is understood to reflect on their community of origin and may affect the degree to which their home convention is seen as an attractive destination or one which has earned reciprocal attendance.

Southern singers also do sometimes convey messages about clothing or other forms of decorum in one-on-one conversation, but do so in such a subtle way that the criticisms implied are sometimes missed by the intended recipient. Comments on "cute" items of clothing, for instance, are often meant critically, but it takes an experienced ear to hear that. At the more blatant end, one New York singer was approached during the break at a singing by an elderly woman she did not know, who looked at her tank dress and said, "That's a cute dress. It would look nice with a top." More typically, though, such criticisms are either far more subtle or are delivered by friends, in the vein of "I'm helping you out by giving you this friendly advice."

Clothing is not the only area in which such interactions take place; for instance, leading styles can also send significant signals. As with clothing, Shelbie Sheppard addresses leading styles in her singing schools, saying,

When you get up and lead, you don't need to make all these monkey motions in the center of the square where your body is gyrating all over the place. . . . You want to conduct yourself in a manner when you're in the square that's becoming to a religious event, because that's what it is to us. When it is not treated that way, some of us get offended.[31]

Northern singers may draw their leading styles from contra dance, classical choral conducting, or other traditions that involve more extravagant motions than are involved in Sacred Harp leading as it has long been done in the South and as it is taught. A style that departs radically from this simple, though refined and graceful, movement, may be seen to be disrespectful in the way Shelbie outlines, or may be cause for laughter, or draw other negative reactions that can distract from the singing (though a leader who is cause for laughter can draw those in on the joke into a form of solidarity).

Again, though, leading styles are rarely if ever criticized directly outside of singing schools. The same is true of other possibly problematic behaviors, but these violations of decorum do have ramifications for the offenders. A singer who transgresses too egregiously at one of their first southern singings, or who does not pick up the subtle cues offered as to appropriate behavior, may simply be relegated to a status in which no

overt criticisms are made and certainly no hostility is expressed, but neither is the best possible hospitality offered. Such people, for instance,
might be called to lead their songs at less good times of day, even if they
are competent leaders and have traveled a distance to be there; will not be
sought out for welcome by host singers; or will not be urged to return to a
singing. None of these things seek to drive offenders away, but neither do
they seek to draw them in. Observant visitors may notice either the ever-
so-slightly cool reception or the behaviors being modeled as appropriate
and change their behavior, in which case they are welcomed particularly
enthusiastically as people who have shown respect for the tradition in
changing their ways.

One of the few behaviors that will draw a direct rebuke is, in fact, vio-
lation of the norm of silence. For instance, in 2002, a man prefaced his
choice of song at the Western Massachusetts Convention by dedicating
it to people incarcerated on drug offenses, which he described as, in the
language of the song he was leading, a form of "tyranny." His speech
was interrupted by the tenor who was pitching that session sounding a
note for the song, which was taken up by the rest of the class. After, he
was approached privately by one of the organizers of the convention and
told that his behavior had been inappropriate. Such a rebuke would only
come publicly in the most extreme circumstances, but the interruption
of his speech by the person pitching conveyed the public message that
such speech would not be allowed.

Just two weeks later, the same man, having apparently learned the
lesson that he would not be allowed to speak out loud, arrived early at
the Georgia State Convention with flyers outlining his opposition to the
war on drugs, which he placed on the chairs as they were being set up
before the convention's start. One of the convention's officers picked up
a number of the flyers and returned them to him, telling him that this
was not appropriate behavior any more than speaking out loud had been.
At both events, the people who foreclosed this man's speech were in at
least partial agreement with him on the injustice of long-term incarcera-
tion for nonviolent drug offenses, but they nonetheless moved swiftly to
protect Sacred Harp from the discord that might emerge from the airing
of controversial views.

Most such events involve transgressions by northern singers who have
come to the tradition as adults and, therefore, were not taught etiquette
while still young enough to be bossed around. Occasionally at a southern
singing, a local person who may have been raised around Sacred Harp but
is not an active singer will cause some disruption by acting as an audience member, making requests or commenting out loud in response to

songs that have just been sung. If such behavior is persistent through a day, local singers will usually speak to the person during a break, asking him not to speak publicly. Similarly, Jeff Sheppard tells of a time the town drunk showed up at one of his family's singings and was told to leave. Lifelong singers, however, are as a group unlikely to aggressively violate behavioral norms they were raised with. Over the years, though, they have engaged in a gradual loosening of the formality of singings, not just allowing less formal clothing but having more flexibility about the degree of expertise required for a singer to sit on the front bench at a big singing and, according to Teenie Moody, Richard DeLong, and others, having a generally lighter atmosphere. Richard says, "My recollection is it was a very strict atmosphere, there was not a whole lot of laughter"; while according to Teenie, since her own generation became the dominant arbiters of appropriate behavior, "It's been a more open, relaxed atmosphere than it was when I was growing up, and a lot more fun." These changes, though, happened over a period of years and pertain more to the degree to which private conversations between two or three singers are permitted between songs, or eye contact leading to shared laughter is allowed during songs, than to public speech or other actions attempting to engage the class as a whole.

In one-on-one relationships, however, the insistence on silence dissolves, albeit gradually. Singers begin their relationships with each other within the framework of Sacred Harp singings, but the interactions they have during breaks and lunch hours may lead to dinners together on the evenings after singings, stays at each other's houses, and, most of all, opportunities for deeper conversation. Sacred Harp, therefore, provides a substantial new backstage area in which many potentially controversial subjects—including politics—can be addressed even between people who might otherwise have little to say to each other.

In one such instance, two men from rural south Georgia, were talking with Minja Lausevic in Minnesota. One was discussing a gift he'd been sent by another Sacred Harp singer who had visited China, which arrived wrapped in a Chinese newspaper. He made a joke about how of course the newspaper had no comics in it, because it was a communist newspaper and communists have no sense of humor. Minja, who is from the former Yugoslavia said, "You know, I'm a Communist," at which the man turned slightly red and said, "It looks a little different when it's sitting across the table from you."

Out of such moments, or out of a series of subtler moments, the sorts of relationships that form would lead the members of Liberty to offer space in their cemetery to Karen House's family and Rod Ivey to dig her grave himself. Some singers never get past their perception of difference to actually discuss the content of those differences, but nonetheless form close enough relationships to include gift giving, shared meals, and the exchange of regular e-mails and phone calls. Others move still further to discuss their differences—their Primitive Baptism and their Communism, their thoughts about race and the civil rights movement from the differing perspectives of white northern liberals and white southern conservatives. Sacred Harp by no means makes such relationships automatic or inevitable, but it makes them possible.

National Singings

What I call national singings are the major venues that bring people together across their many differences. Some singings are almost entirely local, with no expectation that they will draw visitors from farther than an hour or two's drive. Others, though, work to draw and then welcome visitors from greater distances and in larger numbers; these I label as national. This is where reciprocity comes in, with local singers going to other people's singings and promoting their own, writing personal notes to people they particularly want to attend, and otherwise using their capital within the broader Sacred Harp community to promote a particular singing. During the singing itself, efforts are typically made to make visitors feel at home, which can entail setting aside specifically local traditions for more generic Sacred Harp practices.

For the most part, the adjustments that the hosts of a singing make to welcome visitors from other communities might seem subtle or inconsequential. They do not involve major public statements of accommodation or changes to the basic structure of a day of singing, but they can accumulate to reorient the singing toward making visitors feel at home and thereby promoting national community rather than solely local community. These adjustments are most visible in communities that hold more than one all-day singing or convention each year, with different orientations.

A month after the Decoration Day singing discussed in chapter 3, Liberty holds its annual two-day convention, formally called the Henagar-Union Convention but equally often referred to as the July singing. In many respects it is similar to Decoration Day—both are attended by many of the same local singers, David Ivey serves as chair, and other tasks tend to be taken on by the same people—but where that is oriented to extended family, the July singing is oriented to the broader Sacred Harp community. This outward orientation has been intensified since David Ivey and Jeff Sheppard began Camp Fasola in 2003, bringing singers from around the country to spend four days in singing schools and more typical summer camp activities. Camp is timed to lead up to the July singing and many of the campers stay for at least one day of singing. Even before Camp Fasola was started, though, this singing drew many out-of-state visitors, so the introduction of the campers has simply increased existing tendencies.

We might think of singings at Liberty as being populated by a core of local singers who can be counted on to work on setting up, cleaning, bringing food, and other such tasks. However, the three annual all-day singings there each have their own character: The singing on the first fifth Sunday of the year, recently named the Ivey Memorial, is mostly composed of this core (though it draws some long-distance travelers and some locals who don't sing regularly); Decoration Day adds to the core a large number of family and church members who do not sing often; and the Henagar-Union Convention adds a large number of long-distance travelers.

In preparation for these visitors, who unlike the family members at Decoration Day do not bring food for dinner on the grounds, the core singers have to cook extra. Where copies of the Cooper Revision of *The Sacred Harp* are left easily available throughout the church for the fifth Sunday and Decoration Day singings, so that family and church members can choose longtime favorites from that book, before the July singing Rod Ivey and Shane Wootten often gather up all the Cooper books and put them in a corner of the room to discourage their use, stressing that this is primarily a singing from the 1991, or Denson, Revision,[32] as opposed to one drawing on local traditions including more books. Where a lifelong member of the local community always acts as the arranging committee at the other two singings of the year, at which knowledge of local people's leading habits is crucial, at the July singing I did the arranging for at least one day during several years of my research period, as I was familiar with both local and visiting singers.[33]

Singers visiting from many locations (there were people in attendance from at least sixteen states and Canada) increase the size of the singing and are joyfully welcomed. However, there is quiet debate over whether they actually strengthen the quality of the singing. Sacred Harp singing produces an extraordinary level of musical quality given that it entails amateur, unauditioned singers (some of whom may be unable to carry a tune) singing together without rehearsal, allowing anyone to lead their choice of song at the pace of their choice. But it is also the case that the sound produced by singers who are accustomed to singing with each other is tighter and more blended. There is a tenuous balance to be struck between this fact and the desire to produce a fuller sound with the largest possible number of singers. Few local singing communities have enough singers to have a really good, convention-level singing without visitors,[34] but too many people unfamiliar with singing with each other, and with the extensive repertoire of songs contained in *The Sacred Harp*, can produce raggedness, no matter how skilled each is as an individual.[35] Especially since the inception of Camp Fasola, the Henagar-Union Convention sometimes tips over from benefiting from large numbers of singers to losing some of its musical coherence as a result. This effect is reduced on Sunday, when some travelers go to Georgia and west Alabama for one-day singings and others begin the trip home.

But whatever their effect on the moment-to-moment singing quality, these visitors are understood and valued as important for the long-term quality and health of Sacred Harp, and their treatment in every particular reflects this understanding. David Ivey, as chair, emphasizes the extent of the welcome when he says, as he frequently does in giving a public welcome, that "everybody looks like home folks" or "nobody looks like a stranger."

Another indication of the focus on visitors came Saturday evening, when Coy and Marie Ivey held a social. Saturday evening socials are much more the norm at northern conventions than at southern conventions, since they were founded with the understanding that the goal was to get visitors from as many places as possible, creating a group of people new to town and perhaps unknown to local singers, such that socializing would be a unique opportunity. When I first sang at Liberty at the 1999 United, there was no formal social. Some people were invited to drop by Coy and Marie's house, but not all that many and this was extremely informal. In 2000, they again had a small informal gathering the Saturday of the Henagar-Union Convention, but over the next few years this became more public and more elaborate. After some singers became offended they had not been invited, the invitation was made general. In response to this, though, a somewhat overwhelming number of people showed up for an event at which the food served was mainly snacks and leftovers from the singing. The social was then moved away from the house to their large garage, used not just for cars but for tractors, and nonsinging family members put together more substantial food, including grilling hot dogs and hamburgers.

Music at this social, too, has evolved. The first year a general invitation was issued to everyone at the singing, several singers brought their guitars, banjos, and autoharps and played together informally. Because playing together required finding points of commonality in their repertoires, the songs of *O Brother, Where Art Thou?* featured heavily in 2001 and 2002. Over the next few years, the number of musicians grew; then, in 2005, a more organized ensemble of local musicians was brought in for a performance rather than participatory music.[36]

The Liberty July singing remains deeply personal and local for many of its home singers, but at the same time they have carefully constructed it as an event for singers from around the country, as the comparison with their Decoration Day singing a month earlier shows. Such careful accommodations help to create the conditions of possibility for the formation of a Sacred Harp community that transcends locality. Singers are drawn into commitment to Sacred Harp through the participatory nature of the music, requiring that they reach out to others to effectively produce Sacred Harp song and through the intense experience of singing it. The reverence many northern singers have for the perceived authenticity of lifelong southern singers draws them into ongoing relationships in which the culture among northern singers as much as among southern ones involves an expectation that northern singers will be respectful and appreciative of southern traditions, including the spirituality that is so central to Sacred Harp, not only for most southern singers, but also for some northern ones. Finally, this commitment to Sacred Harp established, the prohibition on controversial public speech enables people with a wide range of beliefs to sing without fear that distasteful differences will be thrust in their faces and to develop trust in each other, which, in some cases, leads to more open discussion in private.

Pictures of Sacred Harp singers reveal few of the differences between them, but looking below the surface, you might find that of two women smiling next to each other, one is a devout Christian and the other an atheist Jew, or a row of people in matching Camp Fasola T-shirts might include a gay man, an Amish man, a Polish woman, and an Anglican from Canada. Given these largely invisible but culturally meaningful differences, how do we understand not only their mutual interest in a somewhat esoteric tradition but also their desire to practice it together?

In constructing community across difference, singers first use meaning-making processes and the meanings they attribute to Sacred Harp; second, spirituality; third, the goal of authenticity; fourth, the structures of Sacred Harp singing itself; and fifth, silence on potentially controversial issues. As discussed in chapter 4, meanings such as spirituality and authenticity are inscribed in local Sacred Harp practice, with ongoing implications for the types of local communities that are formed; similarly, both widely held understandings of Sacred Harp and specific local ones go into the formation of national community.

At the local level, singers tend to have much in common demographically and share any localized understandings of proper Sacred Harp function, but commitment levels vary; in fact, commitment is the greatest variation within a given locality and poses one of the greatest challenges for community building. How do people for whom Sacred Harp is a deep-seated identity and people for whom it is either a five-times-a-year hobby or a not-altogether-welcome family obligation work smoothly together and feel connected? Some singers travel to faraway singings, others do not; this is as true on Sand Mountain, where some people attend one singing that is associated with their family or church each year but do not treat Sacred Harp as a distinct tradition to which they are committed, as it is in Chicago, where some attend only the Midwest Convention.

At the national level, there is significant diversity among singers, as people from different places come together, bringing their characteristic demographics and their local norms. Commitment levels, however, are more consistent, with traveling a near requirement of participation. Here, local norms must be overcome, which happens in a number of ways, usually through a combination of obliviousness and intentional compromise. Again, the question of whose authority, whose power, and whose authenticity will matter most comes to the fore, but now, the communities people come from are part of the grounds on which they are evaluated as authentic, authoritative Sacred Harp singers. In general, southern singers are given respect by northern ones on the assumption that they have been singing all their lives and have deep knowledge of the music and associated traditions as a result. (Not infrequently, these judgments are made in ignorance of whether the singer in question is in fact a longtime singer and of how status is perceived within the South.)

A significant literature has shown music to be important in ideas and enactment of community in situations ranging from the Depression-era southern textile workers[37] to choices of national anthems.[38] Recently, Tia DeNora has used historical studies to theorize about the ways that music, as a "resource for—rather than medium about— world building, . . . helps to structure such things as styles of consciousness, ideas, or modes of embodiment."[39] She demonstrates, for instance, how the introduction of Beethoven's piano compositions gendered piano playing in late-eighteenth- and early-nineteenth-century Vienna; to engage in the style of physical comportment associated with performance of Beethoven was enough "to risk one's decorum as a feminine being."[40] Just as gender was affected by how "the physical configuration of musical events is itself a resource for what music may come to afford,"[41] so does the physical configuration of a Sacred Harp singing afford certain notions of community.

First, as I have emphasized, Sacred Harp is participatory music, which cannot be done effectively alone or even necessarily with a group of relatives or close friends. Larger groups are better, which pushes singers to find and form lasting ties with other singers, at least in the present day as families grow smaller and geographic mobility increases such that even those singers whose families have sung together for generations cannot count on kin to continue to provide the basis for a full-sized singing.

A second important factor is the democratic structure of singing in the hollow square shape, with singers separated into their vocal sections and a leader—who changes with each—standing in the center of the square. While there are hierarchies involved in where a singer sits and even at what time of day they lead, these are not formalized or rigid, so there is a sense of equality and togetherness produced by this physical structure, especially as opposed to the more common situation of a performer and an audience, or even choral singing in which a single director is in charge of the pace and flow of singing and designates some singers as soloists.

The fact that singers are facing each other is important as, through the course of a day of singing, people have the chance to observe each other in some detail, which underscores trustworthiness and creates a sense of shared experience. The combined physical intensity of the experience— the effort involved in singing in full voice for a day should not be underestimated, especially in summer heat—and the psychological impact of singing lyrics about death and salvation and other fairly encompassing topics heighten the sense of shared experience and of the construction of intimacy. This is meaningful in a local context, but more so in the national context where singers have fewer opportunities to establish these kinds of trust and intimacy through daily contact.

These aspects of the physical structure of a Sacred Harp singing push northern and southern—new and lifelong—singers alike to reach out to people who would not otherwise be in their lives and who may be very unlike themselves. Other factors in the production of national community appeal more to one type of singer or the other. The desire for authenticity, for instance, induces many people who come to Sacred Harp as adults to travel South to participate in Sacred Harp in its "traditional" settings with lifelong singers.

SIX

Going Hollywood

Sacred Harp functions overwhelmingly without reference to mass-marketed popular culture. Though most if not all singers are consumers of some form of popular culture, and may make reference to other musical genres in discussing their attraction to Sacred Harp, the act of singing and the organization of singing communities are remarkably detached from commercial considerations. Singers spend money to travel to distant singings or to help host local ones without any expectation of ever profiting financially from their participation; the assumption that others in the community will adhere to these practices is part of the way the authenticity of the tradition as a tradition is constituted and reproduced.

Although they do not require substantial commercial success for the tradition, they do value publicity. This is valued not because it brings financial benefit or fame to individual singers but because a tradition based in participation requires participants. Like many folk traditions, Sacred Harp's decline and eventual death has been forecast many times. In 1944, George Pullen Jackson wrote, "The Sacred Harp *may* persist another century. But it will be a wonder if it does,"[1] and in 1978, despite the beginnings of a northern revival, Buell Cobb wrote, "The future of the Sacred Harp is not assured, and in some areas the prospects already appear dim."[2] In this context, finding ways to attract new singers is a goal for many. Through the 1980s and into the 1990s, expanding Sacred Harp to new areas of the country was one major focus of this effort, but more recently the focus has been equally on shoring up Sacred Harp in its traditional areas of strength.

What happens, then, when the possibility of Sacred Harp making money or attracting significant publicity, through engagement with commercial mass media, is introduced? How would these communities formed in the absence of such possibilities respond? From 2002 to 2004, Sacred Harp singers faced these questions (though ultimately not the challenges that would have been posed by great commercial success), with the inclusion of two Sacred Harp songs in the film *Cold Mountain*. This event provided a natural experiment, allowing me to observe the effects of this outside influence on the singing communities I was already studying. And the years that have passed since provide perspective on the intricacies of such effects, showing that what initially seem to be minimal effects may play out more robustly in time.

Though Sacred Harp music had been marketed and sold in various ways, such commercialization had always been small scale and localized, either geographically or within very small market segments such as folk festivals and field recordings, and had been conceived of more as a means of cultural preservation than of profit making. Similarly, it had been the subject of a number of newspaper articles and radio stories over the years, but these came at a trickle and were too dispersed for a coherent public narrative about the tradition to emerge, let alone one that canonized particular singers or communities as, for instance, the spiritual had earlier been canonized by the Fisk University Jubilee Singers.[3]

A LexisNexis search of major newspapers for the term *Sacred Harp* is instructive. Though it by no means encompasses all of the coverage Sacred Harp has received, which may well have been concentrated in smaller newspapers, it reveals the absence of a dominant narrative about Sacred Harp. Although each year from 1991 to 2003 shows some mentions of Sacred Harp, the contexts are widely varied. Of 139 references,[4] only 36 place Sacred Harp as a distinct tradition, and only 15 of those are full-length articles. The rest are expanded versions of announcements of upcoming singings and columns in which Sacred Harp features (the latter are entirely drawn from southern newspapers, predominantly the *Atlanta Journal-Constitution*).

Other references to Sacred Harp usually place it under the umbrella of another art form, whether as part of a folk festival, performance, or recording; part of a classical performance or recording (groups including the Boston Camerata and Chanticleer have performed some Sacred Harp songs over the years); or part of a dance performance, play, or art show. Occasionally it appears in relation to a church or historical event, and it shows up in obituaries of singers.

All this means that before the release of *Cold Mountain*, Sacred Harp was rarely given enough attention to allow it to be framed as a distinct tradition, rather than merely part of a folk or classical repertoire or of an encompassing category, such as religion or history. How would the entry of Sacred Harp into a public and commercial framework, with particular singers or communities elevated into the public eye, affect the national and local singing communities?

Cold Mountain, which grossed approximately $173 million world-wide,[5] was Anthony Minghella's film adaptation of Charles Frazier's National Book Award–winning Civil War novel. The movie was intended to be Miramax's major Oscar contender for 2003; while it received seven nominations and Renée Zellweger won the best supporting actress award, it was not nominated for top awards, such as best picture or best director. These equivocal results on the awards circuit were mirrored at the box office, where the film was seen as a moderate failure, given its production and marketing costs.

Music is an important part of the film, and the music and sound track were done by T Bone Burnett, the enormously successful producer of the *O Brother, Where Art Thou?* sound track, which *Cold Mountain* clearly attempts to emulate. Tim Eriksen contributed three songs to the sound track as the singing voice of one of the movie's characters and facilitated the recording of Sacred Harp music for it. Sacred Harp singers were included in several events, including a show at UCLA's Royce Hall, which was subsequently televised on the cable network A&E; the Academy Awards; and a concert tour (called the Great High Mountain Tour). For each of these events, the usual practice of Sacred Harp was altered somewhat, producing new pressures on its communities and the ongoing relationships within and between them.

This case provides an excellent opportunity to study—from beginning to end—what happens when a noncommercial genre comes into contact with major commercializing institutions. In particular, the participatory rather than performance-oriented nature of Sacred Harp singing meant that Sacred Harp singers and commercial culture producers had very different agendas for the interaction and different definitions of what would constitute success for the genre. While in direct interactions between Sacred Harp singers and Miramax pictures or Sony Music, the priorities of the latter generally prevailed, Sacred Harp singers were often able to use this contact to advance their own agendas through local media and in appealing to potential new singers. These competing agendas came into play during five events or series of events: the initial recording of Sacred Harp songs for the sound track; the time between the recording and the release of the film and sound track; the period of publicity around the film and sound track release and the concert at Royce Hall; the Academy Awards; and the Great High Mountain Tour. Each point in time produced a different balance between commercial and performance imperatives and attention to Sacred Harp and observance of its traditions. Throughout these stages, the ability of singers to influence events was inversely related to the amount of profit that might be expected to result.

Recording

The inclusion of Sacred Harp singing on the *Cold Mountain* sound track was shaped by a series of coincidences and slightly improbable moments of individuals pushing for Sacred Harp. This process began in June 2002, when Tim Eriksen was hired as the singing voice of the character Stobrod.[6] When he learned of plans to have a choir record a Sacred Harp song for the movie, Tim suggested that actual Sacred Harp singers could be brought to the studio to record a song rather than using a professional choir. However, when he called David Ivey, David suggested that a recording session could be put together at Liberty, which is just three hours southeast of Nashville, where major recording of music for the film was taking place.

Minghella and Burnett agreed to record at Liberty, and Tim collaborated with David and Rod Ivey to pull together a singing with only two weeks notice. The singing was scheduled for late in the afternoon of Friday, June 22, so that few local singers would have to leave work early to attend. Sixty-three singers gathered—including Tim and ten others who traveled more than five hundred miles specifically to attend this singing[7] and an additional two out-of-towners who were already in the area.[8] Apart from these thirteen, all the singers at the recording session were from Alabama or Georgia and predominantly from the Sand Mountain area.

Though the local singers were excited about the prospect of recording for a "Hollywood movie," it was not clear in advance exactly what the scale of the project was. Some, but by no means all, singers arriving that Friday afternoon knew what book the movie was from, that Nicole Kidman was in it, that Academy Award–winning director Anthony Minghella was directing, and that *O Brother, Where Art Thou?* producer T Bone Burnett was also producing this sound track. Even for those who knew all this, it was difficult to grasp the scale of the movie itself, and singers engaged in little speculation about the role Sacred Harp would have in the movie. Singers began to reassess the importance of what they were doing when Minghella, Burnett, and actor Brendan Gleeson arrived for the recording session along with the expected sound engineers; similarly, the $200 payment each singer received served as a marker that this event might be meaningful to the filmmakers, since the investment of well over $12,000 in Sacred Harp singing was unprecedented.

Susan Harcrow had called local newspapers to notify them about the recording session but not out of an expectation that the event would be anything more than an opportunity to garner local publicity. Rather, she explains that she "did have enough presence of mind to at least know it was kind of a big deal, for the singing and for a small town," but that "the first clue I consciously had that there might be something more to it was when Tim introduced the director" (which preceded the singers being paid). She notes, though, that many local singers did not know or care who Anthony Minghella was. At this time and for months thereafter, it remained uncertain whether Sacred Harp's role in the film would survive the filming and editing processes.

Despite this uncertainty, however, there was considerable excitement throughout the Sacred Harp community, as well as some resentment on the part of those who had not been invited to the recording session (resentment which was in some cases short lived and in other cases periodically resurrected over a year or more). Since Sacred Harp events are almost always open to anyone who wants to attend, the fact that invitations were issued for the recording session—however informal the invitation process was—meant that this event was outside the norm and therefore could be questioned by those who felt left out.

Although this event was going to be recorded, to be released to a (presumably) wider audience than Sacred Harp had ever known, and although the number of singers requested was limited to fifty, for the most part the invitation process was consistent with tradition in its dependence on the central value of participation, as opposed to musical proficiency, as the determining principle of inclusion. The values according to which Sacred Harp singings are usually conducted were in no way challenged or questioned in the organization of the recording session. Tim invited a few people he knew, but for the most part he relied on David to assemble a group of singers, and David in turn worked with Rodney. Rod's focus in issuing invitations to the recording session was on people who had been supporting a recently started night singing in nearby Fort Payne. As a new singing with no connection to a particular church or family of singers, participation in the Fort Payne singing showed loyalty to Sacred Harp singing and singers specifically rather than some combination of Sacred Harp and church or family. Insofar as attending the recording session was a reward, then, it was a reward for already being an active singer; as such it was more in line with the democratic ethic of participation than if the invitations had been given out on the basis of natural singing talent or practiced excellence.

With the few exceptions of singers disappointed or resentful of not having been asked to the recording session, singers I talked to were excited about what had already occurred and at the prospects for the future. However, the movie's Christmas 2003 release date seemed impossibly distant, and the short supply of concrete information limited speculation. Many singers kept in mind the possibility that Sacred Harp would be eliminated from the film in the editing process, self-consciously avoiding inflated hopes.

Waiting

Once the initial flurry of excitement and resentment over the recording session itself died down, singers were left for a year and a half with a nebulous sense of hope—and occasional fear that they would be overrun by celebrity seekers with no interest in Sacred Harp itself. Hope predominated, though: In early 2003, I told Betty Shepherd and Elene Stovall—middle-aged women raised in Sacred Harp by their parents—that according to Tim, the role of Sacred Harp in the movie had been increased somewhat. We began discussing the possibility of greater publicity and attention to Sacred Harp coming out of *Cold Mountain*. During this conversation, first Betty, then Elene, began crying. "My father worked so hard to keep the singing going . . . if he could have seen this," Betty said. "I just wish he would have seen it spread like this." Such a response would have been echoed by many singers, as it subsequently was by Elene in that conversation.

The approach of the release of the movie and its sound track brought an entirely different scale and type of publicity from local newspaper coverage and, with it, new benefits for and pressures on the singing community. Shortly before the release of the sound track, National Public Radio's *All Things Considered* did a thirteen-minute segment on Sacred Harp focusing on the Ivey family, with Melissa Block attending and recording the Alabama State Convention. The *New York Times* also sent reporter Randy Kennedy to the Alabama State Convention and subsequently ran a feature on Sacred Harp.[9]

Sacred Harp was getting national attention because of *Cold Mountain*, but its treatment remained focused on the participatory nature of the tradition and on its routine practice. The NPR story followed Coy, David, and Rodney Ivey getting ready to go to the Alabama State Convention and did not mention *Cold Mountain* until eleven minutes into a thirteen-minute story. Both stories described the hollow square and the way each song is led by a different person, as well as the dinner on the grounds and the mix of lifelong southern and more recent northern singers in attendance. Both reporters drew most substantially on their conversations with core, widely respected community members, but, in describing the mixture of southern and northern singers, both also emphasized the exotic to some degree. One woman appeared unnamed in both stories—NPR referred to her nose ring, while the *New York Times* quoted her self-description as an "atheist Jew."

December to February

Attention to Sacred Harp soon shifted from a focus on its routine practice to putting it into performance contexts. The night after the Los Angeles premiere of *Cold Mountain*, a concert titled The Words and Music of *Cold Mountain* was held at UCLA's Royce Hall. Thus placed in an academic venue, the show included clips of the movie; a discussion between director Anthony Minghella and a film historian; performances by well-known musicians Jack White, Alison Krauss, and Sting, all of whom sung on the sound track, along with other musicians from the sound track, including Tim Eriksen and Cassie Franklin, a local Alabama singer; and actors from the film reading from the screenplay and novel *Cold Mountain* and from sources that had been inspirations for the writing of both. The time devoted to reading from a variety of texts echoed the practice of authors' readings at bookstores and further certified the evening as a literary event—and the film therefore as a serious one. The evening closed with the Sacred Harp song "I'm Going Home" sung by some forty-five Sacred Harp singers joined by Nicole Kidman, Jude Law, and other members of the film's cast.

The inclusion of Sacred Harp, and what form that inclusion would take, had been uncertain until just days before the show. Throughout the planning process—which took place before the sound track was released and reviews praising the Sacred Harp component came out—Tim pushed for some form of Sacred Harp to be included, and there was general agreement that it would be. However, it was initially unclear whether Miramax would pay for singers to attend.

Ultimately, perhaps influenced by the release of favorable reviews, Miramax paid for a small group of singers to be flown to Los Angeles for the movie's premiere and the Royce Hall performance. Additionally, some thirty other singers from Alabama, Georgia, Illinois, Massachusetts, Rhode Island, and New Mexico paid their own ways to sing at the Words and Music event, having been invited through informal social networks originating with Tim.[10]

Significantly, though one singer had told the *New York Times* that "you could stand Nicole Kidman or Jude Law up in the middle of the room here, and a lot of these people would not know who they were. And if they did, they wouldn't care anyway," almost everyone who was invited to attend the event did so even though the invitations came at very short notice. Indeed, the lure of appearing on a stage with Nicole Kidman drew a few singers' family members who rarely appear at ordinary singings but successfully sought inclusion in the concert nonetheless.[11]

Most of the singers in attendance would have couched their desire to be present largely in terms of preserving Sacred Harp through helping it attain greater exposure. Some acknowledged their excitement at the proximity to celebrity, but others downplayed it. Whether acknowledged or not, though, this desire for celebrity—through being near the very famous, appearing in media depictions of Sacred Harp, or being chosen to have one's expenses paid—was one of the issues at the core of some minor tension over this event. Despite the informality of the invitation process, which drew on the typical openness of Sacred Harp events, and despite the continuing rhetoric of bolstering Sacred Harp rather than deriving individual benefit, individual singers' investment in prominence had risen along with the increased prominence perceived to be available.

Singers were told to arrive several hours before the show's start, although actual onstage rehearsal time was limited. They spent much of that day in an isolated rehearsal room, where they did what Sacred Harp singers do, and sang in a square, for themselves as a group. During this time of informal singing, a production staffer asked for volunteers to serve as stand-ins on stage while the lighting and sound were checked. Two of the usually nonsinging family members present immediately volunteered, and after further requests, a few regular singers agreed to do so as well.

At the Royce Hall event there was difficulty finding an appropriate configuration for the singers to perform in, a configuration that would be consistent with both Sacred Harp tradition and entertainment conventions, which assume that performers must face the audience. Tim had talked to the show's producers about having chairs so the singers would be in Sacred Harp's traditional inward-facing hollow square, but this detail, central to him but peripheral and apparently confusing to them, was repeatedly overlooked (intentionally or not), and ultimately the singers stood in a loose horseshoe shape to perform. The show producers' incentive to find a way to make a hollow square was also low, because in a horseshoe, Nicole Kidman and Jude Law could be clearly seen standing with the singers, where sitting in a square they would barely have been visible to the audience. Instead, after the initial performance, the singers waited offstage while chairs were set up in a hollow square for a reshoot (without the actors), which was ultimately included on the DVD release of the film in a brief, more ethnographically framed, segment on the Sacred Harp tradition. When the singers went back to their rehearsal room, they sang one last song, "Idumea," standing wherever they happened to be when the pitch was sounded, singing for themselves alone once again.

The Royce Hall event and the release of the sound track were followed by many local newspaper stories—in Alabama, stories ran in the *Birmingham News*, *Fort Payne Times-Journal*, *Rainsville Weekly Post*, *Huntsville Times*, *Decatur Daily*, *Anniston Star*, *Gadsden Times*, and *Tuscaloosa News*.[12] The *Knoxville News* sent a reporter and photographer to Liberty, a Huntsville television news station did a segment on Sacred Harp, a group of singers were featured on a Birmingham television morning show, and singers were interviewed on a local radio station. Such local stories could have given exposure to a significant number of different people by focusing on singers in the newspapers' areas, but instead, most of these stories focused on the same group of Alabama singers—those from Liberty, in particular those who had not only appeared at the Royce Hall show but who had also attended the premiere—and on Tim Eriksen, who spoke about his experiences recording several non-Sacred Harp songs for the sound track and teaching Nicole Kidman and Jude Law how to sing one of the two Sacred Harp songs, but who relentlessly threw the focus back onto Sacred Harp singing and singers rather than putting himself in a central role in the articles.

Outside of Alabama, the *Chicago Tribune* ran an article on Sacred Harp focusing on Tim, who was visiting the city to teach a Sacred Harp singing school and perform; the article also contained parts of an interview with a Chicago Sacred Harp singer and gave information on local singings. The *Atlanta Journal-Constitution* also ran an article based on interviews with local singers who had been at the sound track recording and the Royce Hall event. Other newspapers followed suit, either running wire-service stories on Sacred Harp or producing their own focusing on local singers.

While these stories appeared in many locations and relied on interviews with numerous singers, the overwhelming focus on the singers from Liberty and on Tim Eriksen created a center to a field that ordinarily has none—longtime Sacred Harp singers could assess this focus on particular individuals and singing communities based on their own experience, but newer singers and especially people being introduced to the tradition through this press coverage could not make similar judgments. The group of singers featured in these articles, therefore, had the opportunity to frame Sacred Harp according to their collective priorities, and they simultaneously emphasized its local, participatory nature and the positive response that the music and the singers had gotten from celebrities, such as Jude Law and Nicole Kidman, creating a narrative that they were respected by movie stars and famous musicians simply for singing their music.

This narrative relied both on the widespread acceptance of the importance and desirability of contact with celebrity and on Tim's insistence on placing Sacred Harp equal with or before his own solo career. Given that he had, at that point, had substantial contact with both Kidman and Law, teaching them how to sing Sacred Harp for the movie, he could have worked to parlay this "anointing" by the film elite[13] into personal benefit. Rather than portraying himself as a cultural middleman in the style of Alan Lomax with expertise in multiple genres, or promoting himself as a performer—both roles he could rightfully claim—he stressed his own immersion in and subservience to the tradition of Sacred Harp singing and his reliance on the judgment of Sacred Harp singers.[14] The message was that the tradition and the mass of participants were more important than the most prominent individual associated with them. At this point, the agendas of the Sacred Harp singers were relatively uncomplicated. While many would eagerly seize on any public recognition they could get individually, their overwhelming desire was for publicity that would draw participants to Sacred Harp singing events, bolstering the tradition for years to come. Concern for the group and the music was paramount, with the individual secondary.

Academy Awards

The apex of commercial exposure for Sacred Harp came two months after the Royce Hall event, at the Academy Awards. Two songs from *Cold Mountain*, "You Will Be My Ain True Love" and "The Scarlet Tide," both sung by Alison Krauss, were nominated for Oscars, and the decision was made to have Sacred Harp singers provide backup to the final choruses of the latter song. Through the weeks leading up to the event, the number of singers invited and the extent of their planned performance fluctuated, but in the end some forty singers from ten states[15] went to Los Angeles, not only to sing on "The Scarlet Tide," but also to subsequently sing "Liberty," a song from *The Sacred Harp*.

"Liberty" was ultimately cut from the show, apparently for time reasons, but its intended inclusion was revealing of the ways Sacred Harp was being framed by its culture-industry boosters. Usually only nominated songs are performed at the Academy Awards, but that year all of the nominated songs were rather downbeat, even depressing, and Joe Roth, the show's producer, wanted a "showstopper" to liven things up. T Bone Burnett worked to persuade him that an up-tempo Sacred Harp song, sung by Sacred Harp singers joined by Alison Krauss, Sting, Elvis Costello, and Annie Lennox—all of whom were performing nominated songs in the same segment of the show—could be such a showstopper. There was more to the choice of Sacred Harp for this role, however. While the decision whether to include any Sacred Harp singers in the show at all was in its initial stages, Janet Jackson's breast made its much-publicized Super Bowl appearance. Burnett used this to argue that featuring Sacred Harp singing would be an opportunity to partially redeem American culture by presenting it in a wholesome, uplifting way for an international audience. Sacred Harp was, therefore, valuable not for commercial reasons but because it could stand as a representative of an American culture supposedly purer and cleaner than mere commercial products.

Although the actual Sacred Harp song was cut from the show (apparently being valuable for noncommercial reasons was not enough in this instance), the singers did back Alison Krauss, Elvis Costello, and Cheryl White on the final two choruses of "The Scarlet Tide," some carrying their *Sacred Harp* books with them onstage on the chance that it would be shown onscreen. Echoing the issue of how sound track reviews and articles labeled the singers, a behind-the-scenes battle was also waged—successfully—to have the singers introduced not as "*the* Sacred Harp singers from *Cold Mountain*" but simply as "Sacred Harp singers from *Cold Mountain*," a difference that would be meaningless to most viewers but which was intended by the singers to emphasize the broader, inclusive nature of the tradition. The designation "from *Cold Mountain*" was unavoidable given the context.

The Academy Awards represented a further shift in the way inclusion was structured. The recording session had drawn mainly on singers in the Henagar area, with particular attempts made to include people with strong ties to Liberty and people who made a regular effort to support the Fort Payne night singing; it therefore adhered as much as possible to the ethic of inclusiveness while still limiting numbers. The Royce Hall concert divided people, with some having their way paid and others not, and still others not invited, but the invitations for people to pay their own way were distributed relatively broadly within a few communities with which Tim Eriksen had ties. Although he asked people with whom he initiated contact to exercise discretion in issuing further invitations, the process was informal, and the major lines between those who were invited and those who were not were drawn between communities rather than individuals. By attempting to broaden the communities into which Oscar invitations extended, he inadvertently made the selection process more exclusive on an individual level.

In contrast to Royce Hall, where singers were left substantially to their own devices, at the Academy Awards the singers' efforts to put aside the unusual environment and just sing were less successful. Substantially more rehearsal time was required, the spaces provided for singers to spend the time between rehearsals were less appropriate for singing in a square, and interruptions were frequent. Additionally, the scale of the event was so much larger that it was more difficult to relax and just sing without thought of the circumstances, not simply because of concrete demands on the singers' time but because the Oscars are such an established and glamorous part of American culture: it is one thing to focus on Sacred Harp in a basement at Royce Hall, another to do so as a cart of Oscar statuettes is wheeled down the hall and singers are coming in and reporting sightings of Julia Roberts.

Great High Mountain Tour

The final in-person contact that Sacred Harp singing and singers had with the culture industries was on the Great High Mountain Tour, an attempted "rebranding" of the highly successful Down from the Mountain Tour that came out of *O Brother, Where Art Thou?*. Tim Eriksen was one of the regular performers on the tour, and he persuaded T Bone Burnett and the tour managers to allow him to invite local singers to open each show by singing, with the cast musicians, the two Sacred Harp songs included on the *Cold Mountain* sound track. Many of the singers then stayed and participated in the show's finale, in which Ralph Stanley led the cast in "Angel Band" and "Amazing Grace."

The fact that the tour provided a recurring performance medium with a consistent cast of musicians and backstage personnel produced still another relationship between Sacred Harp and performed commercial music. As at the Royce Hall show and on the Academy Awards, the opening Sacred Harp songs were sung by people standing in a rough horseshoe shape, not sitting in a square. The singing was therefore reconfigured for performance, but in each case the singers' amateur, nonchoir status was marked visually by their nonmatching dress and occasionally ragged entrances and onstage blocking. At Royce Hall, the singers had been introduced by T Bone Burnett, and on the Great High Mountain Tour, Tim played this curatorial role, speaking briefly about the tradition, highlighting the presence of local singers and noting that "like any two-hundred-year-old American singing tradition, it has its own website" and giving that URL—www.sacredharp.org—for interested audience members. Local singers were also given the opportunity to leave flyers advertising their singings at tables in the tour venues. The concessions made to the performance medium were therefore lessened in this (nontelevised) context, with the local, nonprofessional aspects of the tradition, if not the hollow square and lack of audience, emphasized.

The concessions made to performance were also lessened in the process of determining who would be invited to sing and what their backstage status would be. Singers were often invited at the last minute, as Tim struggled to stay a day or two ahead of the tour schedule in finding a local singer who was willing and able to assemble others for the show. The invitation process was therefore different from place to place. In some cases, the person Tim contacted simply put out a general invitation to all local singers, following the principal of inclusivity. This was most pronounced in Huntsville, Alabama (the show closest to Sand Mountain), where over seventy singers attended, including a large number of children, brought along in the self-conscious hope of extending their participation in Sacred Harp.

In other cases, some local singers were excluded, either because of their lack of singing ability or because the person coordinating attendance had personal conflicts with them. Even in many areas where invitations were highly inclusive, the organizers still had to struggle with extremely marginal singers wanting to participate. More than one person who could not read shape notes volunteered to attend the Chicago concert, while a woman in another state told me, "There's a few people who don't sing much that have suddenly got really interested in Sacred Harp since this concert came up." Personal conflicts aside, the inclusiveness or exclusiveness tended to reflect first, whether local singers had any kind of existing informal authority structure that would enable one person to exclude others, and second, whether the goal of local singers (or the representative contacted by Tim) was more oriented to incorporating and making into active singers people on the fringes of the tradition or to trying to attract new singers through presentation of an attractive sound.

Depending on how much room was available backstage and in the audience, during the show singers were either sent to find empty seats in the theater or stayed backstage, usually watching the show from the wings. In either case, they were present for at least an hour before the show began, during which time they sang in a rehearsal room or other space. Having so many nonprofessionals wandering around backstage involved significant adjustment by all of the professionals involved with the tour. As Tim Eriksen described it, "At first, they wanted a list with everyone's name. But eventually, if you showed up with a *Sacred Harp*, that was good enough." At most venues, singers were given freedom to move around the backstage area, and though Tim asked them to be considerate of the performers, many were able to collect autographs.

The desirability of collecting autographs, though, was not uniform to Sacred Harp singers, varying in part by region. To many singers, performers such as Alison Krauss and Union Station, Ralph Stanley, the Cox Family, the Whites, Norman and Nancy Blake, and the Nashville Bluegrass Band were significant musical figures long before the Great High Mountain Tour. But this was not universally the case: At the Wolf Trap in Vienna, Virginia, I was standing by a local singer when Union Station performed "Man of Constant Sorrow," with Dan Tyminski singing. His rendition of this song on the *O Brother, Where Art Thou?* sound track had won a Grammy for country collaboration and the Country Music Association award for song of the year in 2001, so is familiar to many people who are not bluegrass fans. The singer standing near me, though, turned to me and said, "Who is he? He has a neat voice. I've never heard this song done like this."

Other singers placed the tour within somewhat different popular-culture frameworks. One Washington, DC–area singer was disappointed to learn that the New York show had been at the Beacon Theater rather than at Town Hall, since that was where the film *A Mighty Wind* was set.[16] Far from implying that the Great High Mountain Tour was so parodic as to evoke *A Mighty Wind*, she seemed unaware that the suggestion that the real-life tour and the film parody were similar might be taken as an insult. Rather, her familiarity with the film, and its Hollywood aura, offered a way to understand and validate the tour within the context of popularized "folk" music.

Accommodations and Tensions

At each moment of opportunity provided by *Cold Mountain*, there were opportunities for tension or resentment within the Sacred Harp community. As in any community, among Sacred Harp singers are people who like and dislike each other, who are competitive or jealous, or who have a sense of their own stature within the community that exceeds the generally held sense of their importance. It is extremely rare that such tensions ruffle the surface of a singing, but the unusual stakes of brushes with fame, and the new avenues of authority emerging for both individual singers and singing communities, heightened tensions normally existing far below the surface, such that there were occasional ripples of discord. They were, though, so minor and receded so quickly that recounting them in detail from this distance would seem picayune in the extreme. Nonetheless, the surfacing of *any* tensions, however minor, was a noteworthy part of the *Cold Mountain* experience given the Sacred Harp norm of silence.

The main source of tension came from violations of the almost universally held norm of open participation; in most cases, invitations to sing at events were spread as widely as possible, but limits on the number of participants were imposed from outside the singing community. This pattern was set with the initial recording session, as I've discussed. That experience of unforeseen resentments being produced by the invitation process served as notice when time came for invitations to be issued for later events. With each event, the rationale for choosing singers changed, as the singers (always singers) extending the invitations sought the formula that would avoid upsetting their peers.

For the recording session, it was regular singers local to Sand Mountain and in particular to Liberty and the new Fort Payne night singing. For Royce Hall, the initial invitations, and invitations to having expenses paid and attending the premier, went to Tim Eriksen's most immediate personal network and the inner core of Liberty singers he had relied upon to set up the recording session, with a slightly broader set of Alabama and Western Massachusetts singers getting their invitations through these same networks. For the Academy Awards, an attempt was made to expand the local singing communities to which invitations were extended, with the result that within those communities, invitations were more limited than had been the case within the communities in which invitations to the earlier events were circulated.

That is, essentially only singers from Alabama and Western Massachusetts were invited to Royce Hall, but a regular singer in those areas had a good chance of going if they so chose. For the Academy Awards, singers from Alabama, Georgia, Illinois, Massachusetts, Michigan, Minnesota, New Mexico, New York, Rhode Island, and Texas were included, but only a handful of singers from each of those areas were invited, leaving others in those localities potentially feeling that *they* should have been the ones onstage at the Oscars. At Great High Mountain Tour concerts, finally, invitation rationales were locally determined—which meant that resentments were kept local, but also that when they arose they were close and fresh.

To the extent that exclusions produced resentment, it was in degrees shocking to Sacred Harp singers accustomed to the tradition's usual conviviality but minuscule to outsiders considering the stakes. Secondly, it tended to occur where there had already been tension, however minor and unadmitted to (and usually personal in nature), below the surface. Though the *appearance* or discussion of tension, in other words, felt new and was played out in a new territory, the substance of it tended to be preexisting.

The compromises singers had to make were more significant. The inclusion of Sacred Harp in a product of commercial culture and its subsequent promotion depended on people in positions of some power within culture-producing institutions, people who had very different ideas about what constituted success than did Sacred Harp singers and whose ideas about success might change from moment to moment. Bielby and Bielby note of television programming that

a decision to develop a series for prime time is simultaneously a choice about a commercial commodity, an aesthetic endeavor, and a social institution. As a result, those making programming decisions will be variously evaluated according to perceptions of their business judgment, their aesthetic tastes, and the values they impart.[17]

The question of commercial success is a complicated one, since Sacred Harp singing constituted two out of nineteen songs on the *Cold Mountain* sound track, itself a component of the film. Barring runaway sales for the sound track, Sacred Harp was unlikely to be seen as a commercial music form that would yield substantial financial profit. Its usefulness was more likely to be located in its aesthetics and the values it imparted; however, the sponsoring institutions (Miramax Films, Sony Music) and their representatives (T Bone Burnett, Anthony Minghella, Harvey Weinstein) were primarily responsible for turning a profit. The aesthetic benefits of promoting Sacred Harp, therefore, had to be weighed against financial concerns.

As Richard Peterson has shown, and as discussed in chapter 4, there are six requirements for the perception of authenticity.[18] Sacred Harp singing fits these requirements strikingly well: it is a tradition more than 150 years old, many of whose practitioners come from families that have participated in it for nearly that long, yet it has changed with the years, and singers today do not see themselves as engaged in reenactment or imitation—Sacred Harp singers do not, for instance, dress in period costume or eschew air-conditioning for the sake of historical accuracy.[19] Rather, they understand their participation in this tradition within the framework of contemporary lives very much involved with mass media and popular culture.

Even if Sacred Harp could not itself be a major commercial success, it was well suited for the task of conferring authenticity upon its institutional sponsors. As a British screenwriter-director of Italian extraction, Anthony Minghella was under a great deal of pressure to treat the American Civil War accurately. Including in his film a musical tradition dating to the Civil War and still practiced today, which had not been used in previous Civil War films, was one effective way of signaling his immersion in and respect for the subject matter. T Bone Burnett's recent career has been largely structured around the production of folk authenticity in bluegrass and related genres, such that sponsoring clearly noncommercial music might lend weight to other music he sponsored, suggesting that his judgments are truly authentic, that whether or not the act is commercially successful, his choice was made on aesthetic grounds.

Although my analysis of their actions primarily considers Burnett, Minghella, and others, including Harvey Weinstein, as seeking to maximize profit, whether financial or moral, in their dealings with Sacred Harp it is important to note that both Burnett and Minghella, who attended the recording session at Liberty Baptist Church, seemed to be sincerely moved by and appreciative of the music and the singers. Clearly their institutional positions guided their priorities and the uses they chose to make of any type of music, and analyzing such decisions can yield important sociological insight into the popular culture industries. At the same time, their sponsorship of Sacred Harp cannot reasonably be attributed entirely to calculation and reflects a level of personal investment and care that was much appreciated by the Sacred Harp singers who came into contact with them and ought to be recognized here.

Burnett was a particularly prominent part of marketing the sound track because of his recent and stunning success with the sound track to *O Brother, Where Art Thou?*, a project that the *Cold Mountain* sound track clearly set out to emulate (Burnett and Minghella's protestations to the contrary notwithstanding). With the release of a second sound track focusing on traditional, or at least traditionally noncommercial music, Burnett had achieved something of the status of a cultural middleman, as described by Filene: "Eager to promote the authenticity of the performers they worked with, the middlemen depicted themselves simply as cultural funnels channeling the musicians' raw, elemental power to popular audiences."[20]

Burnett was distinct from earlier roots music middlemen, though, because of his openly commercial, popular culture institutional placement and identity. He positioned his work on the *Cold Mountain* sound track, with the eager participation of music critics and other journalists alike, as being traditional music with the emotional directness of rock music, saying, "To me, we were just making rock and roll. Rock grew out of this, out of rebellion and defiance and a spiritual quest." As the most unambiguously "authentic" songs on the sound track, the Sacred Harp songs became an important verifier of songs performed or composed recently by commercial musicians. At the same time, though, Sacred Harp singing was not likely to be a future commercial success for him, and Sacred Harp singers, with the possible exception of Tim Eriksen and Cassie Franklin, a young Sacred Harp singer who contributed a solo song to the sound track, were not musicians in whose careers he was going to be involved. His understanding of success for and his agenda for Sacred Harp were therefore quite complicated.

The engagement between Sacred Harp singers and culture producers associated with *Cold Mountain* was characterized by uncertainty. In the face of this uncertainty, persistence by individuals often tipped the balance in favor of Sacred Harp. Sacred Harp singers rather than a choir singing a Sacred Harp song transcribed from a recording were used only because Tim Eriksen, a musician hired for another type of music entirely, happened to be invested in the tradition and willing to speak up. The recording session happened to turn into a particularly good singing—by no means a foregone conclusion—and made an impact on Anthony Minghella and T Bone Burnett, such that the role of Sacred Harp in the movie was increased rather than being cut altogether, as it could well have been. The invitation of singers to the Words and Music concert was last minute, following, once again, initial consideration of professional musicians to sing the song rather than Sacred Harp singers. The inclusion of singers in the Academy Awards was originated by the advocacy of T Bone Burnett and was increased by additional advocacy by T Bone and Tim. While the Sacred Harp song was ultimately cut to provide more time for profit-producing commercials, the very presence of Sacred Harp singers on stage would reverberate within their home communities.

Additionally, the contact between Sacred Harp and commercial institutions involved cooperation between individuals and groups with differing agendas and differing motives for their promotion of Sacred Harp. The effects of the interaction occurred at multiple levels, with differing dynamics at each. Sacred Harp singers had very little ability to influence events at the institutional level—whether, for instance, the producers of the Academy Awards would want Sacred Harp singers to perform—and what influence they did have was mediated through Tim Eriksen, a professional musician with deeper connections to the movie and to people in positions of institutional power.

Tim in turn looked to other singers, such as David and Rodney Ivey, to get a sense of what was possible and desirable in the contact with commercial culture. In suggesting that the recording session happen at Liberty, David acted as something of an entrepreneur promoting both Sacred Harp as a living tradition and his home church as a central location in that tradition. Susan Harcrow, too, acted in a semientrepreneurial fashion by getting local newspapers to cover the recording session even before she knew that Minghella and Burnett would attend, let alone that any songs would be included in the final movie. She and other singers also used their association with large-scale culture producers to influence more local culture producers, such as local newspapers, to give Sacred Harp favorable publicity, in accord with their priority of reinvigorating Sacred Harp in its areas of traditional strength.

The ways that Miramax employed Sacred Harp are also telling: Its value came from its ability to impart authenticity to the film's Civil War story, to the more commercial music with which it was packaged on the sound track and the Great High Mountain Tour, and to the Academy Awards, which were seen as being in need of specifically wholesome, value-laden authenticity. Authenticity must therefore be considered as a market value that Sacred Harp (and presumably other cultural forms) carries.

For these purposes, Sacred Harp had to be reshaped as a performance genre. There was one direct debate over how the values of normal performance style and the values of Sacred Harp practice would be balanced: The negotiation at Royce Hall that ended with singers performing while standing in a horseshoe shape then being reshot seated in the hollow square. That event, The Words and Music of *Cold Mountain*, has to be understood in the context of Miramax's Oscar campaign for *Cold Mountain*. Miramax had established itself as a powerhouse and had been bought by Disney in 1993, in large part due to its ability to market traditionally low-grossing independent films with aggressive publicity campaigns like mainstream Hollywood films, working hard to get them distributed beyond the usual art cinemas to the multiplexes and promoting them to Oscar voters. *Cold Mountain* was part of a later development in which Disney's money made it possible for Miramax to move beyond acquiring already made pictures (which it continues to do) to producing its own films.[21]

Cold Mountain was intended to be Miramax's annual best picture nominee at the Oscars, and the Words and Music event must be understood as part of the nomination campaign.[22] It self-consciously presented the film as stemming not only from a best-selling and National Book Award–winning novel, that is, a prestigious work of literary fiction, but also from Minghella's extensive historical research, highlighting source materials and interspersing them with readings and scenes from the film. The framing was of *Cold Mountain* not simply as entertainment but as highbrow culture.[23] In that context, with the research underlying its depictions of the Civil War era standing as one of the movie's claims to authority, Sacred Harp singing was a small but crucial validator; the fact that an authentic presentation of it gave added value to the film's ambitions undoubtedly served as a bargaining resource for Tim Eriksen and others who wanted to promote it without sacrificing the integrity of the tradition as they understood it.

Outside of that campaign for critical recognition, though, there was less room for negotiation. Authenticity had less value; therefore, there was no question of standard performance values being upended in its name. At the Academy Awards and on the Great High Mountain Tour, singers appeared standing in a loose horseshoe shape, without attempts at a hollow square presentation. Instead, the push for authentic representation of Sacred Harp after that point centered around things like who would be invited, what the singers would be called, and, on the Great High Mountain Tour, with Tim Eriksen's brief introduction to the tradition.

Looking Back

In 2003 and early 2004, when singers considered the possible impact *Cold Mountain* would have on Sacred Harp, commercial success was what they focused on. When it became clear that neither *Cold Mountain*'s sound track nor Sacred Harp would achieve significant commercial success, it then seemed that the film's impact on the tradition would be limited. Increased attendance at singings could not be expected to continue once the glamour of Hollywood had worn off, and further opportunities for commercial exposure seemed unlikely. There was, though, a more subtle hope, and one without the attendant fears of overexposure or excessive crowds of people interested more in celebrity than in Sacred Harp.

For southern singers, the hope was to keep a new generation in the tradition by giving adolescents a way to understand—and explain to their friends—their participation in Sacred Harp as something other than entirely old-fashioned, by giving young children and teenagers alike a memory of glamour to attach to singing. In the ever-less-automatic choice members of southern singing families face between Sacred Harp and not, *Cold Mountain* was a weapon for Sacred Harp, and one that could even work on adults who had drifted away from the tradition but could be pulled back under the right circumstances.

For northern singers, it was a question of taking advantage of a moment of expanded opportunity for the process by which they always sustain their numbers: Pulling people in by ones and twos as they are first exposed to the music, giving them space to learn and become part of the local and then the national singing communities, and hoping that a reasonable number of them stick with it.

In both North and South, this hope was realized more in some communities than in others, depending on the degree to which they took advantage of opportunities for publicity, oriented their singings toward hospitality to new or returning singers, and were already populated with diverse enough age ranges to appeal to the widest possible range of newcomers. Communities that were already vibrant, in other words, were more successful—their singing sounded better and was more fun, they were more accustomed to welcoming newcomers and making them feel comfortable, and they were more likely to include at least one person with whom any given newcomer might identify or feel kinship.

The heightened appeal to newcomers in both regions was based in the culture of celebrity. One reason participation in Sacred Harp among its hereditary constituency has declined is that it is seen by some as being old-fashioned and countrified. For many children being brought to singings, it is something that their parents and grandparents do, not an activity for the young or something they would discuss with their friends as they might discuss popular culture. Association with celebrity can help dispel such an image; as Gamson observes, among celebrity watchers (a category in which many people are counted at one point or another), "satisfaction is garnered not so much from recognition by a particular star but from acknowledgement by any celebrity. . . . The celebrities are treated, if not as a traditional power elite, as an elite with the power to anoint, however briefly."[24]

Each of the events connecting Sacred Harp and *Cold Mountain*—the initial recording, the Royce Hall show, the Academy Awards, the Great High Mountain Tour—brought with it some form of acknowledgement, or anointing. Sacred Harp singers therefore used the cachet of association with the glamour of Hollywood to provide certification of the tradition's value, in the hope that it would contribute to the ongoing vitality and/or revitalization of Sacred Harp as a regional tradition—a very serious goal for many of those involved, although one that at times seemed to be subsumed by the singers' own excitement at this association.

As much as the taste of celebrity attracted new singers directly or re-committed existing ones, it provided a hook for the media. Sacred Harp for the first time had its own complete public narrative, which not only enabled coverage of singing directly related to the film but also created an ongoing identity that local singing communities could use to attract reporters' attention and frame a narrative for media coverage for years to come.

In reaping long-term gains and in garnering immediate local public-ity, then, *Cold Mountain* provided a set of opportunities that different communities responded to and benefited from differently. But in most places, the benefits are subtle and difficult to isolate—one or two people who came to Sacred Harp because they heard it in *Cold Mountain*, an existing singer who recommitted to Sacred Harp as a result, events being easier to publicize even five years later, a clearer way to explain the music to strangers to the tradition.

Perhaps most critically, it opened up space for the success of two ventures that had their genesis earlier and bear no evident debt to *Cold Mountain*, but were brought to fruition during the years when it was a no-ticeable force in the Sacred Harp world. In 2003, the first session of Camp Fasola, the summer camp teaching Sacred Harp singing and tradition, was held. And in 2006, *Awake My Soul*, a documentary film on Sacred Harp, was released. Both Camp Fasola and *Awake My Soul* were successful contemporaneously or post–*Cold Mountain*. But both also represented exactly the kind of effort that had gotten the role of Sacred Harp in *Cold Mountain* into local newspapers around Alabama and around the country: Dedicated singers pushing open doors that had not even appeared to exist.

The first session of Camp Fasola was held in the summer of 2003, after the *Cold Mountain* recordings had been made but before the movie was released. Originally conceived as a children's camp, to draw young people into the tradition, it initially drew predominantly adults, with fifty-one adults and twenty-two youth in its first year, evening out to sixty-one adults and forty-five youth in its second year, with separate classes for youth and adults. In 2008, Camp Fasola was split into two sessions, one for youth and one for adults, to provide an experience tailored to each group rather than trying to balance the amount of recreation desired by teenagers with the amount of teaching desired by adults taking their limited vacation time to learn Sacred Harp.

The first years of Camp Fasola were truly organized as a summer camp—campers slept on bunk beds and ate in a cafeteria, attending singing classes and engaging in recreation, such as swimming and arts and crafts, during the day, with a more traditional Sacred Harp singing each evening. It took dedication for adults to sleep in those beds and stand in line for the shower each morning. But the increase in young people from year to year was what excited singers around the country and particularly in longstanding singing areas that had been witnessing a slow decline as their own younger generations fell away from the tradition.

No benefit can be directly attributed from *Cold Mountain* to Camp Fasola. The idea for such a camp had first emerged in the 1990s, according to camp organizer David Ivey, and the crucial moves forward in its planning had been logistical, not tied to the movie. Camp attendance the first year, before the movie was released, was an unexpected success, and the second year's growth was not unreasonable in the context of the first year's attendance. And yet, it is possible to see how *Cold Mountain* created conditions of possibility for some of the greatest early successes of Camp Fasola.

As I discussed above, one of the great challenges of keeping young people from singing families in the tradition is the perception that Sacred Harp is old-fashioned. Inclusion in a widely released movie, even one not high on the viewing lists of most teenagers, served to combat this sense. At the first two sessions of Camp Fasola, almost all of the young people were from singing families, but a few were not, having been introduced to Sacred Harp by their singing friends and encouraged to go to camp. Some such introductions are often taking place, but in the years *Cold Mountain* was recorded and released, and camp was started, there were an unusually high number of teenage singers' friends attending their first singings or attending camp and sticking with the tradition.

If camp had not been held and had not been both a clear and comprehensive introduction to singing Sacred Harp and fun in summer camp ways, with swimming and rock slides and teenage flirtations, these teenagers from outside the tradition would not have become Sacred Harp singers. The outcome in which several Sand Mountain–area teenagers who had not previously been exposed to the tradition went with friends to a singing and ended up attending singings for years would not have happened based on *Cold Mountain* alone. Yet it might not have happened based on camp alone, without the point of entry afforded by the movie, the chance for teenage singers to explain their weekend activity as something contemporary and exciting and bring friends along for it. Certainly, the increase in singing attendance in 2003 and 2004 of young people from longtime singing families who did not attend camp increased supports the notion that *Cold Mountain* had made Sacred Harp a more appealing pursuit for this age group.

The impact of *Cold Mountain* on *Awake My Soul*, the documentary produced by Atlanta-area singers Matt and Erica Hinton, is even more tenuous, but the documentary fit into a cultural space available to Sacred Harp that had been slightly expanded by the publicity surrounding *Cold Mountain*. The Hintons had begun filming years earlier and did not move up their production schedule to take advantage of *Cold Mountain*. They did not find funding for their project as a result of it. And in the end, when *Awake My Soul* was released, they sometimes found that publicity they had worked hard to get for their documentary ended up featuring *Cold Mountain*. In these direct senses, *Cold Mountain* was irrelevant to or even a distraction from their project.

But *Awake My Soul*, which ultimately aired on more than 150 PBS stations and was featured in film festivals, especially throughout the South but in other regions as well, and drew coverage in *Time* magazine and others, was released not into the world of 1991–2003, when a LexisNexis search found only fifteen full-length articles about Sacred Harp, but into a world in which Sacred Harp had been featured in the *New York Times*, the *Atlanta Journal Constitution*, and papers around the country via an Associated Press article. *Cold Mountain* did not directly open doors for *Awake My Soul*, in other words, but publicity surrounding it—again, publicity often garnered by determined singers promoting their local singing communities and events—had established a narrative for Sacred Harp as something other than a curious minor subgenre of folk or religious music. *Awake My*

Soul in turn expanded that space dramatically and created a resource and a pathway into Sacred Harp for still more people.

———

The events connected with *Cold Mountain* did not introduce any dramatically new dynamics to Sacred Harp. Had the movie or sound track been an enormous success, a greater amount of attention to Sacred Harp could have had a farther-reaching or longer-lasting impact, but as it was, existing dynamics were simply made more visible. The fundamental practices of Sacred Harp singing were never changed more than momentarily; unlike some groups that, finding themselves in a media spotlight, conform to the image the media casts them in, Sacred Harp communities took performance opportunities without moving toward performance as a more usual practice. Some people were raised to brief prominence by the media, but they did not represent themselves as leaders and emphasized a broadly agreed-upon narrative of the participatory, inclusive nature of Sacred Harp.[25]

The ascendance of Liberty as a singing location and community was highlighted when the recording was done there and heightened as several of its singers sang at Royce Hall and the Academy Awards and were featured in newspaper coverage. Tensions that had been simmering below the surface of the relationships of some people became apparent as one went to the movie premiere or the Academy Awards and another did not. The cultural differences of singers in different places were revealed as some saw Alison Krauss as a star and others did not, and their differing orientations to authority showed up in the invitation processes for the Great High Mountain Tour.

While all of these things became briefly visible, and a few effects, such as the increased cycle of strength at Liberty, have continued to the present, the resilience of Sacred Harp singing communities was also demonstrated in the lack of widespread disruption of singings. Even when publicity drew many new people to a singing, it proceeded according to plan, with the newcomers invited to join in singing rather than being allowed to understand it as a performance medium. Similarly, tensions receded back to their base points and relationships normalized, as silence norms prevented public argument, while singers' shared commitment to Sacred Harp brought them together regularly to share a beloved activity, literally, in harmony. Singers managed to extract lasting strength for Sacred Harp by pushing for publicity and creating opportunities for expansion, but otherwise emerged unscathed.

Conclusion

Sacred Harp singers gather somewhere in the United States almost every weekend of the year to sing with each other. On most weekends, the gatherings are overwhelmingly local, but on a few, people travel from all around the country to go to one little church in Alabama, one college hall in Chicago, or one history museum in Minnesota. Singers ranging in age from their teens to their seventies or eighties; ones for whom one weekend of travel a year is a significant expense and ones who are able to travel when and where they want; Republicans and Democrats; devout Christians, Jews, Buddhists, and atheists; farmers and college professors, all come together to sing a music in which individual voices are at once allowed to be themselves, not rendered smooth and featureless through classical training, but at the same time are subsumed in a mass of sound so that no one stands out. Sound rises and swells and bounces off the walls, physically tangible at times and catching the singers up in a consuming momentum. Sweat-stained clothes and speaking voices revealed by break-time conversation to be hoarse show the physical effort of singing, but singers' expressions—their joy and their grief—as they sing show the power this music and the experience of participating in it has over them. Through singing, they become a community.

This national Sacred Harp community, composed of singers from many places and backgrounds, is the most obvious level at which community must be intentionally constructed, but it is not the only one. Local communities must first be created as building blocks of national community—

hosting singings, drawing in and nurturing new singers, and encouraging those new singers to travel. These local communities partake of the broader culture of their contexts, with practices changing over time in all locations, as how even in the most conservative southern churches dress standards have changed. Outside the South, and to some extent in the urban South, the different contexts mean adhering to Sacred Harp tradition in significant ways but also diverging to, for instance, allow women to offer public prayer, or adapting to the necessities of singing in public, rented spaces.

Everywhere it is sung, Sacred Harp is a choice. For people who do not encounter it until adulthood, the choice is entirely obvious, but given the high proportion of people who grow up with Sacred Harp but sing rarely if at all as adults, even fifth-generation singers must be understood as having chosen the music and the community. Even for them it is not a casual choice. It is a choice to attend church irregularly, to regularly spend hours driving to sing, to spend days before their own singing cooking and getting ready for guests. It is also a choice that brings them into sustained interaction with people very unlike themselves.

Although Sacred Harp singers are in many ways typical of their regional, cultural, educational, and class backgrounds, they also puncture many stereotypes of those backgrounds, at least for each other. A Jewish Democrat from Chicago whose main associations with the South are the civil rights movement and white southern racism may come to see a more complicated picture and to care deeply about the Republican Baptist singing next to her. A Primitive Baptist from rural Alabama who has preconceived notions when he first views a man wearing an earring and several bracelets may come to value that man's strong singing voice and then his friendship.

Asked why they sing, most singers point to the music and the fellowship, each of which may be framed in more or less religious terms, and which have to be understood as inextricably linked. The music provides the groundwork for the fellowship—singing the same songs, looking across the square at each other and seeing that you are sharing a profound experience—but the fellowship also strengthens the music, as people learn each other's favorite songs, learn to follow each other's leading, and learn to blend voices successfully.

Though they explicitly identify it less often, many singers—especially new singers—also clearly seek a sense of authenticity and connection to history from Sacred Harp. Singers from the urban North who may move frequently and do not live near extended family can find in Sacred Harp a greater sense of rootedness. As discussed in chapter 4, their identification with Sacred Harp singing and traditional singers can be understood as part of a centuries-old pattern of urban elites identifying with a romanticized notion of the rural "folk"; in this case, though, the "folk" are not an invented category and speak and act for themselves. That twist fundamentally changes the nature of "revivals" of Sacred Harp, recreating it as actual, rather than imaginary, boundary crossing.

But for lifelong singers, the sense of history and authenticity can also be powerful. Singing can involve a sense of affiliation not only with Sacred Harp but also with the way things used to be, with the people today's singers grew up respecting. For people who have chosen to remain in rural areas, living within miles or even yards of the houses they grew up in, Sacred Harp can be a powerful part of that choice; for those who have moved away, it can represent a continuing connection to family and home.

These localized, situational appeals of Sacred Harp are part of the sets of beliefs singers bring to Sacred Harp and around which they organize it. To take an obvious case, people for whom Sacred Harp is a religious practice place more importance on prayer: Almost every all-day singing features prayer at specific times, but in places where it is more explicitly religious, even shorter local singings begin and end with prayer. Such localized practices draw on the shared beliefs of singers about religion, authority, and authenticity and, in turn, contribute to community cohesion.

This local cohesion must to some extent be overcome or set aside when singers from different communities join together to sing. An event at which one area's practices dominate too strongly can be off-putting for visitors; this possibility is mostly prevented by the fairly specific framework—prayer at the beginning, the end, and to bless a large potluck lunch; elected convention officers who then appoint arranging, memorial, and other committees; all attendees welcome to lead a song; and so on—adhered to by most all-day singings, but occasional challenges do present themselves.

These challenges are surmountable—indeed go unnoticed by many singers—because of the ethic of silence that prevails at singings. Singers may whisper to their neighbors and carry on real conversations during breaks, but they do not speak publicly about anything that may be controversial, even aspects of Sacred Harp itself. This silence does not produce apathy, as Nina Eliasoph might suggest.[1] Rather, it provides space for singers to be fully and deeply engaged with the music and the community before they confront possible controversy. Shared commitment to the music pushes singers to seek out people unlike themselves to fill out the sound they produce and to ensure that the tradition continues for generations; shared joy in singing it pushes them to actually become close to and seek to understand these other people.

Notes

1. McPherson and Rotolo 1996; McPherson, Smith-Lovin, and Cook 2001.
2. Putnam 2000; Vaisey 2007; Brint 2001.
3. Similarly, Janet Lever (1976) found that boys' involvement in team sports broadens their social circles because large numbers of players are required.
4. Durkheim 2001; Ammerman 1997; Wuthnow 1998b.
5. Vaisey 2007; Etzioni 2001. {LC: Please supply an entry for both citations in the works cited list.}
6. Roy and Dowd 2010.
7. Heider and Warner (2010) similarly give attention to the physicality of Sacred Harp singing—specifically the "bodily co-presence" of singers at singing events—using a Durkheimian and interaction ritual theory approach.
8. Small 1998.
9. I am indebted to Roy and Dowd (2010) for a succinct statement of this distinction. One might also note that the concept of musicking parallels significant sociological efforts to change nouns to verbs, such as West and Zimmerman's (1987) celebrated article "Doing Gender," which argues for a reconceptualization of gender as a constituting activity.
10. Roy and Dowd 2010, 189.
11. Grazian 2003; Peterson 1997.
12. Finnegan 1989, 219.
13. Small 1998, 218.
14. Peterson 2005, 1083.
15. Grazian 2003; Beverland 2005; Graham 2001; Peterson 1997.
16. Grana 1989.
17. Peterson 2005, 1086.

18. Roy and Dowd 2010, 197.
19. Grazian (2003, 10–11) defines authenticity as "the ability of a place or event to conform to an idealized representation of reality . . . [and] the credibility or sincerity of a performance and its ability to come off as natural and effortless."
20. Grazian 2003, 11; also see Peterson 1997.

CHAPTER ONE

1. Since the first Saturday and first Sunday in a month might fall on different weekends, Sacred Harp convention is to identify annually recurring singings by the Sunday on which they occur.
2. Coy and Marie have two other children who do not sing regularly. One lives on the same street as them and attends at least part of most singings held at Liberty; his daughter is sometimes brought to other singings by Coy or Rod. The other lives several hours away and only attends one or two singings a year while visiting her parents. The fact that Coy and Marie have two children who sing and two who do not underscores the point that even for people raised in the tradition, Sacred Harp singing remains a choice and not an automatic part of life.
3. Hunter (1991) argues for a sharp division between the worldviews of groups he labels "orthodox" and "progressive." The coherence of these divergent worldviews is a crucial piece of the theory, in contrast to other sociological theories suggesting that people have access to multiple outlooks that are invoked by and applied in response to particular situations or social roles. A number of scholars have produced findings that undercut the strong version, at least, of this theory. While cultural politics may be a source of division, they do not produce clearly defined oppositional groups. See for instance DiMaggio, Evans, and Bryson (1996); Evans (1997); Demerath and Yang (1997).
4. Laumann et al. 1994; Wuthnow 2003; Blackwell 1998.
5. Putnam's (2000) *Bowling Alone* and Putnam and Feldstein's (2003) *Better Together* are well-known examples of this strain.
6. See DeNora 2000 and 2002, Small 1998, and several of the pieces in Bennett and Peterson 2004.
7. DeNora 2002, 25.
8. See Roscigno and Danaher 2001; Roscigno et al. 2002; Cerulo 1989; Lieberman 1995; Marini 2003; DeNora 2000.
9. Occasionally young children and the extremely elderly are allowed to lead songs that have already been led, since they may know (or remember) fewer songs and it is deemed most important to give them an opportunity to lead.
10. Interview with Elder Ricky Harcrow on January 1, 2003, in Ider, Alabama.
11. Roy 2002.
12. In an interview with me, sociologist and Chicago singer Stephen Warner

suggested that perhaps the most notable thing about the Chicago sing- ing community is that it is overwhelmingly composed of single people and a few couples without children. There seem to be increasing numbers of couples and people with children among the Chicago singers, but his observation remains generally apt and a particularly strong contrast with southern singers on average.

13. "New" and "lifelong" are vastly oversimplified terms for very complicated concepts, as are "northern" and "southern" or "revivalist" and "tradi- tional." Each of these terms gets at certain aspects of the more complex reality, which deserves more discussion than it can receive here, and I use each advisedly at different moments.

14. Peterson 1997, 5.

15. Stevens 2001, 121.

16. Anderson, quoted in Clawson 1989, 76.

17. Eliasoph and Lichterman 2003, 737.

18. Clawson 1989, 76.

19. It is worth noting here that many Sacred Harp singers are also Freema- sons—but equally many belong to religions that proscribe Freemasonry.

20. Eliasoph 1998, 7.

21. Stinchcombe 1965, 153.

22. Frith 1991, 103.

23. Cobb 1989, 12.

24. Randy Kennedy, "For a Timeless Song Style, a Chance at the Big Time," Music, *New York Times*, December 23, 2003; Harrison Creel, quoted in Marini (2003, 72).

25. A group of singers is referred to as a "class," a song led as a "lesson."

26. Small 1998, 8.

27. The art world of European classical music has long been founded on notions of individual genius, but Small (1998, 1999) is one of a growing number of scholars who interrogate that foundation, seeing such beliefs as objects of analysis. Other scholars doing work in this vein include Ruth Finnegan (1989) and Tia DeNora (2000, 2002).

28. Small 1998, 10.

29. DeNora 2002, 21.

30. Roscigno and Danaher 2001; Cerulo 1989.

31. Wuthnow 2003, 16.

32. Wuthnow 2003, 70, 76–77.

33. Ammerman 1997.

34. Ammerman 1997, 54.

35. Bellah et al. 1985, 143.

36. Bellah et al. 1985, 144.

37. Bellah et al. 1985, 50.

38. Wuthnow 1998a, 3–4.

39. Bellah et al. 1985, 143–144.

40. Wuthnow 1998a, 169.
41. Grazian 2003, 12.
42. Grazian 2003, 21.
43. In fact, the song, "Not Made with Hands," *is* in the Cooper revision of *The Sacred Harp*; at the time, I was only familiar with the Denson revision of the book, and while two of the sites I deal with in this book—Sand Mountain and Minneapolis-St. Paul—do occasionally use the Cooper book, when I refer simply to *The Sacred Harp*, I mean the Denson book, which is most widely used.
44. Contra dance is a folk style common especially in New England. It has similarities to square dancing but is done by couples standing in lines facing each other.
45. I am also lucky to be able to draw on interviews with seven singers from Chicago and one from Georgia conducted by Anne Heider, who has generously shared them with me.
46. Cobb 1989, 155.
47. Cobb 1989, xv.
48. Eliasoph and Lichterman 2003, 739.
49. "Stafford," *The Sacred Harp* 1991, 78.

CHAPTER TWO

1. Finnegan 1989, 325.
2. Stinchcombe 1965.
3. Such an ideal of authenticity can be found in many musical genres or scenes. See for instance Grazian 2003; Peterson 1997; and Thornton 1996.
4. While there is Sacred Harp singing on the West Coast, for logistical reasons I have not been there. Outside of fieldwork for this project, most of my singing experiences have been in the Northeast and mid-Atlantic regions.
5. I first heard and sang Sacred Harp in Western Massachusetts, at a time when local singing was done in a private home, once a month, with rarely more than twelve people attending. Today, the annual convention that started in 1999 draws around three hundred people, and weekly night singings draw thirty-five to forty on a regular basis. Because of the area's large number of college students and recent graduates, many of its singers go on to found or revitalize singings elsewhere, such that some singers outside the area refer to it as "the incubator." The stunning growth of the Western Mass singing over the past ten years, the dominance of young people in the community (though there are also participants in their fifties, sixties, and even seventies), and its incubator status would have made it a natural choice for this book. Unfortunately, given my history there, I felt too close to Western Massachusetts Sacred Harp to choose it as a research site. As noted in the main body of the text, however, I will draw on my experiences there in understanding and fleshing out observations from other sites.

6. Eric Hobsbawm, "Introduction: Inventing Traditions," in Hobsbawm and Ranger (1992).

7. Covington's (1995) book was generally well reviewed and was a National Book Award finalist; he drew praise for treating the area "sensitively" and going deeper than stereotype. Be that as it may, I would take issue with its depiction of Sand Mountain defined by the most stereotypically "white-trash" class of people there, and what I would argue are exoticized descriptions of, for instance, "the lean, kept look of southern Appalachian women," a peculiar choice of words considering the prevailing obesity rates throughout the South.

8. From http://www.census.gov. Specifically, http://quickfacts.census.gov/qfd/states/01/01049.html, http://quickfacts.census.gov/qfd/states/01/01071.html, and http://quickfacts.census.gov/qfd/states/01/01095.html.

9. For a discussion of independent churches in the South, see Tyson, Peacock, and Patterson 1988, 203–12.

10. Pollan 2006, 65–84.

11. For discussions of social networks and social capital today, see Putnam (2000) and Wuthnow (1998b). Many of Erikson's (1976) observations on community in Buffalo Creek, though more extreme than I find on Sand Mountain, are relevant. I also devote more attention to this question in my 2005 article, "'Everybody Knows Him': Social Networks In the Life of a Small Contractor in Alabama"—some of this account of Sand Mountain draws on that paper as well.

12. Dunaway (1996) argues that southern Appalachia, including northeastern Alabama, operated as part of the world capitalist system as early as the colonial era.

13. This is not to deny that racial coding never occurs. In addition, recent decades have seen the emergence of a Mexican immigrant population; it's not clear how that will play out in terms of the region's racial formation. See Murphy, Blanchard, and Hill 2001.

14. I was never entirely sure at what moments being associated with a famously elite school like Princeton affected people's thinking about me. Every now and then it was hauled out, usually in the course of someone introducing or explaining me to someone else; in these situations, the word was audibly capitalized: "She goes to PRINCETON." At other times, it seemed to fade from memory.

15. The local accent is closer to mountain southern than coastal southern accents; in addition to pronunciation issues, there are a number of word usages that differ from other areas of the country.

16. For a greatly amplified picture of these and related traditions, see Tyson, Peacock, and Patterson (1988); Peacock and Tyson (1989); Leonard (1999); and Beverly Patterson (2001).

17. Primitive Baptist and some other small denominations reject Bible study and Sunday school for theological reasons thoroughly discussed in Peacock

and Tyson (1989); taking up these practices is a move toward the Protestant mainstream.

18. At most southern and many northern singings, the ethic is that there should be nearly as much food left over as has been eaten. When this is not the case, it is either a sign of a failure of hospitality or a sign that many, many more singers have attended than expected.

19. "Food is love" is part of the mission statement of God's Love We Deliver, the New York City organization Bender (2003, 25) studies that delivers meals to people with AIDS. Not only does the organization employ the phrase, but the volunteers Bender writes about also use it in a range of ways tailored to their own understandings of what it is to feed people with AIDS. Similarly, Sacred Harp singers bring different meanings to their cooking, as to their singing, but many would agree on the message that food is love.

20. Sack 2001, 97.

21. Before I brought graduate school friends to an Alabama singing, I attempted to convey to them the magnitude of dinner on the grounds. In describing their experience at the singing, they agreed that their response to me had been "yeah, yeah, we know what a potluck is"—and that they had in no way anticipated what they experienced.

22. The food isn't actually very good, but they talk a good game about local and organic ingredients.

23. The Denson Revision's immediate successor, the 1991 Revision, is the most widely sung version of *The Sacred Harp*, but the Cooper Revision remains in active use and singers in some areas do sing from both books.

24. These churches, and Sacred Harp singing in West Georgia, are subject to many of the processes and pressures of changes including suburbanization and aging detailed in Ammerman (1997); the rise of exurban megachurches and their effect on existing religious institutions are also covered by Eiesland (1997, 2000).

25. Bealle (1997, 201) relates both these stories—of the founding of the New England and Illinois State Conventions—which have become enshrined in a substantial oral tradition and are often retold by the New England and Chicago singers involved. The Chicago story is by now so well known that in a late-1990s interview with Anne Heider, Ted Mercer referred to "the famous conversation."

26. Miller 2002, 203.

27. In using the term *mythology*, I do not mean to imply that these idealized pictures of the past are entirely untrue—certainly there used to be many more singers in west Georgia than there are now, for instance—but it is important to remember that, whatever the truths of certain specifics, the picture as a whole is idealized.

28. Eiesland 1997, 2000.

29. Vegetarians can have trouble finding food at southern singings, and in

much the same way southern singers report not being able to tell what northern dishes are, northern vegetarians may have difficulty establishing what dishes contain meat as a minor ingredient.

30. Camp Fasola, discussed in chapter 6, may have begun to reverse this trend, with some Georgia youth attending and thereby gaining a set of friends who serve as incentive for them to go to more singings.

CHAPTER THREE

1. Zerubavel 1981, 70.
2. Zerubavel 1981, 102–3.
3. Gieryn 2000, 481.
4. The number of songs sung per day:

	Saturday 2003	Sunday 2003	Saturday 2004	Sunday 2004	Saturday 2005	Sunday 2005
Midwest Convention	72	77	80	78	84	75
Minnesota Convention[a]	79	69	82	77	74	73
Holy Springs[b]	86	92	104	88	103	108
Henagar-Union Convention (Liberty)[c]	98	87	107	89	101	88

[a]Because Minnesota typically has lower attendance than the Midwest, they can allow all leaders two turns while still leading a relatively low number of songs. However, upon hearing that interpretation of these numbers, one Minnesota singer told me, "Don't give us too much credit," pointing to a year when, faced with somewhat higher attendance, in order to give everyone a chance to lead both days, they had to call large groups of Minnesotans to lead together.
[b]In 2005, due to declining attendance, Holly Springs switched to having leaders choose two songs per turn, which increases the number of songs per hour as there is less time spent waiting for people to get from their seats to the center of the square.
[c]This convention runs half an hour longer on Saturday than on Sunday, accounting for some of the difference between days each year. More generally, memorial lessons are held on Sundays, reducing the amount of time devoted to singing.

5. Again, this is a product of the racial patterns of folk revival participation detailed by Roy (2002), Filene (2000), and others, not a phenomenon specific to Sacred Harp. The emergence of the Wicker Park neighborhood as a center of Chicago bohemian or counter-cultural life follows a trajectory from the 1960s Old Town neighborhood, associated with folk and blues revivals, to the 1970s Lincoln Park neighborhood. In each case, countercultural artistic and musical innovation initiated a process of gentrification, prompting a shift to a new epicenter of low rents and subculture formation. For folk, blues, and the alternative rock that characterized Wicker Park in the 1990s (Liz Phair, Smashing Pumpkins), the establishment of musical performance venues (i.e., clubs) was one of the hallmarks of emerging neighborhood hipness. As a nonperformance, noncommercial genre,

Sacred Harp could not be an obvious part of this place-based development cycle.

6. See Miller (2004) for a more detailed account of this engagement.

7. Morris dance is a type of English folk dance that involves rhythmic stepping (sometimes with bells on the dancers' lower legs) and often uses sticks or other props.

8. Gerstel and Sarkisian (2006) argue that marriage can be a greedy institution, limiting other social ties.

9. Lieberman (1995) and Filene (2000) ably document the roots of this linkage between folk music conceived as such in the first half of the twentieth century; Cantwell (1996) and Roy (2002) extend the view into the great popular revivals of the 1960s and 1970s.

10. It is interesting to note that in both Chicago and the Twin Cities, the newer groups of singers were established with a core of undergraduate ethnomusicology students.

11. Tim has a shaved head and wears an earring, bracelets, rings, and a necklace; the color scheme of his clothing tends to be dark, but the individual items of clothing run to button-down shirts and black jeans. The overall impression he creates often leads to wildly distorted descriptions of him. I have heard any number of singers describe him as wearing leather, chains, or a dog collar—none of which is true. After he spoke in her class, one of Minja's students described him (in writing) as wearing a shirt unbuttoned to the navel and a large cross necklace—again, not something he would ever wear, let alone to teach a class.

12. Although Minnesota and Chicago singings are both characterized by a lot of talking between songs, I do not generalize this to all northern singings. In Western Massachusetts, for example, although the officers and committee members often extend their announcements and committee reports beyond the minimum necessary, there is almost no other talking between songs—no more than in most southern singings. As a result, the numbers of songs led per day in Western Mass is close to the numbers led at Liberty or Holly Springs, while Chicago and Minnesota lag by ten or more songs per day.

13. Songs are called by their page numbers to facilitate everyone quickly finding the correct song.

14. Some singers seem to gain a sense of belonging or distinction by having particular songs or particular ways of leading those songs identified with themselves; others emphasize their skill and knowledge of the music by leading a wide variety of songs.

15. Wuthnow 1998a, 8.

16. Some singers refer to this process as pitching, others as keying, others interchangeably. I suspect that it is partially regional, but if I am correct in this, it is microregional in ways that I have not been able to fully disentangle. I use the terms interchangeably.

17. They may practice at less formal night singings, at small all-day singings,

and often begin their learning through an informal apprenticeship model, in which an experienced keyer privately works with a promising singer.

18. The "talkiness" of northern singers, in contrast to the terser style of southern conventions parallels Lichterman's (1995) observation of the differences between the expressive, discursive style of upper-middle-class environmental activists and the more instrumental conduct of anti-toxics activists based in a black church. See also Bellah et. al.'s (1985) discussion of "expressive individualism".

19. Sack 2001; Bender 2003; DeVault 1991.

20. Grazian 2003, 10–11.

21. The Sacred Harp Musical Heritage Association publishes the minutes of all Sacred Harp singings. These can be found at http://fasola.org/minutes/. This list is from *Sacred Harp Singings 2004 and 2005* (p. 223).

22. Bellah et. al. 1985.

23. It appears that there was ample blame to go around for this emergency. None of the outgoing or incoming cochairs (all of whom were Old Guard, north side singers) had contacted the University about the booking until two days before the convention; the Hyde Park area singers who were ostensibly registered as a student group were in fact not so registered, having failed to continue to draw students to their regular singings; and the University employees who had given the booking away had apparently not made much effort to reach the contact person and were in any case notoriously incompetent, leading to difficulty with booking Ida Noyes several times over the years.

24. In this case I have used a pseudonym.

25. He had previously attended the 1999 Midwest Convention, which was his most recent appearance in the minutes book.

26. For discussions of the role of humor in both creating group bonds and establishing internal boundaries and hierarchy, see Coser (1960, 1966).

27. Some southern singings also do not take up collections at singings attended by out-of-towners, preferring to take on the expense as part of hosting a singing. For instance, Liberty's fifth Sunday or Decoration Day singings may include collection, but the two-day convention in July never does.

28. *Sacred Harp Singings 2005 and 2006*, 133. My own notes correspond very closely to this recording, but are slightly less complete as by this time in the memorial I was struggling to keep up.

29. It is by no means only people ignorant of this etiquette who lead anthems at problematic times of day. Some singers who know full well do so as if to suggest that by being the exception to the rule, they demonstrate their status. For discussions of the ways social order is maintained and enforced through informal means, see Whyte (1943).

30. It could be argued that, as cochair of the convention, Marcia Johnson ought herself to have taken on the task of interrupting.

31. In saying that it is bureaucratized, I do not mean to imply that it has the ruthless efficiency of Weber's bureaucracy. Rather, it observes many pieces of bureaucratic language and organization while often needing to be effortfully reconstructed from year to year.
32. Wuthnow 1998a.

CHAPTER FOUR

1. Stevens 2001, 110. Cadge (2004) similarly examines a case in which two groups pursue the same activity separately.
2. DeNora 2002, 19.
3. Bellah et al. 1986; Wuthnow 1998a.
4. Roof 1993, 243–47.
5. The geographic range of this tradition is not completely clear; Decoration Days are widespread in northern Alabama but are not held in the southern part of the state.
6. See Lareau (2003) for a vivid picture of how contemporary middle-class families struggle to coordinate children's activities and cope with incessant time demands.
7. See Wuthnow (1998a, 4–9) for a discussion of spiritualities of dwelling and seeking.
8. This is similar to the characterization of one of the volunteers in Courtney Bender's (2003, 107) study of God's Love We Deliver of the "certain spirit" of that setting: "You can call it the spirit of cooperation or the spirit of a cause, or the Holy Spirit, or whatever kind of spirit you would think about calling it. There's definitely a spirit there."
9. I have heard Georgia singer Teenie Moody express this sentiment in almost exactly the same words.
10. That is, Sacred Harp is often characterized as "sacred" or "religious" or "Christian" music, but it is not assigned to a more specific genre within those broad categories. At the same time, despite its location in the folk world, Sacred Harp lacks many of the presumed characteristics of folk music, including its reliance on a written, notated text. For definitions of folk as a genre, see Filene 2000 or Cantwell 1996.
11. Grazian 2003, 145.
12. Roy 2002, 467.
13. Filene 2000, 11.
14. Filene 2000, 25.
15. Roy 2002, 467.
16. Roy 2002, 468.
17. Roy 2002, 461.
18. See Bayton (1990) for an account of how women who come to rock music with formal training in other genres must often unlearn or divest themselves of their previous techniques.

19. Hobsbawm and Ranger 1992, 1.
20. Peterson 1997; Grazian 2003.
21. For instance, in addition to the work by Peterson and Bigenho cited in this section, Jones and Smith (2005) use the concepts "creative authenticity" and "national authenticity" to analyze the relationship of the *Lord of the Rings* movies to New Zealand.
22. Peterson 1997, 206–9.
23. Bigenho 2002, 16.
24. Bigenho 2002, 17–18; emphasis added.
25. Bigenho 2002, 18; emphasis added.
26. Bigenho 2002, 20; emphasis added.
27. I deal with singers' thoughts about history separately below, so have shortened Bigenho's term to "cultural authenticity."
28. I have seen such things questioned in only one or two other, much more extreme, cases, as when a group of Atlanta singers appeared on the public-access cable show of a Black Israelite who asserted, among other things, that 9/11 had been God's punishment on the United States.
29. Wuthnow 1998a.
30. Marini 2003, 92.
31. Posted September 9, 2004.
32. Bigenho 2002, 18–17.
33. Stevens 2001, 110.
34. Stevens 2001, 118.
35. Swidler 1979, 100.
36. Swidler 1979, 90.
37. The Sacred Harp Publishing Company, which prints and distributes the songbook and revises it periodically, is an institution with a formal hierarchy, including an executive secretary, a president, vice presidents, and a board, but while these roles are certainly recognized and draw some respect outside the operations of the publishing company, they do not confer any kind of control over the general practice of singing from *The Sacred Harp*.
38. Lichterman 1995, 514.
39. Women, including Chicago's Judy Hauff, may occasionally key the music at the National Convention, but the National is in many ways similar to a nonsouthern singing. In another exception to the men-only rule, when Cassie Franklin was fifteen to sixteen years old, she did key at a handful of singings. She subsequently stopped doing so, however, and though she may key songs during informal singings with friends, she does not do so in formal settings. There are at least a few other women who I know to be capable of keying who do not do so in public settings.
40. The front of the tenor section is considered most important because the tenor line is the melody of the song, and leading is done while facing the tenor.
41. For other literature discussing ways that communities regulate behavior through recognized authority and control mechanisms not dependent on

formal office, see Auyero (2000); Brodkin Sacks (1988); Carr (2003); and Ehrenhalt (1995).

42. Wuthnow 1998a, 5.

43. Bellah et al. (1985) may again be relevant in understanding this tendency toward individualism even in the context of community; Stevens (2001), though, captures these dynamics exceptionally well in his depictions of the "other" homeschoolers.

44. http://www.stlfasola.com/moharm.htm.

45. http://web.mit.edu/user/i/j/ijs/www/thenorumbegaharmony.html.

46. Miller 2005, 258.

CHAPTER FIVE

1. Although I variously refer to this community as "nationwide" or "national," I imply nothing about nationalism. In fact, it could be referred to as an international community; I do not do so because that seems to overstate its internationalism, which is derived from a few singers from the UK and Canada who travel regularly to sing.

2. See Gardner (2004) for description of bluegrass festivals as another kind of national community formed around music.

3. Travel both as a concrete action and as a metaphor is such an important part of Sacred Harp singing that the ethnomusicologist Kiri Miller (2007) titled her book *Traveling Home: Sacred Harp Singing and American Pluralism*.

4. Word of mouth is a less easily controlled way of drawing travelers.

5. Reciprocity is much discussed in gift theory literature. According to Mauss (2000), gifts are not meant to be given freely but are meant to be *exchanged*, with reciprocity a core value of gift exchange, building up community and solidarity within the community. See also Bourdieu (1977) and Gouldner (1960).

6. I was not yet doing fieldwork in this period, so I do not know if Wilton Donaldson accompanied his wife to sing during these years. It is possible that he did so but did not lead; his appearance in the minutes may be a result of Miss Ivalene's declining health, as he most frequently led with her rather than on his own and may have wished to provide physical support should she become unsteady on her feet. (Among Sacred Harp singers, including adults, "Miss" is often used preceding an older woman's first name as a sign of respect and affection. "Mister" may be used in the same way for men. This is applied inconsistently, though I feel it is used more frequently for people who are perceived to be somewhat frail.)

7. See Cheal (1988) for why Miss Ivalene's illness might have intensified the reciprocal response to her attendance: Cheal argues that gift transactions are importantly part of the moral economy, and that gift morality includes a strong impulse to give to others to express love.

8. I count myself among the singers from Massachusetts. Some of these visi-

tors stayed for Camp Fasola that week, but though Richard's singing was not their only destination in the South, they had arrived early for it and chose it over another possible singing.

9. Bealle 1997, 201.
10. Interviewed by Anne Heider 1998.
11. See Sack (2001) for the importance of shared food in American Protestantism.
12. Interviewed by Anne Heider 1998.
13. Interviewed by Anne Heider 1998.
14. Interviewed by Anne Heider 1998.
15. Interviewed by Anne Heider 1998.
16. Interviewed by Anne Heider 1998.
17. Interviewed by Anne Heider 1998.
18. Interviewed by Anne Heider 1998.
19. Interviewed by Anne Heider 1998.
20. Interviewed by Anne Heider 1998.
21. Eliasoph 1998.
22. Indeed, there probably are some people who avoid Sacred Harp singing because of the religious content or their perception thereof. My analysis obviously cannot capture people who never participate in Sacred Harp at all, but the fact that some atheists and other non-Christians participate in it shows that religion does not become an absolute bar to participation.
23. For instance, a singing held on the Fourth of July (or the Friday before or Monday after) at Muscadine Church in Alabama is typically more casual than other singings, because the church is uncomfortably hot and the singing is not held on Sunday. At that singing, it is considered appropriate for a woman to wear Capri pants and a T-shirt.
24. See Huisman and Hondagneu-Sotelo (2005) for another account of differences in dress practices between "dressed-down" New Englanders and a population cultivating a more formal style.
25. These differences may be contrasted with the bluegrass festival scene described by Gardner (2004), where participants may also differ from one another in education, occupation, and religious and political views, but where informal norms governing dress uniformly hold sway.
26. A substantially similar recounting of this event was previously published in *Poetics* (Clawson 2004).
27. Transcribed from video shot by Bill Windom.
28. Interestingly, he never seemed to distinguish between the feminine style of the woman in the lightweight pale blue outfit and the obviously butch lesbian style of the other woman; indeed none of the southern singers commented on that distinction in my hearing, though the incident was discussed for weeks.
29. Eliasoph 1998; Bender 2003, 18.
30. Goffman 1959, 108–7.

31. Said at Camp Fasola in 2004. Similar comments are a standard part of her workshops on leading at camp and elsewhere. Especially in her invocation of "monkey motions;" it is possible to read a racial subtext and to understand these comments as racial boundary work. Indeed, the history of folk and related musics has often involved substantial racial boundary work (Filene 2000; Peterson 1997; Roy 2002). However, in the moment it was said in direct response to watching a middle-aged white man leading with a motion bearing no discernable relationship to black dance or worship movements; my reading of it, therefore, is relatively uninvolved with racial subtexts, though I will not entirely write that off as a possibility.

32. This does not prevent someone, frequently Rod's father Coy, from passing out Cooper books so that he can lead from it.

33. I first arranged in 2001 when the Young People's Singing was held at Zion Hill, about an hour from Liberty but still on Sand Mountain. That singing was attended by two vanloads of people from my home singing in Western Massachusetts and the theory ran that I would know their leading habits and also how to pronounce unfamiliar names. The same theory holds true of the campers and other visitors to the Henagar-Union Convention; it has also emerged that I am good at arranging (which I maintain essentially calls on the skills required to do ethnography, including attentiveness to how different singers are likely to behave and interact with the class and what type of song they are likely to lead with what degree of skill).

34. In fact, Sand Mountain is one of these places—even local singings there tend to be excellent. Western Massachusetts is another.

35. The ability of large groups to produce high-quality, although unrehearsed, music is made possible by the participation of a decisive number of singers with previous familiarity with the song repertoire and experience singing them while following competent leaders. For comparisons of performance practices across genres see Finnegan (1989) and Becker (1982).

36. See Gardner (2004) for the practice of informal jamming at bluegrass festivals where audience members bring instruments and play music in the campgrounds following the onstage performances.

37. Roscigno and Danaher 2001.

38. Cerulo 1989.

39. DeNora 2002, 21.

40. DeNora 2002, 30.

41. DeNora 2002, 26.

CHAPTER SIX

1. Quoted in Cobb 1989, 158.

2. Cobb 1989, 161.

3. Filene 2000, 27–29.

4. Excluding unelaborated announcements of singings, letters to the editor, and passing references with no classifiable context (overwhelmingly from the *Atlanta Journal-Constitution*).
5. http://www.boxofficemojo.com/movies/?id=coldmountain.htm.
6. Stobrod, the vagrant father of Ruby (Renée Zellweger), was played by the actor Brendan Gleeson.
7. These nine singers all had personal ties to Tim, four having known him since college.
8. I was spending the summer on Sand Mountain, doing research, while one Chicago singer had arrived early for the weekend's regularly scheduled singings.
9. Randy Kennedy, "For a Timeless Song Style, a Chance at the Big Time," Music, *New York Times*, December 23, 2003. This was a significant article, beginning on the front page of the arts section, with pictures both on the front page and on an interior page.
10. These singers did receive minimal reimbursement from Miramax at the event but made their plans with no expectations of this.
11. Here, as frequently throughout this chapter, Gamson's (1994) analysis of the power of celebrity in contemporary culture is relevant.
12. This produced excellent coverage of the northeast quadrant of the state, where Liberty Baptist Church is located and where Sacred Harp singing is arguably strongest, but the coverage was not restricted to this area— Anniston is in east central Alabama, Birmingham is centrally located, and Tuscaloosa is in west central Alabama.
13. Gamson 1994, 132.
14. In this, he positioned himself between the archetypal folk-revivalist roles identified by Benjamin Filene (2000): Where Lomax was interested in finding and preserving old styles of music, but not necessarily in expanding their performance, and Pete Seeger was engaged in "an effort to break down the passivity that often marks Americans' encounters with music" (Filene 2000, 194) but not necessarily to preserve specific forms or repertoires, Tim emphasizes both in much of his performance and, in the case of Sacred Harp, emphasizes that, though old, it is also an active form for which he is only one of many possible spokespeople.
15. Alabama, Georgia, Illinois, Massachusetts, Michigan, Minnesota, New Mexico, New York, Rhode Island, and Texas.
16. *A Mighty Wind* was director Christopher Guest's 2003 film satirizing folk music artists and fans.
17. Bielby and Bielby 1994, 1290.
18. Peterson 1997, 206–9.
19. They are not, that is, reenactors like the "hardcore" Civil War reenactors who struggle for complete historical accuracy, as chronicled in Horwitz (1999). Tim Eriksen sometimes points out in singing schools that the street clothes

in which students have arrived from work or leisure *are* period clothes—that is, that the "period" to which Sacred Harp belongs is the present.

20. Filene 2000, 6.

21. This story is in a broad sense generally known, but, here, I have drawn heavily on the presentation and interpretations in Biskind (2004).

22. It was not, in fact, nominated for best picture, which Harvey Weinstein publicly attributed to that year's accelerated awards show schedule, with the Oscars and Golden Globes moved up a month, allowing less time for Miramax's campaign to have its usual effect ("Miramax's Run of Best-Picture Contenders Stops with *Cold Mountain* Snub." *USA Today*, January 27, 2004, http://www.usatoday.com/life/movies/news/2004-01-27-miramax_x.htm?csp=34).

23. It was not, of course, genuinely highbrow culture—rather, the show was making an argument for this piece of upper-middlebrow culture to be considered highbrow. And in fact, in his *New York Times* review of the movie, A. O. Scott ("Lovers Striving for a Reunion, With a War in the Way," December 25, 2003) said that it "follows in what has become a Miramax holiday tradition of highly polished, and often lifeless, literary adaptations, including *The English Patient* (also directed by Mr. Minghella), *The Cider House Rules*, and *Chocolat*," but "distinguishes itself from such middlebrow conversation-stoppers."

24. Gamson 1994, 132.

25. This stands in marked contrast to Gitlin's (1981) analysis in *The Whole World is Watching*, in which Students for a Democratic Society, another participatory group, was ultimately transformed by media attention—both actively, by changing its emphases and practices to gain further media attention, and passively, as new members joined in expectation of finding the group as it had been portrayed in the media.

CONCLUSION

1. Eliasoph 1998.

Works Cited

Ammerman, Nancy Tatom. 1997. *Congregation and Community.* New Brunswick, NJ: Rutgers University Press.

Auyero, Javier. 2000. "The Logic of Clientelism in Argentina: An Ethnographic Account." *Latin American Research Review* 35:55–81

Bayton, Mavis. 1990. "How Women Become Musicians." In *On Record: Rock, Pop, and the Written Word,* ed. Simon Frith and Andrew Goodwin, 201–19. New York: Pantheon Books.

Bealle, John. 1997. *Public Worship, Private Faith: Sacred Harp and American Folksong.* Athens: University of Georgia Press.

Becker, Howard S. 1982. *Art Worlds.* Berkeley: University of California Press.

Bellah, Robert N., William M. Sullivan, Ann Swidler, and Steven M. Tipton. 1985. *Habits of the Heart: Individualism and Commitment in American Life.* Berkeley: University of California Press.

Bender, Courtney. 2003. *Heaven's Kitchen: Living Religion at God's Love We Deliver.* Chicago: University of Chicago Press.

Bennett, Andy, and Richard A. Peterson. 2004. *Music Scenes: Local, Translocal, and Virtual.* Nashville, TN: Vanderbilt University Press.

Beverland, Michael B. 2005. "Crafting Brand Authenticity: The Case of Luxury Wines." *Journal of Management Studies* 42 (5): 1003–29.

Bielby, Denise D., and William T. Bielby. 1994. "'All Hits Are Flukes': Institutionalized Decision Making and the Rhetoric of Network Prime-Time Television Program Development." *American Journal of Sociology* 99 (5): 1287–1313.

Bigenho, Michelle. 2002. *Sounding Indigenous: Authenticity in Bolivian Music Performance.* New York: Palgrave Press.

Biskind, Peter. 2004. *Down and Dirty Pictures: Miramax, Sundance, and the Rise of Independent Film*. New York: Simon and Schuster.

Blackwell, Debra L. 1998. "Marital Homogamy in the United States: The Influence of Individual and Paternal Education." *Social Science Research* 27 (2): 159–88.

Bourdieu, Pierre. 1977. *Outline of a Theory of Practice*. Cambridge: Cambridge University Press.

Brint, Steven G. 2001. "Gemeinschaft Revisited: Rethinking the Community Concept." *Sociological Theory* 19 (1): 1–23.

Brodkin Sacks, Karen. 1988. *Caring by the Hour: Women, Work, and Organizing at Duke Medical Center*. Urbana: University of Illinois Press.

Cadge, Wendy. 2004. *Heartwood: The First Generation of Theravada Buddhism in America*. Chicago: University of Chicago Press.

Cantwell, Robert. 1996. *When We Were Good: The Folk Revival*. Cambridge, MA: Harvard University Press.

Carr, Patrick J. 2003. "The New Parochialism: The Implications of the Beltway Case for Arguments Concerning Informal Social Control." *American Journal of Sociology* 108 (6):1249–91.

Cerulo, Karen A., 1989. "Sociopolitical Control and the Structure of National Symbols: An Empirical Analysis of National Anthems." *Social Forces* 68 (1): 76–99.

Cheal, David. 1988. *The Gift Economy*. London: Routledge

Clawson, Laura. 2004. "'Blessed Be the Tie that Binds': Community and Spirituality Among Sacred Harp Singers." *Poetics* 32 (3–4): 311–24.

———. 2005. "'Everybody Knows Him': Social Networks in the Life of a Small Contractor in Alabama." *Ethnography* 6 (2): 237–64.

Clawson, Mary Ann. 1989. *Constructing Brotherhood: Class, Gender, and Fraternalism*. Princeton, NJ: Princeton University Press.

Cobb, Buell E., Jr. 1989. *The Sacred Harp: A Tradition and Its Music*. Athens: University of Georgia. (Orig. pub. 1978.)

Coser, Rose Laub. 1960. "Laughter Among Colleagues." *Psychiatry* 23:81–95.

———. 1966. "Role Distance, Sociological Ambivalence and Transitional Status Systems." *American Journal of Sociology* 72:173–87.

Covington, Dennis. 1995. *Salvation on Sand Mountain: Snake Handling and Redemption in Southern Appalachia*. New York: Penguin Books.

Demerath, N. J., III, and Yonghe Yang. 1997. "What American Culture War? A View from the Trenches as Opposed to the Command Posts and the Press Corps." In *Cultural Wars in American Politics: Critical Reviews of a Popular Myth*, ed. Rhys H. Williams, 17–38. Hawthorne, NY: Aldine de Gruyter.

DeNora, Tia. 2000. *Music in Everyday Life*. Cambridge: Cambridge University Press.

———. 2002. "Music into Action: Performing Gender on the Viennese Concert Stage, 1790–1810." *Poetics* 30 (1–2): 19–33.

DeVault, Marjorie L. 1991. *Feeding the Family: The Social Organization of Caring as Gendered Work*. Chicago: University of Chicago Press.

DiMaggio, Paul, John Evans, and Bethany Bryson. 1996. "Have Americans' Social Attitudes Become More Polarized?" *American Journal of Sociology* 102 (3): 690–755.

Dunaway, Wilma A. 1996. *The First American Frontier: Transition to Capitalism in Southern Appalachia, 1700–1860*. Chapel Hill: University of North Carolina Press.

Durkheim, Emile. 2001. *The Elementary Forms of Religious Life*. New York: Oxford University Press. (Orig. pub. 1912.)

Ehrenhalt, Alan. 1995. *The Lost City: Discovering the Forgotten Virtues of Community in the Chicago of the 1950s*. New York: Basic Books.

Eiesland, Nancy L. 1997. "Contending with a Giant: The Impact of a Megachurch on Exurban Religious Institutions." In *Contemporary American Religion: An Ethnographic Reader,* ed. Penny Edgell Becker and Nancy L. Eiesland, 191–220. Walnut Creek, CA: AltaMira Press.

———. 2000. *A Particular Place: Urban Restructuring and Religious Ecology in a Southern Exurb*. Brunswick, NJ: Rutgers University Press.

Eliasoph, Nina. 1998. *Avoiding Politics: How Americans Produce Apathy in Everyday Life*. Cambridge: Cambridge University Press.

Eliasoph, Nina, and Paul Lichterman. 2003. "Culture in Interaction." *American Journal of Sociology* 108 (4): 735–94.

Erikson, Kai. 1976. *Everything in Its Path: Destruction of Community in the Buffalo Creek Flood*. New York: Touchstone Books.

Etzioni, Amitai. 2001. "Is Bowling Together Sociologically Lite?" *Contemporary Sociology* 30 (3): 223–24.

Evans, John. 1997. "Worldviews or Social Groups as the Source of Moral Value Attitudes: Implications for the Culture Wars Thesis." *Sociological Forum* 12 (3): 371–404.

Filene, Benjamin. 2000. *Romancing the Folk: Public Memory and American Roots Music*. Chapel Hill: University of North Carolina Press.

Finnegan, Ruth. 1989. *The Hidden Musicians: Music-Making in an English Town*. Cambridge: Cambridge University Press.

Frith, Simon. 1991. "The Good, the Bad, and the Indifferent: Defending Popular Culture from the Populists." *Diacritics* 21 (4): 101–15.

Gamson, Joshua. 1994. *Claims to Fame: Celebrity in Contemporary America*. Berkeley: University of California Press.

Gardner, Robert. 2004. "The Portable Community: Mobility and Modernization in Bluegrass Festival Life." *Symbolic Interaction* 27 (2): 155–78.

Gerstel, Naomi, and Natalia Sarkisian. 2006. "Marriage: The Good, the Bad, and the Greedy." *Contexts* 5 (4): 16–21.

Gieryn, Thomas F. 2000. "A Space for Place in Sociology." *Annual Review of Sociology* 26:463–96.

Gitlin, Todd. 1981. *The Whole World is Watching: Mass Media in the Making and Unmaking of the New Left*. Berkeley: University of California Press.

Goffman, Erving. 1959. *The Presentation of Self in Everyday Life*. New York: Anchor Books.

Gouldner, Alvin. 1960. "The Norm of Reciprocity: A Preliminary Statement." *American Sociological Review* 25 (2): 161–78.

Graham, Colin. 2001. "'Blame It on Maureen O'Hara': Ireland and the Trope of Authenticity." *Cultural Studies* 15 (1): 58–75.

Grana, Cesar. 1989. *Meaning and Authenticity: Further Essays on the Meaning of Art*. New Brunswick, NJ: Transaction Publishers.

Grazian, David. 2003. *Blue Chicago: The Search for Authenticity in Urban Blues Clubs*. Chicago: University of Chicago Press.

Heider, Anne, and R. Stephen Warner. 2010. "Bodies in Sync: Interaction Ritual Theory Applied to Sacred Harp Singing." *Sociology of Religion* 71 (1): 76–97.

Hobsbawm, Eric, and Terence Ranger, eds. 1992. *The Invention of Tradition*. Cambridge: Cambridge University Press. (Orig. pub. 1983.)

Horwitz, Tony. 1999. *Confederates in the Attic: Dispatches from the Unfinished Civil War*. New York: Vintage Books.

Huisman, Kimberly, and Pierrette Hondagneu-Sotelo. 2005. "Dress Matters: Change and Continuity in the Dress Practices of Bosnian Muslim Refugee Women." *Gender and Society* 19 (1): 44–65.

Hunter, James Davison. 1991. *Culture Wars: The Struggle to Define America*. New York: Basic Books.

Jones, Deborah, and Karen Smith. 2005. "Middle-Earth Meets New Zealand: Authenticity and Location in the Making of *The Lord of the Rings*." *Journal of Management Studies* 42 (5): 923–45.

Lareau, Annette. 2003. *Unequal Childhoods: Class, Race, and Family Life*. Berkeley: University of California Press.

Laumann, Edward, John Gagnon, Robert T. Michael, and Stuart Michaels. 1994. *The Social Organization of Sexuality*. Chicago: University of Chicago Press.

Leonard, Bill J. 1999. *Christianity in Appalachia: Profiles in Regional Pluralism*. Knoxville: University of Tennessee Press.

Lever, Janet. 1976. "Sex Differences in the Games Children Play." *Social Problems* 23 (4): 478–87.

Lichterman, Paul. 1995. "Piecing Together Multicultural Community: Cultural Differences in Community Building Among Grass-Roots Environmentalists." *Social Problems* 42 (4): 513–34.

Lieberman, Robbie. 1995. *"My Song is My Weapon": People's Songs, American Communism, and the Politics of Culture, 1930–1950*. Urbana: University of Illinois Press.

Marini, Stephen A. 2003. *Sacred Song in America: Religion, Music, and Public Culture*. Urbana: University of Illinois Press.

Mauss, Marcel. 2000. *The Gift: The Form and Reason for Exchange in Archaic Societies*, trans. W. D. Halls. New York: W.W. Norton. (Orig. pub. 1925.)

McPherson, J. Miller, and Thomas Rotolo. 1996. "Testing a Dynamic Model of Social Composition: Diversity and Change in Voluntary Groups." *American Sociological Review* 61:179–202.

McPherson, J. Miller, Lynn Smith-Lovin, and James Cook. 2001. "Birds of a Feather: Homophily in Social Networks." *Annual Review of Sociology* 27: 415–44.

Miller, Kiri, ed. 2002. *The Chattahoochee Musical Convention, 1852–2002: A Sacred Harp Historical Sourcebook.* Carrollton, GA: The Sacred Harp Museum.

———. 2004. "'First Sing the Notes': Oral and Written Traditions in Sacred Harp Transmission." *American Music* 22 (4): 475–501.

———. 2005. "A Long Time Traveling: Song, Memory, and the Politics of Nostalgia in the Sacred Harp Diaspora." PhD diss., Harvard University.

———. 2007. *Traveling Home: Sacred Harp Singing and American Pluralism.* Urbana: University of Illinois Press.

Murphy, Author D., Colleen Blanchard, and Jennifer A. Hill, eds. 2001. *Latino Workers in the Contemporary South.* Athens: University of Georgia Press.

Patterson, Beverly. 2001. *The Sound of the Dove: Singing in Appalachian Primitive Baptist Churches.* Urbana: University of Illinois Press.

Peacock, James L., Ruel W. Tyson Jr. 1989. *Pilgrims of Paradox: Calvinism and Experience Among the Primitive Baptist of the Blue Ridge.* Washington, DC: Smithsonian Institution.

Peterson, Richard A. 1997. *Creating Country Music: Fabricating Authenticity.* Chicago: University of Chicago Press.

———. 2005. "In Search of Authenticity." *Journal of Management Studies* 42 (5): 1083–98.

Pollan, Michael. 2006. *The Omnivore's Dilemma: A Natural History of Four Meals.* New York: Penguin Press.

Putnam, Robert D. 2000. *Bowling Alone: The Collapse and Revival of American Community.* New York: Simon and Schuster.

Putnam, Robert D., and Lewis M. Feldstein. 2003. *Better Together: Restoring the American Community.* New York: Simon and Schuster.

Roof, Wade Clark. 1993. *A Generation of Seekers: The Spiritual Journeys of the Baby Boom Generation.* San Francisco: Harper San Francisco.

Roscigno, Vincent J., and William F. Danaher. 2001. "Media and Mobilization: The Case of Radio and Southern Textile Worker Insurgency, 1929 to 1934." *American Sociological Review* 66 (1): 21–48.

Roscigno, Vincent J., William F. Danaher, Erika Summers-Effler. 2002. "Music, Culture, and Social Movements: Song and Southern Textile Worker Mobilization, 1929–1934." *International Journal of Sociology and Social Policy* 22:141–74.

Roy, William G. 2002. Aesthetic Identity, Race, and American Folk Music. *Qualitative Sociology* 25 (3): 459–69.

Roy, William G. 2010. *Reds, Whites, and Blues: Social Movements, Folk Music, and Race in the United States.* Princeton, NJ: Princeton University Press.

Roy, William G., and Timothy J. Dowd. 2010. "What is Sociological about Music?" *Annual Review of Sociology* 36:183–203.

Sack, Daniel. 2001. *Whitebread Protestants: Food and Religion in American Culture.* New York: Palgrave.

The Sacred Harp. 1991. Bremen, GA: Sacred Harp Publishing.

Small, Christopher. 1998. *Musicking: The Meanings of Performing and Listening.* Hanover, NH: Wesleyan University Press.

———. 1999. *Music of the Common Tongue: Survival and Celebration in African American Music.* Hanover, NH: Wesleyan University Press.

Stevens, Mitchell L. 2001. *Kingdom of Children: Culture and Controversy in the Homeschooling Movement.* Prince, NJ: Princeton University Press.

Stinchcombe, Arthur L. 1965. "Social Structure and Organizations." In *Handbook of Organizations,* ed. James G. March. Chicago: Rand McNally.

Swidler, Ann. 1979. *Organization Without Authority: Dilemmas of Social Control in Free Schools.* Cambridge, MA: Harvard University Press.

Thornton, Sarah. 1996. *Club Cultures: Music, Media, and Subcultural Capital.* Hanover, NH: Wesleyan University Press.

Tyson, Ruel W., Jr., James L. Peacock, and Daniel W. Patterson, eds. 1988. *Diversities of Gifts: Field Studies in Southern Region.* Urbana: University of Illinois Press.

Vaisey 2007. "Structure, Culture, and Community: The Search for Belonging in 50 Urban Communes." *American Sociological Review* 72 (6): 851–73.

West, Candace, and Don H. Zimmerman. 1987. "Doing Gender." *Gender and Society* 1 (2): 125–51.

Whyte, William F. 1943. *Street Corner Society: The Social Structure of an Italian Slum.* Chicago: University of Chicago Press.

Wuthnow, Robert. 1998a. *After Heaven: Spirituality in America Since the 1950s.* Berkeley: University of California Press.

———. 1998b. *Loose Connections: Joining Together in America's Fragmented Communities.* Cambridge, MA: Harvard University Press.

———. 2003. *All in Sync: How Music and Art Are Revitalizing American Religion.* Berkeley: University of California Press.

Zerubavel, Eviatar. 1981. *Hidden Rhythms: Schedules and Calendars in Social Life.* Berkeley: University of California Press.

Index